The Joy of Linux®

CHECK THE WEB FOR UPDATES

To check for updates or corrections relevant to this book visit our updates page on the Web at http://www.prima-tech.com/updates.

SEND US YOUR COMMENTS

To comment on this book or any other PRIMA TECH title, visit our reader response page on the Web at http://www.prima-tech.com/comments.

HOW TO ORDER

For information on quantity discounts, contact the publisher: Prima Publishing, P.O. Box 1260BK, Rocklin, CA 95677-1260; (916) 787-7000. On your letterhead, include information concerning the intended use of the books and the number of books you want to purchase.

The Joy of Linux®

A Gourmet Guide to Open Source

MICHAEL HALL

BRIAN PROFFITT

A DIVISION OF PRIMA PUBLISHING

A Division of Prima Publishing

Prima Publishing and colophon are registered trademarks of Prima Communications, Inc. PRIMA TECH is trademark of Prima Communications, Inc., Roseville, California 95661.

Important: Prima Publishing cannot provide software support. Please contact the appropriate software manufacturer's technical support line or Web site for assistance. This book is an independent publication of Prima Publishing and is not affiliated with or sponsored by Microsoft Corporation or any other manufacturer mentioned herein.

All trademarks mentioned herein are the property of their respective owners.

Cartoon Illustrations ©2000 GeekCulture, R.R.#1 Meaford, Ontario, Canada, a general partnership under the laws of Ontario, Canada. Printed under license to Prima Communications, Inc.

Prima Publishing and the author have attempted throughout this book to distinguish proprietary trademarks from descriptive terms by following the capitalization style used by the manufacturer.

Information contained in this book has been obtained by Prima Publishing from sources believed to be reliable. However, because of the possibility of human or mechanical error by our sources, Prima Publishing, or others, the Publisher does not guarantee the accuracy, adequacy, or completeness of any information and is not responsible for any errors or omissions or the results obtained from use of such information. Readers should be particularly aware of the fact that the Internet is an ever-changing entity. Some facts may have changed since this book went to press.

ISBN: 0-7615-3151-3

Library of Congress Catalog Card Number: 00-109621

Library of Congress Cataloging-in-Publication Data on File

Printed in the United States of America

01 02 03 04 HH 10 9 8 7 6 5 4 3 2

For Alison
—MPH

For Cindy, who brings me joy
—BKP

Acknowledgments

There are a lot of people who deserve to be acknowledged, because so much of this book has come from individual conversations and interactions over several years.

For starters, Lynette Quinn is owed a great deal, both for conceiving of this book and giving me a crack at it. Lynette's been a paragon of patience and calm. My co-author, Brian, also deserves much thanks for jumping in and throwing literary elbows. Both of them made this book happen and you wouldn't be holding it right now if it weren't for them.

None of the ideas expressed in this book were formed in a vacuum. I'm very lucky to be surrounded by people who bring all sorts of perspectives to Linux, so thanks go to Sam Rowe, Ed Heil , and Brent Heatherwick, who have all shared insights from their own experiences with Linux (and computing in general). They've been a virtual LUG for me, and I've learned a lot from each of them.

While I was working on this book, I was also starting work at the Linux/Open Source Channel at internet.com. Thanks go to both Kevin Reichard, executive editor, and the other editors, writers, and techs there, both for shared insights and patience. They produce some of the best Linux resources available on the Web, and it's a privilege to work with them.

Finally, thanks to Alison, who shared me with this book.

—Michael Hall

You never know quite where to begin with these acknowledgements, since the beginnings of books are often awash in a sea of discussions and outlines. With this book, the beginning is also a bit murky, though the idea for the book is not. That came from the brain of one of my dearest friends, who thought an anthology/history of Linux would be a good thing. My friend, being the slightly lurid, yet lovable, person that she is, wanted to couch the book in the slightly lurid, yet lovable, theme of *The Joy of Sex*.

My initial reaction was that this was a hysterical idea, and I was glad I wasn't doing it. To understand my reluctance, you must understand that I tend to be the one in my circle of friends that gets embarrassed first whenever conversations lurch into double entendre. Putting together a book chock full of innuendo was not something I felt comfortable doing.

Still, the idea was out there. And when I told my friend about a guy from college I knew who was a brilliant writer of Linux-related material, she pounced on him to write this book. I figured I was safe from a three-month blush-fest.

So when Michael called me and wondered if I could help him out on this book, I had some serious misgivings. Not with helping him, but with the whole theme of the book.

Therefore, I must give special thanks to my good friend Lynette Quinn, who managed to drag me out of my Midwestern shell and help me write innuendo and puns with great gusto for the past few months. Because talking dirty is where friends like Lynette are really a big help.

I must also thank my co-author Michael, who invited me onto this project and gave me an opportunity to learn even more about Linux and how to be a better writer. I have been very glad that the tides of time have made us better friends, even if he does call me a "quisling bastard" now and again.

Of course, no book could ever be done without the help of my lovely wife and two daughters, who are each the real joys of my existence. I thank them all for their love and support while Daddy was squirreled away in his office muttering about transvestites and X Window all in the same breath.

—Brian Proffitt

About the Authors

Michael Hall lives in Charlottesville, Virginia at the moment. An editor with the Linux/Open Source channel at internet.com, he contributes to *Linux Today* and writes for *Linux Planet*. He thinks biff should be a more immersive experience.

Brian Proffitt lives and works in the heartland of America, Indianapolis. Despite this, he is a reasonably well-adjusted individual who can function well on either coast. The author of several Linux-related books, Brian is also the Managing Editor of BrowserWatch.com and BotSpot.com, and a Contributing Editor on *Linux Today*. Somewhere in the midst of all this, Brian spends time with his family, preferably flying them around with his new private pilot's license.

Contents

Introduction

PYTHONS AMONG THE SHOWGIRLS, ANARCHO-SYNDICALISTS AND THE RED FLAG OF COMPUTER REVOLUTION

The scene is a hotel room in Las Vegas on the second night of COMDEX, a convention so big it takes two buildings to hold it. I was there to cover it as best I could, but along the way I had to cave in to the urge to buy a toy. Being a compulsive gadget freak, I didn't have a hard time finding something interesting; I settled on a small camera that attached to my pocket computer.

I had been taking pictures with it all day, and I ran up to my room to download the snapshots from the handheld device, thinking surely the images wouldn't be saved in such a way that I couldn't get at them with my Linux laptop. Naturally I was wrong, and I had a good meg of photos that weren't doing me any good. Had I a Windows laptop, of course, there would have been no problem: Everyone makes sure their hardware works with Windows. I spent a few seconds wondering if I hadn't been hasty when I'd wiped all trace of Microsoft from my computer.

Fortunately, in addition to my gadget freak side, I'm an optimist. I did what any good Internet-enabled optimist would do: I fired up the modem and went looking for answers. The product had been out for at least a few months, so I knew in my heart of hearts that there would be a solution.

Enter Tamer Fahmy, a student in Germany. Tamer had the same camera, used Linux, and knew more than enough of the programming language Python to get at the pictures he was taking with the camera. A quick download later and I was in business.

Or not.

Tamer's software was good, but a small bug kept it from working on my machine. I wrote him, politely asking for help in getting to the bottom of the problem, and he was quick to respond. Meanwhile, the pictures sat just waiting to be looked at.

Now, my knowledge of Python is limited, which is a dweebish way of saying I don't really know any Python at all. I did, however, have the source code to Tamer's program, not to mention a burning need to see my pictures. So I opened my second beer of the night, opened Tamer's program in my text editor, and set out to find the problem.

A few hours and beers later, having speed-read a few Python tutorials and engaged in an utterly quixotic session with a debugger, the problem was solved to my satisfaction. I wrote Tamer with the fix.

Tamer was very polite when he wrote back the next morning to tell me that although I had fixed the problem, I had it all wrong, but that it was a good effort and it put him on to where the problem was, and would I please check out the attached version with his fix?

Within 24 hours, I'd bought the camera, found a Linux solution to make it work, discovered a bug, fixed a bug, gotten an education in Python on why one must never, ever directly call the POSIX module, had the camera working, and made a new friend.

The thing that makes Linux work is that it has grown out of thousands upon thousands of interactions just like the one I described. It started out as a way to bring a little bit of UNIX to typical home computers, and now it's hard to name an area of computing where it doesn't have a useful, vital place. That growth, from hobby to phenomenon, has been built by people cooperating to fix small vexations, add new capabilities, and find ways, frankly, to play with a new toy.

Which brings us to an issue, which is my failed history of conveying why I'm a Linux booster.

Not all of us are lucky enough to include admirers of Spanish Anarcho-Syndicalist collectives in their circle of friends. In fact, most people probably believe that if you *do* know someone like that and you call him "friend," he's probably some poor coffee-house eccentric you end up at adjoining tables with now and again, and the "friendship" is more a friendly tolerance. In my case, however, those people would be wrong.

I *do* have a friend who's an admirer of Spanish Anarcho-Syndicalist collectives. Considering the fact we've been in constant contact since eighth grade and even lived together well after college, it's safe to assert that the friendship is more durable than the garden-variety "suffer through the coffee-house loon's rantings until getting to the bottom of the cup" sort of friendship.

This particular friend turns up here, in the introduction to a book about Linux, because he was the first person who ever drew a noticable and awkward blank when I tried to explain why, well, Linux rocks. He may have been the first person I ever tried to explain the whole thing to at all, which makes my eventual defeat all the more unfortunate. It's taken me four years to recover.

Some people might look at an admirer of Spanish Anarcho-Syndicalist collectives and say something like: "This is a post-ideological age! We're not talking about how to bake the societal cake, but how to arrange the cherries on the multi-layered cake of corporate capital and increasingly quaint-seeming states. Anyone who thinks there's room for Anarcho-Syndicalists doing much of anything but standing around looking sour before having the good grace to go register as Democrats is, um, impractical."

My friend isn't impractical at all. If anything, he's more interested in practicalities than most staunch Republicans and certainly more rigorous and disciplined about his politics than the average straight-ticket voter. Which is why, being the newbie Linux advocate I was, I figured I could sway him to at least forebear when I started rhapsodizing about the joy of Linux.

So it was that we were together for the first time in a while, and relating our new enthusiasms to each other, when Linux came up. His partner was putting the finishing touches on dinner and we were engaged in the sort of pre-dinner talk that never amounts to much because a good meal's coming up and it's going to cause a lot of distractions.

When idealists meet, though, there's often room for a strange sort of chilliness when it comes to chatting about their preoccupations. There are as many things to get idealistic over as there are things at all. And when you begin to delve into those things one by one, you start getting into the subatomic world of bits and pieces you and your fellow idealists might be the only ones to see. The more you delve into that world, the more there is to connect together right in front of your nose, and soon you're not convinced the other atoms bumping against your own were ever very useful anyhow.

That isn't to say that idealists are fixated or somehow buried in their world of small and meaningful interconnections. They like the same things everybody else does, unless someone makes the mistake of suggesting that they've maybe missed a connection. Then they furrow their brows a little and do what we do every day to keep all the details from becoming a little overwhelming: They trivialize.

So it went as I, the new Linux advocate, and my friend, the more experienced Anarcho-Syndicalist advocate, made a game attempt at tying my new passion in with his older and more focused desire to run big capital out on a rail before it goes and does something really stupid.

The angle I took with my friend was direct: Linux is cooperatively developed by thousands of people all over the world who do it for free (most of the time) and have actually managed to challenge some of the giants of the computer industry. I reiterated tales of success against the Microsoft juggernaut, the way an operating system that just plain worked better had been seemingly pulled together like some extravagant stone soup of a quality so high that nerds doff their hats at its mention and Bill Gates' lackies paint their doors with lamb's blood in hopes that it will pass over, leaving them (and their stock options) unmolested.

How could an admirer of Spanish Anarcho-Syndicalist collectives fail to see the import!? Written off as impractical by friends and family, Anarcho-Syndicalists are supposed to adore stories that involve the little people getting together and spontaneously making something better out of the poor hand they're dealt by Big Capital.

The attempt ran out of steam after a few minutes, and he politely allowed that if the software industry could learn a little something about behaving in a more instinctively cooperative manner, it might make computers work a little better. In other words: "What the hell does this have to do with anything that matters?"

It was a mercy when dinner was announced and we could get on with the more pleasant task of eating good food and gossiping about things like who was dating whom, and who broke ranks and voted for Clinton despite firm resolve to abstain from entering into a sucker's bet dialog with the hegemonic forces of the state and Big Capital by granting the act of voting any meaning at all.

A recent article appearing on the Web page "Suck" invented a useful word for the part of this anecdote you might be anticipating: hindsleight. *Hindsleight* is all the stuff that you think of after a bad social encounter. It's the heart of the common conversational convention we have of covering over the fact we got creamed by someone, got left looking silly, got straight dissed, by saying "I was like…" and launching into a much more eloquent dissertation of the things we wish we'd said. It's a sort of conversational sleight of hand that invokes a usefully ambiguous, almost verbless phrase and leaves it to the listener to assume we would have won the encounter had we not been utterly distracted by the clumsy stupidity of the person with whom we were arguing.

No hindsleight here. That's the next 300 pages.

I'd utterly failed in my mission to go out among the Anarcho-Syndicalists and convert them to my way of thinking. I would not be arriving at the siege of Microsoft with a legion of hackers waving black and red flags and coding things of such beauty that grown men would weep as they beheld them.

Of course, there are probably Anarcho-Syndicalists out there contributing to Linux in some way, even as I type, and they've been doing it for longer than I've been making everyone happy for the distraction of dinner. There are also legions of staunch Republicans, vaguely centrist Democrats, gun enthusiasts, moms, Hegelians, angry young men, and part-time postal workers out there, doing something useful for the Linux cause, and their efforts are benefitting more and more people every day.

I got another opportunity to make the case for Linux two years later.

It was a cool spring night in Indiana, just after one of those weddings where people walk away convinced. The computer people had all managed to remain standing long enough to get down to the important part of the evening: talking shop.

My friends are successful in their fields. One programs on a Stratus mainframe, truly big iron. He's justifiably proud to be

coding on a machine where uptime is measured in years. The other consults for database giant Oracle: If any company is ever tasked to catalog everything that ever existed, that's who'll handle the contract.

The talk drifted to where Linux was going.

"It's for Intel machines," said the consultant, "not serious hardware. It's a novelty for poor college kids."

"It's been ported to Alphas and Sparcs," I offered.

"Sun already has some sort of UNIX running on Sparcs...why would anyone bother sticking Linux on them? What's the point?"

I suppose my eyes rolled up in my head, though I'll never know. I just know that everyone else in the area realized the party was about to have some sort of unpleasant gravity inflicted on it. We were separated by group consensus, and another opportunity to win over one of the Linuxless was lost.

The statistics shared among Linux enthusiasts (the way Anarcho-Syndicalists enthuse about obscure but wildly profitable collectives up in Basque country) tell a story that indicates Linux is growing a little every day, creeping (or charging) into more and more places in the computing world. Its share in every area of computing is growing, even as some of the poor, dumb giants who thought they had things all sewn up are groping for ways to alternatively ignore or coopt the whole thing.

A thing that was concocted on a 386 to cure a Finnish student's homesickness for the Mother Operating System, UNIX, a thing that once couldn't even be bothered to help boot the computer it was running on, is being crammed into palmtops, extended to run on giant mainframes, tweaked to make old Macintoshes useful, burned on to chips to run industrial machines, and massaged to make it useful to people who thought it was a stroke of computational genius to get America Online installed on a computer they brought home from Sam's Club.

NASA scientists use Linux (one of them wrote the crucial bit of software that spared me from having to go out and buy a new ethernet card for my computer), rebellious teenagers use Linux, Microsoft has even been caught using Linux. At the high school I used to work for, it sparked a subtle realignment among the nerdish boys walking the halls, who went overnight from showing off garish pages they'd crafted with Microsoft FrontPage for the sole purpose of trading Nintendo cartridges to loudly trading shell accounts to their Linux "boxes" among each other and throwing up "This Page Written with the vi Text Editor" banners on their home pages.

Linux is here to stay in the hearts and minds of a lot of people who've invested the time to build it, learn it, and use it daily. They all think it's worth advocating, and I agree with them.

Brian, my co-author, has something to say about the whole thing, too:

TALES FROM THE DARK SIDE

I came to Linux rather late in the game. I was raised in a land where Windows ruled the day. It was a homogeneous land, replete with teal-shaded backgrounds and chiming little noises to signal incoming mail. It was warm and safe in my Windows world, and I felt comfortable in my allegiance to King William and the Court of Redmond.

I even actively participated in the promotion of Windows, editing books that would soothe the brows of troubled Windows users and make their cares blissfully evaporate. But within this little world, dark, ugly things kept popping up, casting shadows on all that was good and pure. These were troll-like little problems, like print spoolers crashing the entire Windows system for no apparent reason, and the need to reboot any time certain applications froze.

At the same time, I had heard of other computer kingdoms, of course. The Land of Macintosh seemed a pleasant enough place, albeit populated by ex-hippies. OS/2 seemed really cutting edge at the time, but the fear pervading that little kingdom was too much to bear.

And then there was Linux. The first person I knew who was using Linux on his home machine was a man who later became a transvestite—which gives you a pretty good picture of how this repressed middle-class Midwesterner thought of Linux at the time. If Macs were for hippies, then Linux was for the truly deviant. I, in my Ward Cleaver little world, would have none of it.

Over time, the trolls in Windowsland got a little bigger, and no longer ran and hid everytime I would try to find them. They were getting bolder and meaner. Windowsland would be upgraded from time to time, and many of the trolls would vanish—to be replaced by trolls that were nastier and harder to spot. These new trolls were learning to blend in with their pretty environment and would be impossible to see until it was too late.

I was getting disenfranchised with computers in a big way. I still used them for work, but now it was no longer a pleasurable experience. It felt like I was fighting the PCs before me. The trolls had taken over, and I had become a knight errant, trying to take back the kingdom I had once loved.

My first steps into the Linux community were, appropriately enough, for the purposes of writing a book. The book I was to write was a text on how to use StarOffice (a Microsoft Office–like suite) for Linux. Normally I prefer to know a lot about the topics I am writing about, but in this case, my needs were great: My day job was relocating its offices to South Carolina and I had no great desire to go with them.

So I parted ways with my employer, got a nice advance from the publisher, and borrowed a friend's extra PC for the sole purpose of learning how to use Linux.

I had several preconceptions about using Linux, since I'd already been exposed to a UNIX system a few years before. I expected it to be awkward and cryptic to use. With these thoughts in mind, I installed Caldera OpenLinux on the computer my friend let me borrow.

It was nothing short of an epiphany!

This was not something that was hard to install, no! It was simple! It was fast! There was no dark little command-line interface; I was getting full-blown, in-your-face KDE, which looked and behaved a lot like my Windows machine did!

I had seen the light, and it was good.

I went on using my friend's PC in his home office for about three more weeks, learning about Linux and its pros and cons while examining the StarOffice suite I was writing about. Then I went out and got a copy of Red Hat for my own PC and set up a dual-boot system at my house. Suddenly, the computer was no longer an enemy; it was a trusted friend again.

To be sure, there were problems. Linux, for all its power and flexibility, is not perfect. But unlike the trolls of Windows, after the problems in Linux get fixed, they stay fixed. They don't come back to haunt you later.

I began to be a Linux evangelist amongst my peers, who just shook their heads and tried to lure me back to Windowsland. I would not go.

Linux would also bring an old friend back into my life. My books were showing up on shelves around the country and lo and behold, one Michael Hall happened to see one on the shelves of his local bookstore one day.

Michael and I met in college, and despite our incredibly different outlooks on life (an idealistic young Democrat who voted every year versus a self-decribed anarchist who was in constant strife with the crypto-facists of the world), we became good friends. We shared a passion and a skill for writing, and when I was the editor of the school newspaper, he was the managing editor. I would try to plan the stories for the next week's paper; he would devise ways of printing the paper off-campus when the college administration would close us down for all the subversive writing we were doing. It was a good balance.

After college, Michael worked with me as a reporter for a time at a community newspaper where I was the editor. Eventually, he went back to school, and I ended up moving to New Jersey.

But Linux brought us into each other's lives once more. Michael, it turned out, had been into Linux for years, and had contributed a little to the GNOME Documentation Project. After I was asked to start writing for *Linux Today*, it was I who recommended Michael to contribute as well. While I continued to write books, he became more involved with *Linux Today*, and today he is *my* editor on that site.

This biographical information is not to bore you with the insipid details of our personal lives. If you ply us with alcohol, you'll get more than enough of that kind of information. But I cannot talk about Linux without talking about the Linux community, for it was that sense of community that renewed a friendship that had lapsed for almost a decade.

Linux has grown beyond a mere operating system hacked together by some Finnish student. Linux is not just a collection of efficient software code. Linux, beyond the dreams of anyone who ever worked on it, and perhaps because of those dreams, has become a place of commonality where tech-heads and normal people alike can get caught up in the romance of the "little operating system that could."

You cannot talk about Linux without talking about the people involved. You cannot avoid discussing the culture and philosophy of these people, either, which goes far beyond the capitalist

mentality of other operating-system purveyors. This fact is self-evident almost as soon as you become involved in Linux.

If you go up to a Linux user and ask her to name just three developers of the Linux kernel, you'd likely get Linus Torvalds, Alan Cox, and Ted T'so. Now go up to a Windows user and ask the same question, and watch them go blank. It is this sense of community that makes Linux a better operating system than anything else that has come out thus far. The people's involvement—not user focus groups—insures its ultimate success.

And it's this sense of belonging, this joy of Linux, that this book is really about.

PART ONE

Do You Know Who Your Millions of Partners Are?

1

The Penguin on Top

February, 2001, New York City

You've got all kinds on the floor of LinuxWorld Expo, the semi-annual convention (one per coast) where the Linux faithful (and not so faithful) meet. Start walking from one end of the exhibit hall to the other, and you'll see the giant penguins hovering over post-adolescents wearing devil horns, corporate types from IBM, teenage boys hunched over laptops, mind-readers, hired models, smirking tech journalists, glad-handing executives, assorted geeks, and the occasional Linux evangelist preaching to his public.

This year's convention is particularly interesting. Beyond the sideshow-like atmosphere of some of the exhibits—not to mention the ill-matched menagerie of suits, nerds, and ad-men—many of us tech journalists sense that we should pursue a final interview with some of the exhibitors, because it may well be the end of the road for the smaller companies. This notion is fueled by rumors of layoffs in some major Linux companies; by an ever-dwindling number of outfits hawking shrink-wrapped distributions on the strength of installation support; and by the largest booths in the building, which are owned by truly giant companies, such as IBM and Intel—indicating that Linux is a market that's been entered, for good or ill, by the people who define computing.

"Look around," one writer says, "half of these people will be gone next year." An older editor makes a crack about the kids being run out of the sandbox. A look over at the Slashdot booth, replete with beanbag chairs (these are *de rigeur* for Linux gatherings, implying the carefree spirit and sturdy backs of youth), Nerf guns, and a Playstation, shows a collection of middle-aged men dressed in corporate-weekender outfits, eyeing the whole thing with mixed puzzlement and condescension. Their hands dip into the pockets of their Polar-fleece vests to produce business cards as the perimeter around the temporary geek-chic habitat holds, itself produced by the corporate largesse of Slashdot's owners.

> "Look around," one writer says, "half of these people will be gone next year."

I take a moment to sit in a beanbag chair alongside a senior executive from a company new to the Linux world. He's building software that makes Linux easier to deal with for housewives, secretaries, and "the end user," a mythical creature widely assumed by true geeks to be the tragic by-product of a lobotomy and an unfortunate youth spent playing in the sun with other children. The executive mentions "the hacker ethic," referring to the loose set of characteristics so many of Linux's pioneers seemed to possess: curiosity, constructive anti-authoritarianism, mutualism, independence, and mistrust of the ready solution or typical answer.

"Your company is new to all this," I say. "And I mean no disrespect, but it's hardly a collection of hackers. You talk about the hacker ethic, but it seems like your company won't really be a success until hackers are a much smaller proportion of the Linux user base."

The executive, perched in his beanbag chair, is quiet for a moment, and then picks his words with care. "It's still early. The hackers are vital to us, creatively vital people...but, well, Linux is bigger than any group." Five minutes later, he's bemoaning the woeful state of quality control present in open-source software, and the slovenly adherence to deadlines observed by the average hacker.

He wants the kids out of the sandbox.

The same day, though, I walk over to a company trying to make its mark with a version of Linux that runs on handheld computers. The people at the booth are excited, their body language is almost frantic. The words of one of the developers I speak to come out in a flood. He excitedly demonstrates a handheld computer performing instant chat over a wireless connection to the Internet. He shows how even the most mundane data can be transformed with his software to make sense in a variety of contexts from handheld computer to desktop machine to processes that don't ever show themselves to users, but communicate amongst each other. There's a high cool factor to what he's preaching, but there's also the point to which he keeps returning: All of it happens with open-source software.

"This is all with open standards," he exclaims. "With open-source software. And it's happening with all the tools we've been building from free software for years. People have been building the foundations to make information take on its own life for years without knowing it, and now we're bringing it together."

Part of it is, to anyone who's been around computing since the first days of the Internet creeping into the awareness of self-annointed Information Age prophets, old hat. Fads come and go. At each conference, we're promised a golden age of intelligent software, or "smarter information," or some other buzzword.

Some maintain that open-source software is itself a fad preached by businesses looking to sound hip even as they figure out ways to share nothing while harnessing the creativity of youth eager to sign up with a revolution or join a movement. But the fact of the matter is, this guy is right. For years and years, people have been building an infrastructure that was surely meant for something besides pushing banner ads, pornography, and corporate brochure sites. Tools have been crafted, sometimes because they had to be to progress any further, sometimes because it was just fun.

Standards have been defended against attempts to close them because a community of Internet users needed those standards kept open to keep their tools working, and the lines of communication open.

The result? Small companies are out to redefine everything with big ideas and the enthusiasm of revolutionaries. Linux was never the meaning of the exercise to them, but Linux is free and open—the perfect base from which they can explore their own ideas without having to reinvent or build from scratch.

It all adds up to paradox after a few hours: Internet visionaries who see Linux as just another tool; industry veterans who predict the demise of more than a handful of Linux companies as the stock market euphoria fades and doomed revenue models they defended prove unviable; graybeards who have come forth from the most hidebound backgrounds to embrace an operating system that was built by hackers but is now in the hands of everybody regardless of cultural allegiance. All the horses seem to be pulling in a direction that indicates the end of Linux as a phenomenon. And yet, it's precisely because of these things that, well, the penguin is on top.

> Small companies are out to redefine everything with big ideas and the enthusiasm of revolutionaries.

TALKIN' 'BOUT A REVOLUTION

Linux poked its head into the world barely ten years ago, not much more than an interesting diversion for a hobbiest, and promising little more than the novelty of booting something very UNIX-like on PC hardware. During the past ten years, however, Linux has gone from toy to contender, putting the fear into more than a few companies as it has found its place as a "glue" operating system. Maybe it didn't perform some tasks that well, but it excelled when it came to doing the sort of day-to-day grunt work network and system administrators rely on to keep things moving.

Alternately lauded and reviled, sometimes by the same people, Linux's progress in the server room and the public imagination has been undeniable. The phenomenon crescendoed in the summer and fall of 1999, when several Linux companies held initial public offerings that set new records as their share prices rose to twenty and thirty times the initial offering price. That explosion died, though, and the very same companies struggle now, still moving toward profitability, but buoyed by buzz no longer.

How is this indicative of a revolution won? If the corporate guys are talking about nudging out the hackers who made Linux happen in the first place even as the public euphoria over the phenomenon fades, where's the victory?

The answer lies in the ubiquity of Linux in 2001.

When Linus Torvalds gave the gift of Linux to the world, he did so (after a false start) under terms that left Linux open to all takers, for good or ill. An implicit understanding of the movement from which Linux derives its license, the document which sets the terms and conditions under which Linux may be distributed, is that software must remain open to modification. That way, if a programmer misses the mark where another's needs are concerned, the next person down the line may do what's necessary to build on the existing work and make it better.

> **A**lternately lauded and reviled, sometimes by the same people, Linux's progress in the server room and the public imagination has been undeniable.

And Linux has missed the mark plenty of times over the years, at first not even able to be booted on its own, then lacking so much as a collection of reliable networking tools. With time, however, each of these deficits has been corrected—the result rolled into the ever-growing, ever-diversifying collection of software and tools that is

Linux, slowly making its way into server rooms and back offices, Web servers and desktops, until we arrive at today, with an operating system that's taken seriously by the likes of IBM and Microsoft (one hoping to profit, the other hoping it will go away before more damage is done).

After ten years of constant progress, Linux is everywhere. It's everywhere in so many forms and because of the efforts of so many people with so many different agendas that it can't go away, because it's not a single thing by a long shot.

> After ten years of constant progress, Linux is everywhere.

As I stand in that convention hall, surrounded by the booths of companies soon to disappear, enclosed by executives who are grateful for all the code they can work with but less so for the hackers who wrote that code, overshadowed by IBM's gigantic booth, I realize something important. Even if the revolution is over, it has left its mark on the computing landscape that won't be removed no matter what sort of marketing hype is brought to bear on it, and no matter how dismally the companies who sought to sell it perform.

The sound and fury of the past few years on the part of Linux evangelists mighty and small came together to buy Linux a place at the table. Whether the hackers carry it forward, or some computing giant ends up driving it, Linux is a fact.

Is There a General Purpose, Time-Sharing System in the House?: The Really Quick and Dirty Story of UNIX

It's impossible to understand Linux at all without knowing where it came from, and that's a story that goes back over 30 years to Bell Laboratories, where UNIX was born.

Two computer scientists named Ken Thompson and Dennis Ritchie were working on an operating system called Multics (*Multiplexed Information and Computing Service*); an attempt to create an operating system for large computers with the means to provide access to many users at the same time. Multics, thanks to its resource hungriness, had earned the disapproval of management, which promptly, in the manner of management everywhere, pulled the plug on the project, leaving the gentlemen without a sanctioned operating system project.

Thompson was eventually granted the use of a DEC PDP-7, and in best computer-nerd fashion, set about to make it a better game machine. That in turn led to the first UNIX kernel. For his part, Ritchie had developed a computer language, which he called "C," for Thompson's new operating system. C is important for the simple reason that it was one of the first proofs of the notion that a programming language can be "cross platform." That is, if you use C to come up with a really good version of "Space Wars" on one machine, you'll be able to run it on a different machine with a different operating system with little hassle.

This is called *portability*, and computer historians agree that there wasn't much of it leading into the 1970s.

So with C in hand, Thompson and Ritchie were tasked with producing an office-automation system for Bell, and they were given better hardware with which to do it—a DEC PDP-11 to be exact. Thanks to C and the wonder of portability, the two rewrote much of the embryonic UNIX and ported it to the new hardware.

Portability allowed UNIX to easily move from its earliest host to its new home, and it also eased the spread of UNIX among computer enthusiasts (who weren't, at the time, quite the same people as they are today, owing to the scarcity of computers outside research institutions and universities). Bell Labs, thanks to the antitrust woes of AT&T, was fairly friendly about the distribution of the UNIX source code for several years, releasing at least one version to universities free of charge, and another for around $100. Businesses and the government had to pay tens of thousands of dollars. For a while, the source code for UNIX flourished until AT&T made moves to halt it, citing its ownership of the proprietary source code.

> This is called *portability*, and computer historians agree that there wasn't much of it leading into the 1970s.

UNIX, however, had caught on.

Books have been written about what made UNIX so popular, and we could spend the rest of this volume mucking about with the gory details. If we did, however, this book would stop being a "connoisseur's guide to open source," and start being an anatomical text. We don't want to go there. Some key items should be listed, though, because they exist in one form or another in Linux as we know it today. For every baggy-pants–wearing kid on a skateboard who runs Linux because it's "kewl," there are plenty of people who first picked it up because it gave them a UNIX they could play with in the privacy of their own home, and that was something they'd wanted for a very long time.

So...the reasons for all that enthusiasm:

- **Portability.** Thanks to C, you could move UNIX from one machine to another without having to rewrite all your favorite programs from scratch.
- **Modularity.** It provided an abundance of very functional, single-purpose tools that were easy on memory and resources, but could be combined to provide big results in a number of ways.
- **Flexibility.** It was flexible without requiring a ton of in-depth knowledge. You could leverage your command of the individual components to produce bigger results through scripting and piping, without needing to come up with a whole new program each time your needs changed.

Portability

UNIX places an emphasis on values that seemingly represent diametric opposites of what you see in other operating systems. For instance, portability is a key value that UNIX enthusiasts share. It's because of this desire to be able to move a common set of tools from one computer to the next that Linux (and its cousins) now run on a staggering array of computing hardware: everything from garden-variety PCs to iMacs to handheld computers to massive mainframe computers.

> UNIX places an emphasis on values that seemingly represent diametric opposites of what you see in other operating systems.

Modularity

Think about a word-processing program and everything it does. It allows text to be formatted, printed, previewed, spell-checked, and generally mangled—and it does it all in a single program that gets bigger and slower as time goes by and more features get chunked in. Word processors are not modular. Now consider a collection of small programs that, on their own, are the functional equivalent of bees in a hive, with a single purpose apiece.

You might, for instance, have a single program for doing nothing more than entering text. It won't check your spelling, or offer a way to make a pretty printout of what you're working on. Once you're done with that program, however, you can then run your file through a spell-checking program that, although it may not do much else, really knows how to spell check. Done with the spell checker? Move the file on to a formatting program that reads your formatting codes and converts the text file into something a printer can understand. From there, you hand things off to a program that handles printing quietly and efficiently with minimal overhead.

> **N**ow consider a collection of small programs that, on their own, are the functional equivalent of bees in a hive, with a single purpose apiece.

To the "modern" way of thinking, this is clearly insane. It implies complexity, because each of these programs must be run on their own—and we all know how bad complex things are. Why bother with a bunch of small, efficient programs when there's a one-stop solution?

We're not going to be OS fascists and suggest that this is a bad question to ask. In some cases, especially considering how inexpensive good computer hardware is these days, it's entirely appropriate to just stick with that big, memory-hungry word processor with more toolbars than there are lost socks in the world and plow ahead.

On the other hand, when you consider that there are hundreds more programs just like the ones I've described, which can do all sorts of other things really, really well in all sorts of combinations, it makes you think. If you're in an environment where processing power is shared, those small programs doing their thing and then quietly exiting end up saving a lot more processing time and memory than a single, huge program.

Flexibility

"Flexibility" in the UNIX world is a simple concept once we take all those single-purpose tools and marry them together. Much the same way a necklace made of many tiny links will appear more supple than one made of big, iron rings, UNIX's "small tools" approach means that there are more small, meaningful relationships a user or programmer can establish between all those tools, and there are plenty of ways to do the same thing, each as "correct" as the next, even if some are more appropriate in certain contexts than others.

The beauty of the UNIX way of doing things is that your knowledge of a fairly small set of all the available tools can be leveraged by compounding their effects and making more tools in all sorts of combinations. And because these compound tools are made of tiny, replacable parts, there's a seemingly infinite array of possibilities when it comes to accomplishing a task. A few features of the UNIX approach confer this flexibility nicely:

Piping

A practical corollary to the modularity of single-task programs within the UNIX way is that they should also act as filters through which you can "pipe" information. Consider, for instance, one of the more tedious tasks of daily corporate life: taking credit for someone else's work.

In this scenario, you, a simple corporate drone with an overpriced apartment and an expensive monthly car payment, have been toiling in the shadow of your neighbor, the ever-industrious John J. Spurworthy, who has spent the last year working on a project you secretly covet. You've got a chance to pass all of his work off as your own...but wait! The rotter has made sure his name is in every file related to that project.

> Consider, for instance, one of the more tedious tasks of daily corporate life: taking credit for someone else's work.

With that *other* word processor (we're not naming names), you could open each file and hunt down his name. Not too bad if he just put it at the top of each file, a trivial task for a moderately experienced Word-pro warrior if it's liberally sprinkled throughout, but a colossal pain if it's not only liberally sprinkled through one file, but all 183 he was working on.

Thanks to your ability to pipe commands with UNIX, help is on the way. You just visit the directory where the mightily gifted and devoted servant to your ungrateful corporate overlords keeps his stuff and type:

```
cat * | sed s/John\ Spurworthy/Dick\ Phillips/g | lpr
```

And out comes his work, having been opened by the cat command (which does one thing very well: shows the contents of files), filtered by the sed command (which does one thing very well: slices and dices text files), and then handed off to the lpr command (which sends files off to the printer), pristine in all its creative glory. Except, of course for the niggling detail that his name is no longer anywhere to be found in the printout, which means you are, um, one gravy-sucking corporate stud-muffin.

Scripting

So you've got small, single-purpose programs that do their one thing well. Added to that, they can talk to each other, making your computer more of a hive of determined and capable bees than a collection of really, really expensive pink elephants with wet-bars tied to their backs. Add the element of easy scripting to the mix, and you've really got something.

Scripting is an easy concept to grasp: Rather than typing a bunch of commands in over and over again, you can write a very simple program (a *script*) that does the typing for you. This capability may remind DOS fans of batch files, but because UNIX was so oriented to the power users of computing in its early days, it developed much more powerful scripting capabilities and, of course, always had many more of those powerful, single-purpose programs to use when it came time to write the scripts they used.

For many tasks, all of those little programs—combined with their capability to filter information before sending it to the next program in a pipe, and further combined with their capability to string together even longer sequences of commands and pipes into a script—mean that there's less need to do what we think of as "programming" for common tasks. You don't need to know C, for instance, to come up with a nifty way to put all of Mr. Spurworthy's work in a secret directory, introduce a few embarrassing typos into a few of his files, and mail your boss mentioning that Spurworthy seems to be

> Scripting can combine all the programs you'd use one at a time into a single script that you can use and reuse.

having a hard time lately, what with all his bad spelling. Scripting can combine all the programs you'd use one at a time into a single script that you can use and reuse. Better yet, your scripts can pipe data amongst each other if they're properly written, which means you can come up with chunks of commands that do much, much more than a single program, in a dizzying number of combinations. This scriptability and combinability gives life to another UNIX value: code reusability.

Using Text-Based Configuration Files

Another element of your typical UNIX is a reliance on text-based configuration files. People roll their eyes and think of the earlier days of Windows when everything was configured in multitudes of INI files. Unroll them, and think about the hell you go through with a single, gigantic registry file.

Thanks to your tiny filtering, inter-operating, scriptable tools, configuring UNIX and all its applications becomes a pretty simple proposition. You can pipe your configuration files through a series of commands that make the changes you need. It may seem trivial for changing only one setting, but if you're a network administrator who suddenly finds that a computer further up the line has changed its name or address and that many of your programs count on knowing where that computer is, the beauty of all those text files and all those little programs is evident.

IS THAT A COMPLETELY FREE RE-IMPLEMENTATION OF UNIX IN YOUR POCKET?

So UNIX was everywhere and people loved it. It was the de facto computing standard for many universities, and many a nerd felt the earth move courtesy of pipes, filters, and scripts. In fact, one man's love for UNIX, combined with his hatred of being kept from modifying computer software when it didn't work as he required, led to a rare thing indeed: a social movement driven by "computer people" that spawned a new way of thinking about licensing software. This new way of thinking seemingly subverted peoples' conceptions of intellectual property as a vehicle for restriction. Along the way, he also built a foundation for Linux to which it may owe everything.

There's certainly no arguing that without his work, Linux would have had a different complexion.

Richard M. Stallman, more commonly referred to as "RMS", was a member of MIT's Artificial Intelligence Lab. Among hackers, the lab is legendary for the role it played in the formative years of computing, and RMS is part of that lab's history.

THE REST OF THE STORY...

To painfully understate the next 20 years of computing history, UNIX went on to become the workhorse of the Internet and a mainstay in corporations and universities. UNIX was the glue that held the Internet together in many ways. Businesses relied on UNIX; it was the operating system of choice for many.

Unfortunately, because of its popularity and the number of ways it was re-created by many different companies, UNIX became a victim of its own success. It's a story for another day, really, but UNIX underwent a period of fragmentation. Because of conflicting attempts to establish standards, leveraging one of its traditional benefits, portability, became so difficult that the UNIX market fell into chaos. In many ways, this gave Microsoft an opening into the server market to which it continues to cling to this day.

Now is as good a time as any to delve into the whole "hacker" issue, briefly, since so many Linux enthusiasts describe themselves as hackers and so many people without cathode ray tans know (as all good law abiding citizens do) that a hacker is nothing more than a computer vandal, which makes the "real hackers" angry.

The classical definition of "hacker" varies depending on the source. The safest bet, though, seems to read something like this:

Hackers are people posessed of a love for things that aren't known. They're curious, and interested in the way things work, and often disinterested in formalism when it comes to figuring things out. Hackers are not tied to computers. Hackers aren't universally disinterested in rules and order. On the other hand, their curiosity is a driving value, and it takes high priority.

> Among hackers, the lab is legendary for the role it played in the formative years of computing, and RMS is part of that lab's history.

There are, of course, a lot of self-styled hackers wandering around these days, thanks in part to the popularity of Linux and its roots among software hackers. We once had the distinct pleasure of reading a message by somebody who had claimed to "hack" a word processor to display page previews correctly by setting the "zoom" level to 10%. What it lacked in ingenuity, one could argue it made up for in elegance...two mouse clicks et voilá! In fact, it's fashionable to be a hacker and there's woefully little in the way of peer review or certification to keep people from claiming the title. But the main thing to keep in mind is that "hacker" doesn't necessarily mean "vandal," and people claiming the title are frequently law abiding enough folk, and certainly not out to get your credit cards.

MIT's AI Lab was a gathering place for computer hackers of the benign sort and RMS was one of them. The culture of the Lab, by all popular accounts, was one of extreme openness for many years. Sharing one's software was the norm among the members of the Lab, as they helped each other solve problems or simply make their computers do, well, cool stuff. RMS relates his own sense of that community in an essay entitled "The GNU Project":

> Hackers are people posessed of a love for things that aren't known.

> *"We did not call our software 'free software,' because that term did not yet exist; but that is what it was. Whenever people from another university or a company wanted to port and use a program, we gladly let them. If you saw someone using an unfamiliar and interesting program, you could always ask to see the source code, so that you could read it, change it, or cannibalize parts of it to make a new program."*

Over the years, though, the AI Lab's open spirit began to decline, RMS himself attributing this to a number of things, including the departure of many of its members to private interests. In addition, the ever-growing computer industry was seeing to it that software stayed a proprietary, closed body of work. To a hacker, curious about the workings of things, this is a burden. To someone who believed that there was a moral imperative to share information for mutual betterment as RMS did (and does), it was intolerable.

So RMS found himself without the community of hackers he'd thrived in, and faced with a larger industry that had identified proprietary secrets as a key ingredient to ongoing growth. It wasn't the world he wanted, and he realized that:

"So I looked for a way that a programmer could do something for the good. I asked myself, was there a program or programs that I could write, so as to make a community possible once again?

The answer was clear: what was needed first was an operating system. That is the crucial software for starting to use a computer. With an operating system, you can do many things; without one, you cannot run the computer at all. With a free operating system, we could again have a community of cooperating hackers—and invite anyone to join. And anyone would be able to use a computer without starting out by conspiring to deprive his or her friends.

As an operating system developer, I had the right skills for this job. So even though I could not take success for granted, I realized that I was elected to do the job. I chose to make the system compatible with UNIX so that it would be portable, and so that UNIX users could easily switch to it. The name GNU was chosen following a hacker tradition, as a recursive acronym for 'GNU's Not Unix.'

An operating system does not mean just a kernel, barely enough to run other programs. In the 1970s, every operating system worthy of the name included command processors, assemblers, compilers, interpreters, debuggers, text editors, mailers, and much more. ITS had them, Multics had them, VMS had them, and UNIX had them. The GNU operating system would include them too."

So RMS had his mission: the creation of a free UNIX-like operating system with which he could rally the previously unnamed "free software" community once again, and restore the openness he'd enjoyed in his time at the AI Lab. He named his project "GNU," a recursive acronym that stands for 'GNU's Not Unix,'" which is not only in keeping with the fondness many hackers have for things like recursive acronyms, but the litigious nature of the computing industry of the time, which would have compelled AT&T to land on the nascent project like a ton of bricks.

IS THAT A RADICAL INVERSION OF OUR UNDERSTANDING OF COPYRIGHT LAW IN YOUR POCKET?

RMS' formula for "free software" is easy enough to follow:

- You have the freedom to run the program, for any purpose.
- You have the freedom to modify the program to suit your needs. (To make this freedom effective in practice, you must have access to the source code, since making changes in a program without having the source code is exceedingly difficult.)
- You have the freedom to redistribute copies, either gratis or for a fee.
- You have the freedom to distribute modified versions of the program, so that the community can benefit from your improvements.

Don't ever try to keep other people from getting at your improvements to the source code.

These principles are elaborated on in the GNU General Public License (known widely as "the GPL"). The GPL is designed to guarantee that once software is made "free" under the above definition, it stays that way. There are lengthy and bloody brawls over licensing esoterica in the computing community, but the gist of the GPL is simple enough to express here, until you can get to the Appendix:

Here's the software. Here's the source code. Do what you want with it. If you improve it, make sure you include all the source code to your improvements and pass it along. Don't ever try to keep other people from getting at your improvements to the source code. We can tell you to do this, because we wrote this software and these are the terms under which we're willing to let you have it.

That's a longish way of getting around to the intent of the whole exercise, which might read, in a less litigious society, more like: "Be excellent to each other."

RUNNING WITH THE DEVIL: A BRIEF DETOUR TO THE OTHER FREE RE-IMPLEMENTATION OF UNIX

RMS wasn't the only person with a thing for UNIX.

During the '70s, the University of California at Berkeley was developing their own variant, based on source code licensed from AT&T known as "BSD." Their own version was very popular...to the point that lawsuits ensued and they embarked on creating a version of UNIX that was "unencumbered" by AT&T's source code.

As one might imagine, the process of stripping all the proprietary source out of an entire operating system is a difficult undertaking, but by the time the legal dust settled and the job was done, Berkeley had given 4.4BSD-Lite to the world. From that code we have a collection of free Unixes in common use today: FreeBSD, OpenBSD, and NetBSD.

When Linux and BSD fans come around each other, there are several key differences that pop to the top once they decide to quit mincing words and pull out the brass knuckles.

Where GNU, the eventual underpinning of Linux as we'll see shortly, was built around the premise of freeing software and restoring the hacker culture to its former heights of openness, BSD was built on the notion of building a better UNIX than UNIX.

Where GNU software requires sharing of source code and redistribution of improvements, the BSD license simply says "take this and do what you like with it, just make sure we're given prominent credit. No need to give back the source."

A lot of snarling goes on over these distinctions, not to mention the occasional flare-up when someone releases a new set of test results showing that some version of BSD is much faster than Linux. The UNIX "purists" in the BSD camp also like to point out that their variant is descended from the mother source itself and that Linux is a mere "imitation."

These are fine points to make, and true for what they're worth. The vitriol you detect between the camps sometimes comes from the fact that despite their "purity," occasional technical superiority, and easier-going licenses, the BSD's haven't caught on with the same ferocity and hype that Linux has. BSD machines are out on the Internet doing the good work, but they aren't as well known. Some people attribute that to the legal issues that kept BSD-Lite from being released earlier, giving Linux a crucial lead. Others say that the nature of the communities surrounding each is radically different, with BSD's being more closed to newbies and outsiders.

> When Linux and BSD fans come around each other, there are several key differences that pop to the top once they decide to quit mincing words and pull out the brass knuckles.

In the end, it's irrelevant. For people who love the essentials of UNIX, both provide a good option at no cost. The differences that make choosing one or the other are hard to pin down, since both the BSDs and Linux are close to ubiquitous across hardware platforms and have different strengths depending on the needs of the user.

If there's a lesson to be taken from this and earlier parts of our narrative, it's simply that UNIX, for a variety of reasons, has enjoyed an unprecedented following. Even when operating systems were at their most closed and inaccessible, people have been working on ways to preserve key pieces of the UNIX experience. It says quite a bit about how important the UNIX legacy is to quite a few people

> **B**SD machines are out on the Internet doing the good work, but they aren't as well known.

that we felt a little guilty only covering four UNIX variants, knowing full well that there are many, many more.

THE BIRTH OF LINUX

So in 1991, whether anyone realized it or not, the computing world was primed for an operating system that would bring the power and flexibility of UNIX to the desktop PC's that were becoming more and more common and inexpensive. Then Linus Torvalds posted a message...

```
From: torvalds@klaava.Helsinki.FI (Linus Benedict Torvalds)

Newsgroups: comp.os.minix

Subject: What would you like to see most in minix?

Summary: small poll for my new operating system

Message-ID: <1991Aug25.205708.9541@klaava.Helsinki.FI>

Date: 25 Aug 91 20:57:08 GMT

Organization: University of Helsinki

Hello everybody out there using minix -

I'm doing a (free) operating system (just a hobby, won't be
big and professional like gnu) for 386(486) AT clones. This
has been brewing; since april, and is starting to get
ready. I'd like any feedback on things people like/dislike
```

```
in minix, as my OS resembles it somewhat (same physical
layout of the file-system (due to practical reasons) among
other things). I've currently ported bash(1.08) and
gcc(1.40),and things seem to work.This implies that I'll
get something practical within a few months, andI'd like to
know what features most people would want. Any suggestions
are welcome, but I won't promise I'll implement them :-)

Linus (torvalds@kruuna.helsinki.fi)

PS. Yes - it's free of any minix code, and it has a multi-
threaded fs. It is NOT protable (uses 386 task switching
etc), and it probably never will support anything other
than AT-harddisks, as that's all I have :-(.
```

The "Minix" he was referring to is a variant on UNIX (still in use today), written by Andy Tannenbaum, a professor of computer science and author of some well-regarded books on the subject. Minix provided something that acted a lot like UNIX on the more and more popular Intel-based computers, but it had limitations.

By virtue of licensing and some of the earliest tools ported to the fledgling operating system, Linux and GNU were closely tied.

Linus, reacting to those limitations, took a small bit of working code he had and used Minix as a guideline and supporting infrastructure in the earliest stages of his project. As his mail mentioned, he'd already begun the work of porting some of the tools Richard Stallman's GNU project had provided (Bash is the shell in most common use on Linux systems and gcc is a program for compiling programs from source code.) For the most part, though, what he had wasn't so much an operating sytem as it was a simple kernel: the part of an operating system that controls the most basic functions of a computer and provides a way for programs to interact with the hardware (in the form of input, output, networking, or other functions) and each other.

Initially, Linus had also intended to release his kernel under a non-commercial license, allowing any and all use by all takers except for businesses who'd use it for profit. He changed his mind eventually, and released it under the GPL originated by RMS and the Free Software Foundation. By virtue of licensing and some of the earliest tools ported to the fledgling operating system, Linux and GNU were closely tied.

With a second message, Linus announced that he was releasing Linux to the world:

From: torvalds@klaava.Helsinki.FI (Linus Benedict Torvalds)

Newsgroups: comp.os.minix

Subject: Free minix-like kernel sources for 386-AT

Message-ID: <1991Oct5.054106.4647@klaava.Helsinki.FI>

Date: 5 Oct 91 05:41:06 GMT

Organization: University of Helsinki

Do you pine for the nice days of minix-1.1, when men were men and wrote their own device drivers? Are you without a nice project and just dying to cut your teeth on a OS you can try to modify for your; needs? Are you finding it frustrating when everything works on minix? No more all-nighters to get a nifty program working? Then this post might be just for you :-)

As I mentioned a month(?) ago, I'm working on a free version of a minix-lookalike for AT-386 computers. It has finally reached the stage where it's even usable (though may not be depending on what you want), and I am willing to

```
put out the sources for wider distribution. It is just
version 0.02 (+1 (very small) patch already), but I've
successfully run bash/gcc/gnu-make/gnu-sed/compress etc
under it.
```

```
Sources for this pet project of mine can be found at
nic.funet.fi (128.214.6.100) in the directory /pub/OS/
Linux. The directory also contains some README-file and a
couple of binaries to work under linux (bash, update and
gcc, what more can you ask for :-). Full kernel source is
provided, as no minix code has been used. Library sources
are only partially free, so that cannot be distributed
currently. The system is able to compile "as-is" and has
been known to work. Heh. Sources to the binaries (bash and
gcc) can be found at the same place in /pub/gnu.
```

So, with a very basic operating system built from Linus' kernel and a handful of GNU tools, Linux was born. It would be appropriately dramatic and narration-minded to leave it at that, but it's important to note one element of the union of Linux (the kernel) with GNU (the attempt to build a Free Software implementation of UNIX) that continues to stir up some conflict from time to time, depending on whether it's a slow news day or not.

> So, with a very basic operating system built from Linus' kernel and a handful of GNU tools, Linux was born.

It had always been Richard Stallman's intent to build a complete operating system, which involves not only software tools, but a kernel. The GNU project's attempts to build that kernel were moving fairly slowly (they continue to this day with the ambitious "HURD" project), and with the arrival of Linus' kernel there was no longer a need to wait: GNU tools could be mated to the Linux kernel, and an operating system was ready to go.

RMS and many others have long argued that since the operating system most people simply call Linux was largely dependent on GNU tools (and since it continues to depend on GNU tools for much of its basic functionality), it's most appropriate to call it "GNU/Linux." RMS says it's giving credit where it's due, others say it's trying to take too much credit when there are plenty of other elements that make up Linux (the operating system) that have nothing to do with GNU at all.

There are a couple of elements at work that have given this debate more life than you might think it would enjoy otherwise:

For one, RMS knows in his heart of hearts that he is right on this issue. People who set out to rewrite an entire operating system because it's the

> **R**MS knows in his heart of hearts that he is right on this issue.

moral thing to do aren't given to backing down on any point, no matter how trivial a point of nomenclature it is to a less involved populace. He's widely respected (as he should be) and a large number of people think his argument resonates.

For two, an equal number of people think he's wrong on this issue, and argue that even if GNU tools are important, they aren't indispensable.

For three, an even larger number than the other two groups combined have no opinion and really don't want to use the phrase "GNU/Linux" where "Linux" will suffice to convey what you're talking about when it comes to "that operating system that Linus Torvalds is associated with."

We've copped out to common usage in this book, but both authors are certain Linux needed GNU tools in its early days to get where it is today. There are some people who have other issues with Richard Stallman and the Free Software movement in general who will disagree: We think they're wrong and believe it serves little to downplay the importance of GNU to the Linux operating system because of issues outside simple history.

LINUX ON THE RISE

There have been a lot of attempts to explain why Linux grew in popularity as rapidly as it did. Only ten years after those first messages announcing it, plenty of people have tried to sum the phenomenon up while it's still underway, and there's no doubt that in twenty years people who write about operating systems will see the whole thing differently. But it's pretty clear that there are a few things that contributed.

First, Linux provided exactly what its creator wanted: a UNIX-like operating system that ran on the Intel-based PC hardware that was growing in popularlity during the early '90s. UNIX was very popular at universities, and the alternative on the most common PC's of the time was Microsoft's MS-DOS, which, though largely derivative of "serious" operating systems in some of its elements, was never built with hackers in mind. Students and computer scientists were picking up PC's for their homes more and more during this period as it became a less than $1000 proposition to own fairly powerful hardware, and they wanted a bit of UNIX on those machines: not something designed for consumers with all the inherent design compromises.

Second, Linux was not only UNIX-like, it was hackable. People could get into the workings of the operating system and make it better if they so chose, or at least have access to the people writing the software to ask for improvements. Looking back over the storied history of UNIX (20 years old at this point), loss of the UNIX source code to litigation and corporate imperatives had been a real blow to many, who had cut their teeth on poring over the very blueprints of an operating system. Linux, though crude, restored some of what they'd lost, and it held the promise of at least providing something they could mold into something bigger and better. In the ensuing years, another related element of Linux's popularity was derived from its ability to run on ubiquitous hardware, which is that it runs very well on hardware others might be ready to discard. Old 486's make great Linux servers, handling mail and file sharing with aplomb while many other commercial products have long since stopped trying to work on all but fairly new equipment.

Third, the arrival of Linux was closely matched to the spread of the Internet. Though around for as long as UNIX, the Net was becoming a daily reality for more and more people. It became easier and easier to download software, communicate,

> Second, Linux was not only UNIX-like, it was hackable.

and collaborate over the Internet with each passing day. By the early '90s, Net connected terminals in student dorm rooms were far from uncommon, and even a university employee could easily connect via a modem to their employer's computers on campus. The development community that sprang up around Linux was global, and the Net held it together.

After the initial flurry of interest in Linux, another interesting facet of Linux culture developed: the *distribution*.

One of the true pains of getting a working Linux machine going was downloading all the needed bits and compiling them, or even just getting them onto a machine. People answered this problem with distributions, which were simply all the pieces of a Linux-based operating system copied onto floppies or CD-ROM's and, well, distributed. Because Linux and the bulk of the software was available under the FSF's GPL (which provided for free and open redistribution of software provided its source code was made available), anybody could download it, set it up in such a manner that it worked out-of-the-box for most people, and redistribute it as a "distribution."

Initially, some of these were crude lash-ups, designed merely to get Linux onto a machine. Others, though, became more and more polished as Linux evangelists began to realize that the easier it was for a second, less expert tier of computer enthusiasts to get Linux up and running, the further it would spread.

Some companies formed around the business of selling Linux distributions, offering incentives to pay for something that could be had for free in the form of convenience and even support via phone or e-mail if something went wrong. Of the current distributions, Slackware is perhaps the one left today with the longest lineage back to the early days of Linux, but in terms of Linux's time on the Earth, Red Hat (the first widely-successful commercial distribution) and Debian (a distribution run entirely by volunteers) are both looking "long in the tooth."

> **A**n early notion of some commercial Linux distributors was that their profit would come from support for installation and administration of Linux computers.

An early notion of some commercial Linux distributors was that their profit would come from support for installation and administration of Linux computers. In shorthand, they'd make money selling shrink-wrapped, pre-packaged products that the general public would feel more secure with than a simple download and no phone support. This notion survived for quite a few years, relatively speaking. We'll see shortly that it probably won't survive the end of 2001.

The Open-Source Explosion

Linux was gaining mindshare at an incredible rate, thanks to distributions, be they companies or not, it was becoming more and more accessible. Their efforts certainly put Linux in easy reach of any moderately motivated hobbiest who was willing to read all the documentation and figure out how to boot his computer from a floppy disk or CD-ROM.

At the same time, though, some in the Linux community were beginning to identify what they considered a problem: The label that RMS had applied to his attempt to reengineer the way we all thought about software, "free software," with all the ambiguity inherent in the English word "free." Stallman never meant that software was to "cost nothing," but rather had coined the phrase to represent the freedom of the source code itself to be copied and redistributed. Among many computer enthusiasts, though, "free software" often carried the connotation of being something a developer wouldn't be able to sell if she wanted to. "Freeware" was typically viewed as low quality or incomplete, something companies gave away to prove to you that you needed to buy something better.

Further, despite the fact many had benefited from Stallman's GNU project, there was a growing sense that the implicit politics of the Free Software Foundation would scare off corporate adoption of Linux, thanks to its language, which less charitable people would characterize as "communistic" in the very least charitable sense of the word.

When you pause to consider how much UNIX hackers loath rebuilding any wheel, what seemed like a constant reiteration of the FSF definition of "free software" was becoming truly irritating to many Linux advocates, who believed Linux had a place as a "serious" operating system if only it could shake off the notion of the less informed that it was a cheap freebie of disposable value.

The Joy of Tech   by Nitrozac and Snaggy

At Earth OS Fest, everyone enjoyed dressing up as their
favorite GNU/Linux celebrity, except for Zap, who always
seemed to get stuck playing Richard Stallman.

One person key to the eventual movement to market this
notion out of existence was Eric S. Raymond, who, like RMS,
goes by his initials. ESR was known for several projects he maintained, including a piece of software for downloading mail (called
"fetchmail"), his dictionary of hackish language (called "The
New Hacker's Dictionary" in its print form and "The Jargon
File" in its online version), and his contributions to a file that
helps UNIX machines understand how to talk to a number of
computer terminals from the days when "dumb terminals" were
the primary way to communicate with large, multi-user computers. ESR is also a self-styled anthropologist of the hacker community, and a "tribal historian" for the same.

According to Raymond, what was required was not a con-
tinual effort to rehabilitate the negative connotations of "free
software," but to invent a new marketing approach. Further, his

own politics were such that the language found throughout the Free Software Foundation's licensing and manifestos was disagreeable; he sought to depoliticize free software.

Along with another prominent figure in the early Linux community, Bruce Perens (former project leader of the Debian distribution), and a collection of others, ESR led a push to market the name *open-source software* as a new way of thinking about the sort of code sharing in which free-software advocates had been engaging in up to that point. They presented the "Open-Source Definition," which created a set of criteria by which software could be determined to be open-source, and monitored the many licenses under which software could be released to determine their compatibility with the Open-Source Definition.

Although the Open-Source Definition clearly paid due respect to the FSF's GPL, open-source supporters also placed a heavy emphasis on the development methodology elements of the Linux and open-source worlds. They played down the political beliefs of early free-software advocates in favor of expressing the benefits of open source as a set of design paradigms that helped eliminate bugs and provided more secure software through the massive peer review of an extended community of hackers.

> ESR is also a self-styled anthropologist of the hacker community, and a "tribal historian" for the same.

The effects of this are still felt today. Whereas many companies would have been revolted at the thought of "giving away their intellectual property," they took to the idea of letting many people work on a project in parallel. That way, the collective creativity of those involved would expose bugs more rapidly and provide solutions to problems more quickly.

Of late, this has led to several takes on open source. These range from "companies giving away all their source code, allowing the developer community to do what it will," to "gated communities," wherein companies maintain tight control of their software. These gated communities admit few, if any, outsiders into their development process, while trying to re-create the organizational model that has served many free/open-source software projects well.

In addition to promoting open-source software, ESR went to work on a series of papers that he hoped would encapsulate the defining characteristics of open-source software development. The most famous was the first, entitled "The Cathedral and the Bazaar," (often referred to as "CatB"), after what Raymond identified as the primary metaphors dominating software development.

> Briefly, software prepared by proprietary interests is typically handled in a "cathedral" fashion, with a single, small team working in isolation to develop the project.

Briefly, software prepared by proprietary interests is typically handled in a "cathedral" fashion, with a single, small team working in isolation to develop the project. The "bazaar" model, on the other hand, involves a large collection of developers working on the parts of the project that most interest them. The bazaar model is characterized by a "take all comers" spirit that pays less attention to the arbitrary definitions of corporate affiliations or workplace product groups and more to the individual merit of the developer approaching a project: If you can contribute meaningfully and gain the respect of those maintaining a project, you can work on it.

CatB was a popular piece of work. It had the benefit of drawing examples from an actual "bazaar style" project (fetchmail), and it summarized in very short form what all the fuss was about with open source. It had an impact on executives at Netscape that sealed its importance when they announced in 1998 that they were releasing the source code to their browser software to the world. Some pegged Netscape's "gift" as more of an opportunistic attempt to exploit the buzz enjoyed by open-source software, but the impact of the move was felt in terms of enhanced prestige for open-source software. If a corporation as prominent as Netscape was willing to try out this development model, maybe there was something to it.

THE LINUX STOCK ORGY AND *LINUX TODAY* MANIA

In the wake of the notoriety Mozilla lent to open-source software, the media began to pay attention to Linux in a way it hadn't before. People could understand what Netscape was, and some would stick around to listen to the new development model it was using. In turn, they were often directed to Linux as "the most successful adherent to open-source methodologies."

> People could understand what Netscape was, and some would stick around to listen to the new development model it was using.

Seemingly overnight, public awareness of the operating system exploded, and a few companies began to position themselves to go public and make some money. Red Hat, the distribution company, and VA Linux, a hardware manufacturer, both had stellar initial public offerings of stock (IPO's) that turned some of their employees and early investors into overnight paper millionaires. The riotous atmosphere surrounding these two companies, fueled by an ever-booming stock market and increasing buzz about Linux itself as it became better suited to more and more tasks, made them seem like the surest bets going.

Other companies began to pile on. If they couldn't offer stock, they just took to announcing "Linux support" or "the open sourcing" of key software. For half a year, Linux stocks rose and rose, and then the bottom fell out. Companies eager to break into public trading withdrew IPO's as analysts began to ask hard questions about how Linux companies would make money, and companies already on the market suffered calamitous drops, going from highs of over $200 a share to lows hovering around $5 a share. A few smaller companies nearly went under, and in the case of Corel, a company that embraced Linux and created its own distribution to complement its WordPerfect product, sold off big parts of their Linux operations.

> **If they couldn't offer stock, they just took to announcing "Linux support" or "the open sourcing" of key software.**

The hardest question people were asking was simply "If this thing is free, and everybody's learning how to use it, and it's getting easier and easier to install (one version allowed you to play Tetris while waiting for Linux to finish installation) where's the revenue for installation support going to come from?" Others wanted to know how long hardware companies specializing in Linux would hold up once giants like Dell and Compaq began to adopt it, as they were at ever-increasing levels.

In many ways, the answer has come from the companies themselves in the form of realignments around new models built to earn money from providing "services" instead of "support." Where companies once proposed to make money with phone support, they now offer remote network management and security auditing. Where it was once fashionable to think simply packaging a lot of extra software on a CD was enough, companies are beginning to realize the real money lies in contracts with giant corporations adopting Linux for use in their day-to-day operations.

So we're left with a wrap-up of our brief history of Linux, back on the convention floor in New York.

The stock hysteria has died, Linux has gone from being a hobbiest's toy to a serious operating system companies are willing to depend on for critical operations. It's also turned up in tiny, embedded devices that control industrial machines, and in handheld computers. The same year that some Linux companies went from booming darlings of the tech industry to near-bankrupt failures, IBM has announced it wants to invest $1 billion in Linux development, and other companies are joining in.

In other words: Linux, born outside of commercial interest, may well outlive many of the first generation of companies that sought to make it a commercial phenomenon. It's a mistake to believe that its success is tied into how well it does in the stock market, or even how well companies pushing it as a sure-fire way to make money fare.

> In other words: Linux, born outside of commercial interest, may well outlive many of the first generation of companies that sought to make it a commercial phenomenon.

As much, though, as Linux is becoming a corporate phenomenon, it's also still a "people" phenomenon. It's great for companies, sure, but it's also wonderful for people. For every company that stands up and proclaims that Linux is useful for something after all, there are hundreds and thousands of people driving its use on personal computers around the world. "The Linux community" might have once been a handful of far-flung programmers working toward the goal of having UNIX on their new 386's. Now it's a far-flung collection of users and hackers of all sorts who use Linux every day. This community is what makes it a joy.

CHAPTER

2

Are You Experienced?

FALLING OFF THE TURNIP TRUCK

If a transcript had been made of my second day with UNIX, it might have read something like this:

[Phone Rings]

Voice: UCS technical support, can I help you?

Me: Erm, I need help with making an alias...I forget all the UNIX commands and want ones like come with DOS.

Voice: [muffled sigh] I'll pass you over to the UNIX guy.

[sound of phone being cupped]

Muffled Voice: Hey. Someone wants to go back to their precious DOS commands on one of the Ultrix machines. You wanna take this?

Faint Voice in Background: Yeah...

[sound of phone being handed over]

Me: Uh, hello? I was just calling about how to set up aliases...

Voice: Yeah. Which shell?

Me: The DOS one.

Voice: No. Which shell in UNIX?

Me: The one it came with.

Voice: [quiet sigh] OK. You're going to have to edit a file called dotcasherk, so open that up with vi.

Me: Spell *dotcasherk*.

Voice: dot cash are see

Me: Cash as in money?

Voice: No! No! Sorry…no…see ess aytch.

Me: The last part? ee are kay?

Voice: [muffled] Sweet Jesus, we have a live one. [louder] No. Sorry…it's dot see ess aytch are see.

Me: OK. [typing and spelling out loud] D…O…T…C…

Voice: Stop. Just stop. That's a period at the beginning. Sorry. So it's PERIOD C S H R C.

Me: Oh. OK

Me: [types vi .cshrc]

Voice: Good. Now all you have to do is add the alias. For a reminder, we'll use a pound sign and a comment so you remember what you did. So type the pound sign on the key over the number three—

Me: [presses #]

Terminal: *beep*

Me: [presses # again]

Terminal: *beep*

Me: [presses # yet again]

Terminal: *beep*

Voice: Did you, uh, press the I key?

Me: No, you told me to press the # key.

Voice: So you don't know how to use vi?

Me: Uh…no.

Voice: You have to press the I key to insert text.

Me: Before I can type I have to press the I key?

Voice: Yes.

Me: That's stupid.

Voice: I know. I use Emacs.

Me: What's Eemix? Is that like Unix without dotcasherk?

Voice: No. Sorry I brought it up.

Me: OK And I just type alias ls 'dir' and I'm OK?

Voice: How did you know that?

Me: Someone put it in this file already.

Voice: Then you're golden. Have a nice day.

Me: Can I make an alias to not type I?

Voice: [dial tone]

By the time I got around to learning how to read my e-mail, there was a harried and terse missive from "Staff" explaining to all and sundry that their friendly support people had taken great efforts to prepare an attractive, beige guide to everything we'd ever want to know about UNIX, including how to make it act more like DOS if we'd just bother to read it. These e-mails came out periodically, each sounding as bitter and frustrated as the last.

> **A**s a thing becomes popular, well, more people have to learn it, right?

Whenever you get an e-mail like that from your own tech-support people, it's the sound of a newbie editing his first configuration file. If it makes you feel any better, if you happen to be a Linux newbie, there are lots of people in the same boat. As a thing becomes popular, well, more people have to learn it, right? The operative word there is *learn*. And it's not getting any easier.

Somewhere along the line, someone realized that much the same way people gravitate toward the comics in their Sunday paper, they gravitate to other brightly colored, simplistic things, like Windows and Macintoshes. Apple ought to be congratulated: They

Support Group for Linux Newbies.

realized that a brightly colored and simplistic operating system is best represented by a brightly colored and simplistic case for the computer it comes in. Witness the iMac.

So although Linux has plenty of options when it comes to getting work done with a pretty GUI, it's still different from what most people are used to. There is, as people like to say, "a learning curve," and most of us start at the bottom.

A FEW WORDS ABOUT "THE LINUX COMMUNITY"

Like just about anything in life with a following, Linux has something of a community around it. In fact, there probably isn't a more frequently used phrase in all of Linuxdom (besides, possibly, "No, you don't have to reboot once a day anymore") than "the Linux community." You'll come across it if you read almost any Linux-related Web site or spend any length of time on IRC chatting with Linux enthusiasts.

Community is one of those words that's fallen into sad misuse because it once said so much to people. We heard *community* and thought of a close-knit group of people who knew each other pretty well, shared many of the same values, and maybe, if we were thrown back to prehistoric times, would take up sharpened sticks to help fight off the people from over the hill.

Now there are communities everywhere. Companies talk about building communities of customers, which is meant to make us feel warm and fuzzy while we're being sold something. Take Jeep, with its special "camp" where proud Jeep owners can gather and bask in the mutual glow of the shared experience of...er...owning a Jeep.

> **C**ommunity is one of those words that's fallen into sad misuse because it once said so much to people.

Or consider Internet companies busy building online communities of users. You know, in case we're ever thrown back to prehistoric times. That way, the America Online clan will take up sharp sticks against the Mindspring clan, while the poor members of the CompuServe clan, nearly wiped out in the plague, huddle in the branches. Which side are you going to be on?

If Microsoft tried to talk about a community of Windows users, we'd have a pretty good laugh and get on with the day. By virtue of its ubiquity, it's hard to imagine that Windows users share much more in common than, well, that Start button they use to turn the computer off. But even if Microsoft products weren't everywhere, there'd be another bar to defining the body of people using Windows as a community, which is that very few of them exercise any real control over what Windows does, and few of them have any stake in how Windows turns out.

Windows is owned by a single company. Unless you get a job there and get a few promotions, you won't ever have a lot of say in the way Windows behaves. Windows, for most people, is just *there*.

Despite the fact that *community* is such an abused word, aimed at our heartstrings in the hopes of getting us to reach for our pocketbooks, communities survive, and Linux has one. The problem is, like any community, it has its share of boobs and self-appointed spokespersons who will tell you what the community wants, or how the community feels about things. What they really mean is "What me and my Linux-using friends want" or "What seems to be the prevailing opinion on Slashdot."

The fact is, there are all sorts of interests and agendas at work in the Linux world. If you're just a user who never does much but surf the Web and write e-mail, you won't much notice or care about the community. If you're a programmer who's participating in a free software project of some sort, you'll care a little more because the way Linux works from day to day will have an effect on your code. If you're in business and want to use Linux as a file or Web server, or as an inexpensive workstation operating system, you'll have your own set of concerns about the direction of Linux. If you hack on the Linux kernel itself, you'll also have some ideas about what's good for Linux. There are also companies with staggering amounts of resources who have invested programming talent and plain old money into building Linux who have their agendas for it, such as IBM, which announced in late 2000 that it had a $1 billion war chest set aside for Linux development and products.

By virtue of its ubiquity, it's hard to imagine that Windows users share much more in common than, well, that Start button they use to turn the computer off.

In other words, there's no homogenous group of people who make up the Linux community. Despite that, there are people others respect and listen to by virtue of their talent, accomplishments, contributions, or simple self-promotion. As you learn your way around the Linux community, you'll come to recognize who seems to have the ear of other Linux users and developers. You'll also recognize that few of these leaders are universally agreed upon, and that some seem to have conflicting agendas.

In the end, because Linux is free software, it's your responsibility to define how you approach it and what you want from it. You should never be afraid to speak up about what you'd like to see Linux do. For every person who violently disagrees with you, there's probably another user who agrees. You should also keep in mind that because Linux is free software, the ultimate responsibility for making it do what you want rests with you. Free software isn't about cost; it's about having the right to work with software so it suits your needs.

> In the end, because Linux is free software, it's your responsibility to define how you approach it and what you want from it.

ASCENDING TO PENGUIN NIRVANA (OR, AT LEAST, LEARNING HOW TO GET GOOD WITH LINUX)

It's pretty easy to get help with your Linux problems without knowing anybody in particular. There's a wealth of Linux-oriented Web sites, IRC channels, mailing lists, and newsgroups that handle massive amounts of traffic per day as more and more people pile on the Linux train. There's usually someone out there who just likes to be helpful who will answer a specific query in very little time.

At the same time, because there are so many new Linux users, and because Linux itself can be very diverse from distribution to distribution, individualized help is a must. Red Hat and

Debian, for instance, do the same thing (run the Linux kernel and many of the same apps), but they have small gotchas and individual quirks that make it hard to track down problems if you're more used to one over the other.

It's also important to remember that the people hanging out online are usually doing so because they like Linux and want to help you like it, too. They're doing it for free, though, so you aren't always going to get a fast answer (though you usually will), and they've all got different perspectives (so you'll likely get a bunch of fast answers that all sound different).

So here goes. When you choose a Linux distribution, you've automatically made a choice that will cause your Linux machine to behave differently from most other machines running Linux. Helpful people will tell you how to make your distribution work. Unhelpful people will use words like "broken" and "brain dead" to describe what you've just invested money, download time, and sweat to install. Getting free technical support is like going to the doctor: Second opinions are welcome. Just don't write the group you queried and say "joe_snuffy@penguinhax0rs.com told me my distribution sucks, but I think he's a moron!" He may be right, and others may reinforce his analysis—in which case you look ungrateful. Alternatively, he may be wrong—in which case you'll have embarrassed someone who at least thought he was being helpful, even if he could benefit from the indirect application of a clue-stick in his vicinity.

> Getting free technical support is like going to the doctor: Second opinions are welcome.

You'll find during your early time with Linux that it's radically different from whatever other OS you're used to. Because it's grown out of a computing tradition that goes back 30 years,

Linux has evolved a different set of behaviors than Macintosh and Windows computers. People who love computers will have a less difficult time than those who "just use them," because they tend to look at computing tasks as an abstraction. Much the same way people who take the time to really understand their native tongue have an easier time understanding a new language, computer lovers have an easier time picking up the "grammar" of a new operating system. Linux is no exception.

If your head's spinning from figuring out how to make something work, and you're cursing GNOME or KDE because it's missing a button or icon you're used to from your Windows days, remember that the missing button isn't really the problem. The problem is figuring out what the button did. Otherwise, you're just complaining because those damnable Spaniards have a different word for *umbrella*.

Once you start thinking like this, it's easier to express what you want

> **P**eople who love computers will have a less difficult time than those who "just use them," because they tend to look at computing tasks as an abstraction.

to the volunteer army of Penguinistas out there waiting to help. "Windows calls dialing a modem to connect to the Internet *dial-up networking*. What's the equivalent in Linux?" goes a lot further to getting help fast than "I can't use Netscape!" Similarly, "Is there anything like WordPerfect for Linux?" is easier to respond to than "I can't write a letter!" (As a matter of fact, there is a version of WordPerfect for Linux—and a bunch of other word processors, too.)

Once you've used all the online help to get to the bottom of the problems that keep you from accomplishing day-to-day tasks,

> Serious Linux Fu involves what the enthusiasts refer to as "building up your sweat equity."

you're faced with a broader issue, which is really learning how to think like a Linux user. Managing to use Netscape successfully or check your mail is, Grasshopper, like being told you get to study at the Shaolin Temple starting next week. Serious Linux Fu involves what the enthusiasts refer to as "building up your sweat equity."

SWEAT EQUITY: WHAT WE MEAN WHEN WE SAY "JUST FIGURE IT OUT"

My ears were burning as I typed that last sentence. As I sit here, it's early 2001, and if the last two years in the Linux world have been about anything in the minds of adoring fans everywhere, they've been about "ease of use" and "enhancing the end-user experience."

Hackers all over the globe have been coordinating their efforts and coding into the night to produce high-quality, user-friendly desktops and applications that will make Linux a snap to use for everybody from the neighbor kid who's never known anything but Nintendo to the grandma down the street. And among those who can't write a line of code, an overnight crop of amateur pundits has sprung up. They sniff the headlines like bloodhounds in an attempt to divine the exact moment when people will troop into their front yards with garbage cans filled to the brim with Microsoft products to usher in the Age of the Penguin.

In the meantime, serious Linux users know that to get to the good stuff—all the power and flexibility and speed you've heard about—you've got to work at it some. There aren't many things you can't do with Linux, but most of the good stuff is rooted in

The Joy of Tech   by Nitrozac and Snaggy

Finally, Joe was officially recognized for all the hours he spent
on IRC telling new Linux users to figure it out for themselves.

that 30-year-old design we talked about a little earlier, and you've
got to do a little digging.

Take this example: I've been following the Mozilla Project
for a few years now. Briefly, Mozilla's the Web browser formerly
known as *Netscape Communicator*. Just before being gobbled
up by AOL like an undersized prawn, the good people at Netscape
decided to release the source code to their browser to all the
world. Linux and open-source enthusiasts flocked to the project,
hoping that, given a good head start with true, commercial-quality
source, they'd have Microsoft and Internet Explorer beaten back
into their rightful 30% share of the market in no time.

Reality fell a little short of the enthusiasm, though, and
Mozilla is now, more than two years later, up to version 0.7—
which is to say that it's over half done, but closer to the halfway
mark than it is to the finish line.

Being a good citizen of the open-source community, though, I've followed Mozilla along, always checking to see if a bug I find has been reported first (they always are) and lending moral support by occasionally putting on a moderate tone and praising the project for the vast progress it's made. After all, if you can't code, you troubleshoot. And if you can't troubleshoot, you shout encouragement from the sideline or announce loudly that you knew it was a bad idea to begin with.

Mozilla wasn't a bad idea to begin with, though. True, some of the early developers on the project have left in a huff. Plus, a lot of early cheerleaders have backed away because they embarrassed themselves with claims that Mozilla would prove once and for all the validity of the open-source model without realizing the sorts of challenges a project that big poses. But the fact is, Mozilla does get a little better each day. If you buy this book hot off the presses, you can download Mozilla while it's still in its "pre 1.0" days and follow along. If you buy this book after it's into its tenth printing and you're kicking yourself because I once asked you for a small loan with high interest and now...you can download Mozilla and marvel at the thought that it ever had a single bug.

> After all, if you can't code, you troubleshoot.

In the past seven months or so, despite its rough start, Mozilla has gotten so good that I've taken to downloading the nightly builds. A *build* of a project is when someone takes the source code of a program and compiles it. When a project like Mozilla is under heavy development, it's not uncommon for builds to be put up on the Internet for download on a regular basis even if the project isn't quite "soup," as they say. In Mozilla's case, a new build is posted once a night just before midnight.

So, there are a few ways to go about downloading something on a regular basis. The first method is what we'll call the "really boring and stupid method." The really boring and stupid method involves getting up every morning, logging on to the computer, visiting the Mozilla site, downloading the latest nightly build, unpacking it from its zip file (well...this is Linux, so we have *tarballs*), and installing it. With practice (and a really, really fast Internet connection), you can do this in a little under two minutes.

The cost of the really boring and stupid way can be expressed in a couple of ways:

- **It costs time.** In seven months of getting that nightly build every single night, I lose two minutes a day. That's an hour a month. That's seven hours off my life. In seven hours I could have gone for a day hike, learned how to conjugate the most common Spanish verbs, read the better part of a hefty book, or actually gotten in a full night's sleep. If Mozilla doesn't hurry up and get done, I'm facing a bleak future of missed opportunities because I'm hunched over my keyboard every morning downloading stuff.

- **It costs pride.** I am not a nerd in any sense that gets me into the best nerd parties (of course, with the downturn in the tech industry, there aren't many of those anymore), but I've got a nerd's pride. It pains me to think that I'm doing this stuff by hand when there's gotta be a way to do it automatically.

So, spurred by a desire to save those precious moments of running through the flowers barefoot, and by a deep shame for actually knowing there's a way to save those precious moments automatically through the miracle of 30-year-old technology, I set out to find a solution.

It's pretty easy to plot out what has to happen:

1. I've got to go get the program and download it.
2. I've got to unpack the archive the program arrives in.
3. Since Mozilla's nightly builds are sometimes broken, I've got to make sure there's a way to keep the previous night's build so I don't manage to automate myself out of a browser.
4. I've got to do a few things to install the program.
5. I've got to do all this before 6:30 a.m., which is when I tell myself I'm going to wake up every morning.

So…what to do?

The first option is obviously to buy a monkey—a very clever monkey—and teach him. Sadly, I have cats. I know intuitively that monkeys, even technical monkeys, and cats don't get along.

The second option is to figure out what tools are at my disposal and cobble something together, even if it's not elegant or clever. All I want to do, essentially, is make the computer type the same stuff I would if I could be bothered on a set schedule.

Since most programmers are, by definition, lazier than all sin, it's a sure bet that the average download program has some way of being told to do something specific without someone being around all the time to tell it—otherwise it wouldn't have been programmed by a programmer, and that's simply not likely. It's part of the UNIX philosophy, to allude to a much-abused and much-cited concept, that programs be easily integrated into scripts and pipes—that is, strings of commands that feed each other input in a sequence. So it's likely that the program that handles the heart of what I'm trying to do, an FTP program, will be scriptable in some way.

So I ask around, being careful to avoid phrasing my questions in the form of "Help! I can't download Mozilla automatically and that means I've lost seven hours of my life this year alone!"

Instead, I ask questions like "Is there a program that I can use to download files automatically instead of having to log in to an FTP server by hand?"

A helpful answer will arrive soon. In this case, it's a program called ncftp. Unlike plain old ftp, ncftp lets you tell it which file you want to download in one swoop, goes out and gets it, and exits. Perfect. I spend a few minutes reading all about ncftp in the helpful manual (which I can read by typing `man ncftp` on my Linux console), and I'm on to the next challenge: doing the whole thing on a set time.

I could type "Help! If I can't do downloads at 5 a.m., I might as well go back to the same practices that have cost me seven hours of my life already this year!" But that's a no-no. Instead, I type "Anybody know how to make a program run at a set time every day?"

A helpful answer will arrive soon. In this case, it's a program called cron. Cron allows you to create a schedule of programs that must happen at a set time (within a minute of their scheduled time, which is close enough for me) at all sorts of intervals, from hourly to daily to weekly to monthly. Perfect. I spend a few minutes reading all about cron in the helpful manual (not as easy as ncftp—there are man page entries for cron, crontab, and crontab again, because there's a program called cron, a file called crontab, and a program called crontab that you use to edit what's in the file called crontab). I learn that by making a line that looks like the following in a file called crontab that I can at least download a copy of the latest Mozilla:

```
0 6 * * * ncftpget -v ftp://ftp.mozilla.org/↵
pub/mozilla/nightly/latest/mozilla-i686-pc-↵
linux-gnu.tar.gz
```

Once more, I don't begin any messages with "Help!" and I ask "I've got a copy of Mozilla that I want to try out, but I don't know how to use it. It came in a file called mozilla-i686-pc-linux-gnu.tar.gz." And the helpful answer will come that, in most cases, to unpack a file like that (referred to as a *tarball*, or, more technically, a *gzipped archive*), all I have to do is type something like

```
tar xzf mozilla-i686-pc-linux-gnu.tar.gz
```

So I've got the part about getting the file down, I know how to do it on a schedule, and I know what to do with it when I get it. The next thing to do is to write a quick script to do all this and I'm on my way. I go through much the same process as the one I just undertook, only this time I'm learning to write scripts in Linux, with lots of helpful people offering sound advice and helpful tips. Maybe, after seven or eight hours of research, I'm ready to, er, save seven or eight hours over the next few months. Glorious progress!

> Part of the joy of Linux is the daily process of figuring out ways to do things more efficiently and powerfully and having a remarkable array of tools at your disposal to do so.

The fact is, though, that along the way I probably learned a lot about Linux. I learned how to download files non-interactively. I learned how to run programs at arbitrary times (very nice for using your computer to turn lights on and off, sending yourself periodic reminders, backing up all your files every night, or even just running a little program that chimes every day at 5:09, but only on Thursdays, and only on odd numbered months). I learned what a tarball is and how to cope with it, which is very important considering most all programs in source-code form arrive in a tarball, and most everybody in the Linux world who sends collections of files to others in any form probably uses a tarball to do it.

I've sweated for my knowledge, and even though I may have saved a little less time overall on this particular simple task, I've gained know-how that will make approaching problems with similar elements remarkably easy the next time around. I've built up sweat equity.

Part of the joy of Linux is the daily process of figuring out ways to do things more efficiently and powerfully and having a remarkable array of tools at your disposal to do so. Yes, other operating systems have lots of neat tools you can use to do neat things, but with Linux, there are more tools lying around than you'll know what to do with, and they run on a platform that crashes very, very seldom.

The Third Way: Get a Guru

There is a third approach to this exercise, besides training a monkey or asking a lot of people about bite-size chunks of the problem: I could have asked my guru.

Most Linux users have a guru. Sometimes a guru is someone who lives nearby and uses Linux, too. Sometimes a guru is someone who lives in Prague and dispenses advice over IRC. Sometimes, people curl up with a book and a few fingers of bourbon and become their own gurus—which is getting easier and easier as Linux becomes more and more widespread and there's more information to be found—but that's a lonely undertaking. Better to just ask someone else who's already figured a lot of it out.

Given my last example, I could have walked up to my guru and said "You know, I'm tired of downloading Mozilla by hand every day. There oughta be a way for it to just sorta happen."

If my guru were any good (and if you ever become someone else's guru, consider this a first piece of advice), she wouldn't write out the script for me, or program cron correctly to run the script at the right time. Instead, she'd tell me what I needed to do, and

The Joy of Tech by Nitrozac and Snaggy

Henry was delighted that he found exactly what he
was looking for –a Linux Guru Appreciation Day card.

some of the tools I might use to do it. If she had a script lying
around that did something similar, she might share it (but not
without first apologizing for the rough edges and numerous instances of bad practice found within). With a guru on hand, the
problem might have been taken care of in less than an hour, which
isn't bad—a mere month of downloading everything by hand.

Gurus are good to have around. Just remember that they're
also being helpful and that if they're taking the time to guide you
along the Linux path with any care, they're teaching you. The
best way to repay your own Linux guru is to take the time to
figure out something for yourself using what she's already taught
you. If you end up stringing together an incredibly over-complex
script that brings your machine to a grinding halt for the simple

purpose of flashing a lamp to tell you that you have mail, your guru will smile with gratification that you tried to apply the knowledge she's imparted. And then she'll laugh really, really hard at your expense, which will also gratify her.

Doing Linux in Groups: Support Your Local LUG

Sometimes, the best way to do anything is in groups and Linux users provide plenty of opportunities in that direction. Part of the Linux phenomenon over the years has been the number and enthusiasm of local gatherings of Linux fans called "Linux User Groups," or "LUGs."

LUGs form because as much as it's nice to reach out over mailing lists or IRC chat or news groups, it can be even better to meet now and then with other Linux fans for presentations, chats, or just a few beers at a good pub. It puts a ton of experience in one place, and because they're local, there are a lot of other benefits.

Take the often-thorny issue of picking an Internet Service Provider (ISP) to use with your new Linux machine.

> The best way to repay your own Linux guru is to take the time to figure out something for yourself using what she's already taught you.

While there's lots of good general advice out there on the Net for how to make Linux connect to the Internet with a modem, cable, or DSL connection, no one's going to know better about which local ISP is the best choice than your LUG. They can tell you who's friendly toward Linux and what some of the ins-and-outs are of all your potential choices. It can make the difference between a friendly visit from a technician to "just plug your box into the wall," or a lengthy ordeal with lots of finger-pointing and false starts. I wish I'd been involved with my LUG when I first got a DSL connection going with Linux: I might have been spared a lot of hassle from a Linux-hostile installation "expert."

LUGs can also point you to the best local hardware and software vendors. Once again, when faced with a choice of several "mom-n-pop" computer shops in my area, I would have loved to know ahead of time that one of them responded to every query about how well their merchandise worked with Linux with a flat "nope" while another had several Linux-friendly technicians on hand who ran Linux on their own computers and were pretty knowledgeable about the things in their inventory that were "must buys" and the things that were best avoided.

Another common function of LUGs is a time-honored Linux tradition called the "InstallFest." Take a room full of Linux enthusiasts with a lot of network cabling, spare mouses and keyboards, and a stack of Linux CD's, hook them up with Linux-curious folks who have a computer they're dying to install Linux on, and you have a day-long event where not only is Linux installed, but helpful classes are given to the proud new parents of Linux machines explaining some of the things to look out for. It's a great way to get started in Linux.

> It puts a ton of experience in one place, and because they're local, there are a lot of other benefits.

Finally, LUGs are great because they bring all sorts of Linux and Unix experience into one place, ranging from simple hobbyists to professors to long-time Unix system administrators. If you're lucky, your LUG might also include BSD enthusiasts, which gives you a chance to learn more about the other "freenixes," though typically your LUG stops being a LUG and starts being a UUG (Unix User Group).

There are so many ways to approach Linux—from a simple file server to a desktop productivity computer to a graphics workstation to a tiny node in a distributed computing cluster—that the more experience you're surrounded with the likelier your chances of getting help with what you're using Linux for are.

Another common function of LUGs is a time-honored Linux tradition called the "InstallFest."

DON'T BOGART THAT ENDLESS FONT OF HELP

There's one tragic phenomenon in the world of computing (it's not limited to Linux, but it's worth noting anyhow), which is the unfortunate tendency older, more experienced users have of coming down hard on new users they perceive to be lazy or selfish. We mentioned it earlier, but it's worth mentioning again: Linux is a grass-roots phenomenon that spread thanks to the enthusiasm of its users, and even though there are plenty of people trying to make money off of supporting new users, the most common place to go is still Net forums, LUGs, and kindly gurus. It can seem, once you know where to look, as if the entire world is a Linux reference library as convenient as directory assistance. The problem is, a lot of new users forget that they're dealing with people who are helping them out because they just happen to like Linux a lot and want to share in their enthusiasm. They aren't paid by "The Linux Corporation," and they don't *have* to help you. Many of them, though they'd like you to enjoy Linux and continue to use it, aren't going to respond well to threats like "help me or I'll just go back to Windows." None of them respond well to people who show no indication of helping others out, or don't even show a faint bit of gratitude for the help they've received.

It can seem, once you know where to look, as if the entire world is a Linux reference library as convenient as directory assistance.

Being a good Linux citizen involves treating the information these people have as a valuable resource you don't want to waste or hoard. Remember to be self-sufficient when you can, and remember that by accepting something with no strings attached, you still ought to keep a sense of obligation to honor the spirit in which help was given by doing the same when it's your turn.

THE UNOFFICIAL GURU QUIZ (WITH ANSWERS!)

So, having covered all the ways you can learn the ways of Linux, it's time for a quick "guru quiz," and unlike messy, painful guru training courses that might get inflicted on you in places like a Shaolin temple, we're providing answers.

1. To edit a text file, you'd use:
   a. vi
   b. Emacs
   c. sed
   d. all of the above
2. The best thing to do before compiling a new kernel is:
   a. make a backup of your existing kernel and modules
   b. make sure you're aware of all your computer's hardware so you can pick the right options
   c. make sure you have a "rescue disk" in case you make a mistake and can't reboot normally
   d. all of the above

3. The very best way to experience Linux is:
   a. with the command line
   b. with a GUI
   c. wearing a rubber suit with a ball gag
   d. all of the above
4. Real Linux gurus:
   a. know all the answers
   b. know how to look inscrutable and say "Well, you *could* do it that way" when contradicted.
   c. understand the immense value of man pages and everything in /usr/share/doc
   d. all of the above
5. Real Linux newbies:
   a. demand answers immediately
   b. provide only vague descriptions of their problems
   c. mock other Linux newbies for the same mistakes they made once upon a time
   d. all of the above.

Answer Key

1. all of the above, sort of. Emacs and vi are text editors, but if you know what you're doing with sed, you can certainly change what's in a file. It's a trick question to the extent that we think sed is really, really neat and encourage you to learn about it. All the best gurus have a weakness for sed, even when firing up a text editor and just changing something might work, too.

2. all of the above. Gurus screw up, too. Compiling a kernel is easy enough, but it's easy to make mistakes. Never confuse gurudom with infallibility, and never assume that you'll restrain yourself from throwing your computer out the window if you put it in a non-bootable state and don't have an easy way out of that. Ask your own guru for some good music to play while you contemplate the complete incompleteness of the half-booted LI... message.

3. all of the above. a and b are matters of individual taste, centered around whether you prefer the more grammatically rich interface of a text command line with all the attendant pipes, filters, and redirects or the graphically helpful cues of a GUI. c is correct because we won't be so arrogant as to discount truly individual taste

4. all of the above. But knowing the difference between when another guru is saying "b" to save face and when she's saying it because she's right is a sure sign that you're at least a good "people person," too. And we need more "people persons" than we need proficient computer users.

5. Trick question. No good Linux newbie does any of this stuff, and not many newbies who behave this way get taught enough to be Linux gurus.

CHAPTER 3

I Don't Do Windows

THE BORG INVADE THE HERMIT KINGDOM, THE AUTHOR LEARNS THE NEW MATH

I was sitting in a PX in the middle of South Korea, eating a slice of pizza and reading the latest Stars and Stripes when I read about Windows 95's release. The Rolling Stones were involved, along with giant video displays and multi-city happenings. Consumers, it was reported, were in a state of near hysteria trying to get their copies. Bill Gates was pictured beaming down on the whole thing, proud to have engineered the first software release ever to play as a cultural event.

I was supremely ambivalent about the whole thing.

The thrust of the whole release was about "ease of use" and "making computing accessible to everybody," and it involved a lot of allusions to the "tiresome and confusing task of setting jumpers on your peripherals." It was going to make getting on the Internet easier, getting stuff done more fun. It was going to deliver the promise of the home-computing revolution right to everybody's doorstep. It sounded boring, and frankly, I was bothered that I might not ever get to play with jumper settings again.

> Bill Gates was pictured beaming down on the whole thing, proud to have engineered the first software release ever to play as a cultural event.

I was pretty soured on Microsoft at that point, anyhow. Part of the time I spent in Korea, I was busy trying to figure out how to fix the unit's personnel database. Whoever had built the thing had fallen prey to keeping the math simple by using two-digit years. Ergo, all the clerk typists of Headquarters and Headquarters Company, 307th Signal Battalion were faced with an angry and obstinate database that insisted our newest incoming soldiers would have been in the Army for 93 years on the day their enlistment was up. The Mighty 307th had fallen victim to the Y2K bug, without even the excuse, in this age of machines that routinely shipped with a generous 8 megs of RAM, that memory was scarce forcing frugal programmers to dole out numbers sparingly.

The Y2K bug wasn't my issue with Microsoft. My issue was that the Army hadn't given us very good machines, but they'd spent a lot on making sure they all ran Windows 3.1 and all the associated Microsoft productivity applications. Merely starting one was an exercise in feeling yourself get older, and sending something to the printer usually gave you a good excuse to go catch a nap. The computers just weren't up to having a giant GUI strapped to their backs, and it offended me deeply that Microsoft had ever told anybody they were.

So Windows 95 seemed to be a promise of more misery to come. More people would be buying machines for the least amount of money possible, and dragging them home to spend a lot of time listening to hard drives grind whenever they so much as looked at their wallpaper, which would keep the hardware people happy because they'd be selling more new computers. Nothing wrong with turning a buck, but it seemed like the extortionary nature of the computer business got a little more pronounced every time Bill Gates decided to make life easier for us.

When I got back to the U.S. a few months later, I fell in with one of the mechanics in my new unit who, it turned out, was heading to Korea shortly. He got it in his head that having e-mail would be a good way to keep in touch with his family. His sister, a prison nurse in Alaska, arrived in town with a gold card and a desire to keep the family together through the magic of the Internet.

The Joy of Tech   by Nitrozac and Snaggy

ARRGGG!!! WINDOWS!!!!

© 2000 GEEK CULTURE, JOYOFTECH.COM

No one in the office could resist slowing down to look at Ted's horrific crash.

I got tapped as the nearest available nerd. They packed me into the family van for a trip to the local appliance superstore, where I was to give advice on the purchase of a computer.

$2000 later, and over my loud protests, we had a new Pentium set up in the bedroom. I got it up and running, prodded at the mouse a little to make sure it all worked, pronounced my job done, and went home.

All hell broke loose when I left.

I was called back a week later. The machine wasn't working right. Not working at all. We turned it on and it booted fine (though it took forever), and I was greeted with a desktop littered and strewn with shortcuts leading nowhere, a color scheme so ugly I had to look away, and sound that sometimes worked, sometimes didn't, depending on whether the plug-and-play sound card had managed to coerce the right settings from Windows at startup. As a matter of fact, anything that was plug-and-play (which was everything that wasn't built in) faced a Darwinian struggle to get configured correctly. The computer had become something Kafkaesque. I spent an afternoon talking to it:

"Okay. You're telling me the sound card needs to have an IRQ setting of 5."

"But I want the modem to be set at 5."

"Okay. But you also said the sound card needed to be set to 5."

"Yes."

"Fine. Let's let the sound card go to 10."

"Okay. But I have to reboot."

"Fine."

Interminable grinding…

"What's the modem set to now?"

"Ten. The sound card should stay at 5."

"So we can leave it like that?"

"Yes."

It became apparent that IRQs, where Windows 95 was concerned, were derived from some numbering system that predated the invention of commonly accepted math. I backed away from the machine, telling my friend that it looked like everything was fine.

The next time he rebooted the machine, the sound card and modem were squabbling again, and I could have sworn for all the world that I could hear Bill Gates cackling somewhere.

THE MICROSOFT FIXATION

For a while, I collected alternate spellings to Microsoft, some of them unprintable in a family book about computers. Here are some good ones, though:

- Micro$oft
- Microcrap
- Microshaft
- Microsloth
- Microsnot
- Microrot
- Mordorsoft
- Monoposoft
- Microborg

Bill Gates himself is alternately referred to as:

- Bill
- Billgatus of Borg
- Gates
- Mr. Gates
- The Cowardly King
- Billy
- Sauron

> Nothing wrong with turning a buck, but it seemed like the extortionary nature of the computer business got a little more pronounced every time Bill Gates decided to make life easier for us.

During the Microsoft Antitrust Trial (capitalized in the way people capitalize "Woodstock"), Gates became the center of a web of evil so immense, insidious, and far-reaching that some seemed to feel nothing escaped his grasp. Armchair industry analysts piled on to examine the far-reaching tendrils of the Microsoft conspiracy, and came up with motivations for every action.

If Gates appeared in denim outdoors while it was hot, one faction maintained that he was signalling to his employees that he remained unflappable and cool in the face of legal woes that would leave him gutted and waiting for the jackals. Another faction would proclaim that he was clearly about to snap, and his fashion sense was just the first thing to go.

> At this point, a reasonable bystander will have determined exactly what Bill Gates and his "minions" have been up to the whole time: They've been subtly driving the Linux community to stark raving paranoia.

When Eric Raymond, the John Reed of the Open Source Revolution, released the now-famous "Halloween Documents," some held forth that Microsoft had deliberately leaked them to show that they had competition in the market. Others, of course, viewed it as further evidence that the Microsoft empire had lost its collective mind and could no longer hide the truth from a world waiting to be liberated from jumperless sound cards. Raymond's own take on the matter was polite enough in its treatment of the "deliberate leak" camp of theorists, but he maintains that Microsoft most likely screwed up.

Maintaining an even keel, though, is hard to do when you're battling the Mordor of the Pacific Northwest:

"He's evil!" proclaimed one person. "Everything he does is for a reason! Don't let your guards down! This means we have to fight harder!"

That prompted others to pile on:

"If we talk about fighting him, they'll use that against us, which is their plan! They want us to talk like that! Then we come off looking like loonies! Everyone act normal!"

At this point, a reasonable bystander will have determined exactly what Bill Gates and his "minions" have been up to the whole time: They've been subtly driving the Linux community to stark raving paranoia.

THE FUD FACTOR

There can be no denying, though, that Microsoft (Microcrap) has had a strange and sometimes unsavory ride to the top. They've even managed to wrestle the phrase "fear, uncertainty, and doubt" from its association with IBM, who used to be considered the worst thing to ever happen to computers before Microsoft (Mickeysoft, Mickeyshaft) ever came on the scene.

Fear, Uncertainty, and Doubt (FUD, for short) is the practice of lying a lot about the horrible things that happen to people who choose anything other than the product the person spreading FUD is trying to sell. It has a long, rich history in the modern computing age, going back to the widely-propagated old saw "No one ever got fired for choosing IBM."

Did you hear the menace in that?

Eric Raymond's Jargon File even has a definition:

> *"Defined by Gene Amdahl after he left IBM to found his own company: 'FUD' is the fear, uncertainty, and doubt that IBM sales people instill in the minds of potential customers who might be considering [Amdahl] products. The idea, of course, was to persuade them to go with safe IBM gear rather than with competitors' equipment.*

> *This implicit coercion was traditionally accomplished by promising that Good Things would happen to people who stuck with IBM, but Dark Shadows loomed over the future of competitors' equipment or software. After 1990 the term FUD was associated increasingly frequently with Microsoft, and has become generalized to refer to any kind of disinformation used as a competitive weapon."*

The whole thing is a wound in the very breast of a hacker, or even someone who just loves technology, because it's an affront to the notion (shared by technicians and others who remain firmly dependent on pesky things like absolutes) that, given a chance, everybody will eventually see their way through to the best of all possible solutions.

If the thought of looking at a putty-colored PC on your desk—resplendent in a look that has remained largely untouched since 1981—and referring to it as "elegant" seems even more bone-chilling than Martha Stewart declaring something "good," you're going to be in for a bit of a stretch. But, if you can think on the idea for a little while and understand how "elegance" might apply to a computer, you'll understand that even engineers have a sense of aesthetics, and so do Linux fans, and that's where all the upset about FUD comes from.

Here's a good example of FUD in action. Once upon a time, a company came up with the notion that if they could make a better MS-DOS *than* MS-DOS, they'd corner the market, make some dough, and retire to some Caribbean island somewhere to live the rest of their days on the beach. In any other market, they would have been on to something. Chevrolet tries to do that to Ford, Kibbles-n-Bits tries to do it to Chuckwagon, and ACME Rodent Suppression Systems tries to do it to ACE Mousetraps.

The Joy of Tech   by Nitrozac and Snaggy

There's some mighty sad tales, up on Never-Boot-Again Hill.

They named their product "DR DOS" after their company (Digital Research), and it was a pretty good one. It handled the expanded memory that more and more machines were shipping with, something MS-DOS couldn't yet claim, and it offered some usability enhancements, too. In some ways, if you were a UNIX fan, it was a good way to swallow your unhappiness with having to work with something other than UNIX because it offered a much nicer shell to work with.

Naturally this caused some consternation in the Microsoft camp. Some of their partners (including IBM) thought the cheaper, better DR DOS was worth considering and made the mistake of saying so in public. Microsoft's finest minds got together to make things, uh, "right."

At the time, Microsoft was readying Windows 3.1. Windows 1 and 2 hadn't gone over so well, Windows 3 was a pretty dubious improvement, Apple was still considered the ruler in terms of ease-of-use, and it was clear Microsoft needed a big win. They had the marketing hype in place, they had a snazzy new logo, and they'd managed to come up with a clunky but working GUI (*Graphical User Interface*) that just might turn things around. They weren't willing to part with their MS-DOS revenue, though, and they couldn't part with MS-DOS itself: Windows was to remain dependent on it.

> The simple fact that we felt compelled to explain what DR DOS is ought to indicate how well the strategy worked.

What to do?

They decided to make DR DOS unusable with their new product. Wrote one Microsoft exec:

> *"It's pretty clear we need to make sure Windows 3.1 only runs on top of MS-DOS or an OEM version of it...The approach we will take is to detect DR DOS 6 and refuse to load. The error message should be something like 'Invalid device driver interface.'"*

Windows 3.1 wasn't even on the market yet; it was still in the hands of the beta testers, people who agree to run software for a company in exchange for bragging rights and the privilege of having their firstborn taken away if they breathe a word of what they've seen. When these people began calling in to complain about the error messages they were getting on their DR DOS systems, Microsoft tech support was on hand to point out to them that they were, after all, running a suspect "third-party" operating system. They might have also politely asked after the children, too, but that never came up in the eventual trial.

The end result was pretty simple. The simple fact that we felt compelled to explain what DR DOS is ought to indicate how well the strategy worked. If its designers are retiring to beaches in the Caribbean, that'll be because they've wisely invested the settlement money they got out of Microsoft years after their product was quietly taken out back and shot.

In the words of Microsoft Senior VP James Allchin, "We need to smile...while we pull the trigger."

In keeping with the current fascination of labeling stuff as "extreme" (we normally draw the line at Taco Bell entrees and anything you can do while seated in a chair), we can probably call this the first-ever case of "Extreme FUD." Not only did Microsoft's merry band of executives identify a crisis and react to it by terrifying their beta testers out of their wits, they managed to manufacture some of the elements they needed to make sure DR DOS stayed right where they buried it.

FUD, though, like Creeping Communism and suspicions of witchcraft in quaint, old New England towns, has a way of cropping up under beds and turning up in closets. How can you tell when you're dealing with the genuine article, or when it's just time to step out for some fresh air and anti-anxiety pills?

A quick game of "discern the FUD" may prove instructive. The rules are simple. Read three assertions and choose the FUD:

> **Assertion One:** "Linux is insecure. If you trust Linux to run your servers, script-kiddies exploiting all the holes in open source software will come find you and erase your hard drive. They'll also call you names. If you stick with Microsoft, which you've been using all along, this won't happen, and if you do you can say you were just following orders...er...marketing." (Source: A Microsoft PR flack)

Assertion Two: "Linux sucks. I tried to install it and something went wrong and I lost everything on my hard drive." (Source: Some guy)

Assertion Three: "Linux is less secure than OpenBSD, which goes over each line of code present in its distribution to make sure there are no security problems." (Source: An OpenBSD advocate) (Those guys again)

Now, Assertion One is easy enough to spot as full-on FUD. A reasonable person (someone who doesn't get too tied up over the whole BSD thing) will also give the OpenBSD folks their due and simultaneously discount Assertion Three as a FUD candidate.

> Microsoft has an unpleasant history of employees turning up in various online fora and spreading a lot of unpleasantness about whoever is trying to compete with them at the time.

Assertion Two is the tricky one, and you have to consider the source, which we thoughtfully obscured. Microsoft has an unpleasant history of employees turning up in various online fora and spreading a lot of unpleasantness about whoever is trying to compete with them at the time. This is called "astro-turfing," and it's part of a broader FUD campaign. On the other hand, sometimes some poor schlep drags home a copy of the latest and greatest Linux distribution, innocently destroys every spec of data on his hard drive, and decides Linux well and truly sucks. Does that make him a Microsoft dupe? Nope. The chances are good he's drawing a legitimate paycheck each week from Uncle Fred's Feed Shack or wherever it is he works, and the last thing on his mind is how well his comments are going to serve his (imaginary) puppeteers in Redmond.

Misused enough, FUD becomes a meaningless word—the geek equivalent of crying "wolf!" or flapping around long lists of suspected Microsoft sympathizers.

"WHEN THEY'RE BAD, THEY'RE TERRIBLE"

Those "Halloween Documents" we mentioned earlier are an interesting indication of what passes for "just a thought" among the folks working at Microsoft, which ought to be enough to make us wonder what they think when they're feeling nasty. Written by a junior engineer at Microsoft as an assessment of the surging popularity of Linux in specific and open-source software in general, they get their name because Eric Raymond released the first one he received on Halloween weekend, 1998.

"Halloween I," the first paper Raymond got his hands on, started off as a fairly sober assessment of the strengths open-source software brings to the table. Judicious in tone, the author spells out what "open source" means, and then quietly flops a slab of red meat out in front of his readers:

> "[Open-source software] poses a direct, short-term revenue and platform threat to Microsoft—particularly in server space. Additionally, the intrinsic parallelism and free idea exchange in OSS has benefits that are not replicable with our current licensing model and therefore present a long term developer mindshare threat."

Sort of like DR DOS.

The author must have been feeling proactive and a little protective of the Mother Company when he sat down to write his thoughts on the whole thing, though, because after spending the bulk of the document saying some pretty complimentary things about how well open-source software seemed to be working, he figured he'd better offer a remedy for all that quality. He strategizes:

> *"Generally, Microsoft wins by attacking the core weaknesses of OSS projects...De-commoditize protocols & applications OSS projects have been able to gain a foothold in many server applications because of the wide utility of highly commoditized, simple protocols. By extending these protocols and developing new protocols, we can deny OSS projects entry into the market."*

If his sentence structure wasn't the most sound, his intent was. Allow us a brief digression to explain. If it helps to imagine, at this point, that we've quietly morphed into the person who's always cornering you at parties so he can spell out why something that happened on his computer today is of utmost importance, it's because we have. We're that person. We're going to make it all clear, and you're going to miss out on that conversation about the effect of yuppies on all the best neighborhoods.

The Internet's one of the most improperly capitalized words around. It isn't a single entity: it's a whole collection of entities, networks, that spend most of their day minding their own business and shuffling files and talking among themselves. The Internet is a common understanding these networks have about what to do when they need to talk to each other in order to better push mail and Web pages and dirty pictures back and forth with other networks. Those understandings are called "standards." Without them, the Internet stops being something you see any sense in capitalizing at all.

These standards are arrived at in a reasonably democratic way by the IETF (*Internet Engineering Task Force*), which is composed of people who spend a lot of time figuring out the delicate balance between existing practice, common sense, and the Next Big Thing. They do a good job: most e-mail gets where it's going, "dot-com" is a ubiquitous (and irritating) part of the language, and people get fired for spending too much time playing around on the Internet when they should be working.

One of the strengths of all these standards is the fact that they're open. The IETF publishes its take on how a standard works, and programmers can sit down to render that standard into software. The net result is pretty clear: An enterprising businessman, for instance, can sit down to a mail program written to comply with the standards regarding e-mail. That program sends off an e-mail that arrives on the doorstep of a mail server that knows what to do with it, which in turn hands the mail off to another server that has the same notions of right and wrong (within the moral confines observed by mail servers). Bit by bit, the mail makes it to where it needs to go and through the magic of standards, you're treated to a new come-on for an herbal weight loss plan or get-rich-quick scheme. Yay standards! The author of the Halloween Document, though, wasn't setting his sights on e-mail.

> The Internet's one of the most improperly capitalized words around.

There are lots of other interactions at work on computers that communicate over a network. The simple act of logging in first thing in the morning invokes a few standards, as does copying a file from a shared directory, reading a Web page, looking at your bank account online, or ordering a book from a Web site. In a world where standards are open and (we'll slip in the phrase) protocols are commoditized, all the various pieces of software that handle these transactions are free to be produced by whomever takes the time to write them. If you're a giant software company in Washington with a will to power that would make Nietzsche blush, however, this won't do. The solution? Get busy making those standards and protocols hard to duplicate, conceal how they work, and blow off the rest of the world.

It was pretty clear to this junior engineer that Microsoft was in a good position to do something about the oncoming wave of pesky, mindshare-stealing software. They had 90 percent of the desktop market and a reasonable share of the small server market. The best thing to do was to ensure that if you wanted to make your computer talk to a Microsoft network, you'd best be running a Microsoft product. It's a process referred to as "lock-in," which means just what it says.

> One of the strengths of all these standards is the fact that they're open.

A few years down the road, Microsoft, ever eager to make its detractors' point for them, tried to do exactly this by quietly "enhancing" a security protocol called "kerberos." Kerberos is in common use all over the place, which made changing it too much a dicey proposition, but try Microsoft did. When someone posted the changes Microsoft had made to the Web site Slashdot, Microsoft threatened with lawsuits. Slashdot won the ensuing legal staring contest, and the open-source community got a good look at just what the Halloween Documents were all about.

...AND WHEN WE'RE BAD, WE'RE RABID

So, having outlined the Problem With Microsoft, we're left with the other side of the coin.

Like I said earlier, it's pretty easy to understand the sort of special pain that FUD can cause an engineer or a programmer. FUD promotes the lesser solution—the "sub-optimal" solution. To people who spend an awful lot of time avoiding repeating themselves (there's a reason copy-and-paste is easier under X Window than any other GUI), and even more time arguing over

The Joy of Tech   by Nitrozac and Snaggy

how to shave microseconds off of a process in the name of efficiency, it's easy to understand the tendency to spit when Microsoft announces a new "innovation."

On the other hand, there's a contingent to which these things just don't matter, and they're still mad about the whole FUD thing, which leads one to wonder why. I have two theories. Theory one is the one I like to refer to as "the charitable theory." It reads like this:

> *"Bill Gates is the Devil. In addition to his crimes against quality engineering, he has spent a healthy amount of time turning up in bedrooms across the country...leaning over the edges of cribs...leering menacingly at the innocent babes within...and pinching them really, really hard. He*

turns up on playgrounds and gives little kids
noogies. His weather-control satellites rain out
"the big game" all over the country. He invented
JarJar Binks. He voted for whichever party you
didn't. His money, by the way, wasn't made from
software sales; it was made trading in harp seal
fur and ivory. He kicks puppies."

Sounds reasonable, then, to despise the man. I'd hate anybody who pinched me in my crib, and I believe my own relatively understanding outlook on Mr. Gates is directly related to the fact that I lived in Texas as a child and he couldn't get to me.

The second theory is a little less charitable, and I call it "The Less Charitable Theory." It goes like this:

"If you like computers, and you don't like pro-
gramming, then you find yourself categorized
fairly neatly as a 'user.' The label of 'user' isn't
the worst thing in the world, really. There are
users in every office, quietly preparing documents,
playing with spreadsheets, sending each other vi-
rus-riddled e-mail, and getting their work done.
It's not very glamorous or sexy. The word user,
spoken by an adequately frustrated tech support
person, sounds an awful lot like 'sheep' or 'drone.'
Users like each other in proportions appropriate
to the normal human levels of liking and not-lik-
ing. Computer enthusiasts who don't have jobs
working on computers, though, are all too aware
that the people who do work on computers don't
think much of them. They yearn to be identified
as uniquely competent…better at the whole com-
puter thing than the 'normals' they once taught
to read e-mail attachments."

Really, everyone's a user these days and lots of people are even good at being users. There's no future in it. Just before I sat down to write this, I witnessed an encounter in a computer store where three teenage girls told the clerk he was full of stuff. The conversation went:

> Clerk: No...you can't share a computer connection like that.
> Girl: Uh, like, I'm going to use that DSL router.
> Clerk: But you can't make the other machines talk to that.
> Girl: Uh, hello, I've got a four-port hub and two NICS for the Linux box. It's called IP masquerading.
> Clerk: Linux doesn't work with DSL. It crashes.
> Girl: Rolls eyes. Leaves.

See? Everyone's good at computers these days, and the people who aren't are proud of the fact. There's not a lot of distinction in knowing how to make a computer work when the secretary down the hall does too, or when the sorority chick down the street is shopping for the best hardware to allow her to set up a heterogeneous network of four nodes using IP masquerading and network address translation to ensure that she can provide herself and her housemates with a secure, networked computing environment.

> **L**inux is built by people you don't hear from much, who look vaguely cornered when you catch them out in public.

So how do you distinguish yourself if you really, really like computers, and really, really want to let everybody know, but it's really important for people to know you're as unique and special as your favorite soft drink? How do you restore the respect you used to get for being "good at computers?" How do you turn on your computer without feeling like you've just set foot in a beige mini-van like Mom and Dad drive? Simple...pick something no one else has heard of or knows only by rumors of its diabolical unfriendliness to newbies, install it, walk around bragging to co-workers (or, more likely, playground chums) so awed with your prowess that they'll leave the room when you show up because it's just too hard to be around someone as good at computers as you, *et voilá!*, you're different again.

A few years ago, one magazine included a Linux disc accompanied by the following, helpful copy:

"Linux is the rebel OS! Install it to impress your friends!"

In other words, don't install it because it represents the refinement of 30 years of software engineering. Don't install it because it works better. Don't install it because you like it. Don't install it to learn. Don't install it to get ahead at work. Don't install it because it's representative of a fascinating paradigm shift in software design.

Install it because you want to be a Pepper, too.

> Some people are compulsive about not being confused with all the other idiots.

Having asserted that they're different from people who use Windows machines or Macintoshes, this particular contingent then sets about adopting a few grotesqueries to further affirm their specialness, including recovered memories of Bill Gates pinching them in their cribs. They also spend a lot of time complaining that there aren't enough games for Linux yet. And because they aren't actually writing software, documenting software, or helping improve software, they spend a lot of time wondering what it means that Bill Gates is wearing denim today.

The uncharitable theory in a nutshell? Some people are compulsive about not being confused with all the other idiots.

Don't judge Linux by this particular group. They'll grow out of it, but Linux has long since outgrown them. Linux is built by people you don't hear from much, who look vaguely cornered when you catch them out in public. They may not think much of Bill Gates, or Microsoft, and it may give them heartburn to consider giving up their beloved Tux for a "crippled" operating system like Windows, but they're too busy building Linux to corner you at the water cooler and hassle you about it.

CHAPTER **4**

Kissing Cousins, Lovers' Quarrels

So, not long after learning enough about UNIX to play around a little, and even managing to get a job working on a UNIX computer, I found myself faced with a terrible problem: Something was going very wrong on the machine I was charged to look after, and I had to fix it. My boss had locked all the manuals for the machine up in her office in order to end a long-standing feud we'd been having over whether we should turn the computer off at night. I admired her apparent faith in books as the only source of knowledge appropriate to solving the world's (or at least our computer's) problems, even if I was a little put off that she thought I'd give up in the absence of a few technical manuals, or suddenly decide I was wrong after all if I couldn't point to a book to prove my point.

Turner-offers are, to my way of thinking, one of the more lily-livered contingents of the computing world. Why turn off your computer at night when you can buy an uninterruptable power supply and enough surge protection to resist the annual output of Three Mile Island and rack up all the bragging points?

> And how are you going to be able to brag about the uptime your single user desktop machine enjoys if it never runs for more than fourteen hours a day?

And how are you going to be able to brag about the uptime your single user desktop machine enjoys if it never runs for more than fourteen hours a day? You can't. Turning off a computer at night is nothing short of depriving yourself of the ability to buy more hardware and brag. It's stupid.

Leave-on-ers are, of course, the only right-minded people in the computer world. In addition to knowing a good opportunity to buy more hardware when they see it, and the sensuous pleasures of saying, "My box has been up for more than three months without going down," leave-on-ers know that turning something on and off wears it out more quickly, or something.

Linux, and UNIX in general, presents an even better argument for leaving a computer on all night: If you don't, and you don't take a little additional care, it messes things up—just a little at first, then in a really, really bad way. Linux, you see, comes awake on many machines at around three in the morning and sets about doing some light housekeeping. It shuffles some log files around, deletes things that don't need to exist anymore, and shakes itself out. Sometimes, if things aren't quite right, it sends mail telling you so. If your machine isn't on during the early morning, it can't ever do any of this stuff. If it can't do this stuff, directories slowly fill with redundant files and scraps of messages the computer sends to itself. The /tmp directory, which you can think of as your computer's appendix, slowly fills up with the nail-bitings and waste products of a computer hard at work. Over time, you run out of space and the computer stops being able to keep the sort of temporary information it needs to do the essentials. That's what ours was doing: quietly strangling on its own rubbish.

There are, of course, ways around this. It wouldn't be any good if you had to live with something as arbitrary as a machine that has to be on at a certain time. At the time, however, I didn't know of any of these workarounds; I just knew my boss was a compulsive turner-offer who'd hidden the only evidence I had to thwart her misguided notions about "wearing out the CPU." So I turned to the Internet and begged for help on a UNIX newsgroup.

The folks there were initially very helpful. One gentleman in particular took care to answer each of my questions in an e-mail exchange, and the kindliness with which he responded made me mist up.

Of course I could make it so the housecleaning took place at a time of day when the boss would allow the machine to be turned on; of course she was crazy to turn the machine off—how was she going to brag about uptime? Of course this was a simple fix—just edit a few files like so…

I reported back to my new mentor the next day, flush with success: All it had taken was a quick session with Emacs and the machine was humming!

Emacs? I'd used *Emacs* to edit a configuration file? Was I some sort of freak!? Did I not know how to use vi? Did I drive cement mixers to the drive-in movies and swat flies with hand grenades? Was I not aware of the simple elegance and power of vi?

I should have left it alone, apologized for my poor choice of tools, and continued to learn at the feet of this sage. As it was, I wasn't aware I'd set foot in the middle of one of the bloodiest and most protracted battles ever fought in the UNIX world, so I replied in kind. Vi, I argued, is for masochists and lickspittles

> Linux, you see, comes awake on many machines at around three in the morning and sets about doing some light housekeeping.

on some sort of bizarre kick that causes second-year college students to run away to monastic cults until they get tired of eating porridge and sweeping the floors with rush brooms that are too short. Emacs, on the other hand, is a comfortable tool meant to be used by people who want a hand in personalizing the text-editing experience, the most important thing a real UNIX user ever does. People who use vi, I posited, are backwards and probably use the word "new-fangled" while they tug on their suspenders.

Vi, I argued, is for masochists and lickspittles on some sort of bizarre kick that causes second-year college students to run away to monastic cults until they get tired of eating porridge and sweeping the floors with rush brooms that are too short.

My ex-guru was careful to forward my thoughtful missive to a few of his friends, who were happy to explain how wrong I was. My inbox stopped smoldering a few weeks later.

ON VIKING MARAUDERS AND RAMPAGING TROLLS

It isn't hard, looking back on the history of UNIX, to see that Linux is the inheritor of more than a technical outlook. It's also the inheritor of a culture. Some of that was covered earlier when we examined where Linux came from and how it came to be where it is, but that's the boring part. Linux has also inherited three decades of UNIX enthusiasts fighting among themselves, which is much more entertaining. Once you're done with this chapter, you'll have the barest essentials required for going out into the world and picking your own fights—and getting stomped by, as a friend of mine puts it, "suspender-wearing UNIX graybeards," who have been fighting about some of this stuff since before you were born.

Before going too much further, I should note that there are several types of conflicts within the Linux community, and they bear some examination.

> **L**inux has also inherited three decades of UNIX enthusiasts fighting among themselves, which is much more entertaining.

The first is informed very heavily by whatever passed for a school of thought among Viking marauders in the Middle Ages. Although these Linux users don't have long ships to pile into, or ferocious seas to cross, or barbarian enemies to crush, they do have computers, the Internet, and everybody who disagrees with them on anything. They also have a wide variety of fairly good microbrews usually within easy driving distance, which isn't quite as good as a flagon of mead after a long day of smiting the enemy, but it'll do. A fight to these hearty souls is sustenance itself. "A vicious flame war is character building," they'll tell you, if they've decided to take time out from flaming each other long enough to explain what the flaming is all about. At work, they'll tell you, is no less than the Darwinian process of separating the weaklings of the herd from the gene pool, ensuring the survival of good ideas, and maintaining the health of the meritocracy that is Linux.

They await your arrival in the Linux community eagerly.

A second type of conflict is characterized by a slightly more nervous disposition about all the scuffling. They remember with unhappiness the near death of UNIX in the '80s and '90s, which they quickly point out was caused by unconscionable amounts of squabbling and scuffling among whole companies, which led to what is spoken of in hushed and fearful tones as "fragmentation." They're aware of history and quake at the thought of repeating it. They pop up in arguments and remind the combatants that although arguing about the merits of one tool over the

The Joy of Tech   by Nitrozac and Snaggy

It was a Wild, Wild Kernel, but *someone* had to tame it!

other is all well and good (and that the same argument has been going on for nigh on 30 years), the rest of the world will take it as a sure sign that use of UNIX stimulates testosterone production, territorial marauding, argumentativeness, and, ultimately, bloodshed. Sometimes these kind souls forget themselves and take to calling others names in their zeal to protect Linux from the same fate that befell the rest of the UNIX world, which pleases those of the "Viking" school of thought to no end.

They, too, welcome your arrival in the community, since there's no point in worrying about fragmentation all the time if new people aren't coming into the fold.

A third school of thought already bears an acknowledged label: the trolls. Trolls thrive in an environment like the Linux community, which lives so much of its life over the Internet, because they're generally safe from physical assault, and they're not required to keep a straight face while they're up to their trolling. As with many things Linux, the Jargon File provides ready definitions, and I'll relate the first two:

> **troll**[1] **(trōl)** *v.* [From the Usenet group alt.folklore.urban] To utter a posting on Usenet designed to attract predictable responses or flames; or, the post itself. Derives from the phrase "trolling for newbies," which in turn comes from mainstream "trolling," a style of fishing in which one trails bait through a likely spot hoping for a bite. The well-constructed troll is a post that induces lots of newbies and flamers to make themselves look even more clueless than they already do, while subtly conveying to the more savvy and experienced that it is in fact a deliberate troll. If you don't fall for the joke, you get to be in on it. See also: YHBT.

> **troll**[2] **(trōl)** *n.* An individual who chronically trolls in sense 1; regularly posts specious arguments, flames, or personal attacks to a newsgroup, discussion list, or in email for no other purpose than to annoy someone or disrupt a discussion. Trolls are recognizable by the fact that they have no real interest in learning about the topic at hand—they simply want to utter flame bait. Like the ugly creatures after which they are named, they exhibit no redeeming characteristics, and as such, they are recognized as a lower form of life on the Net, as in, "Oh, ignore him, he's just a troll."

Your average troll may well have some emotional investment in a flame war, but you'll probably never know what it is. They're more interested in keeping the entertainment the combatants are providing moving along.

You may have figured out from the definition that trolls can be subtle folk, despite the fireworks they seek to provoke, and that discerning a troll can be a tricky proposition. You're right. Determining whether something that makes your blood pressure rise and inspires you to compose an impassioned response on the spot has been issued by someone who is simply disagreeing or by someone trolling is tough to call. That's why it pays to remember that the newer you are to the Linux world (or any online community), the more likely you are to be easy prey for someone out to keep a fight going.

Trolls, of course, exploit something all newbies have in common: the desperate desire to fit in with their new community. If you think you're going to make points by leaping to the fore and smiting someone with a particularly reprehensible opinion, keep in mind that you may just be painting "newbie" in Day-Glo colors on your own forehead.

By the way, trolls also eagerly await your arrival.

So…having covered the Linux community as it relates to conflict, onward with the conflicts themselves. I promise to make no attempt to present any of this fairly.

VI VERSUS EMACS: OF SCALPELS AND CHAINSAWS

Linux is, at root, built around text files. It's configured with text files, and the source code everyone's so happy to get their hands on arrives in text files. Most people who program with Linux use text editors to do their programming; in addition, anyone who's used one of the traditional e-mail programs under Linux such as Elm or PINE has used a text editor to compose their mail. The way a hammer or saw is essential to a carpenter, a text editor is essential to a Linux user.

It makes sense, then, that possibly the most venerable fight in all of Linuxdom—one that predates Linux itself—is over text editors. I'll introduce the contenders.

vi: Fast, Efficient, Perplexing

Vi is as close as the UNIX world comes to a standard editor. It turns up everywhere, and it's been around for a long, long time. Words used to describe vi are "elegant," "powerful," "lightweight," "frustrating," "irritating," and "inscrutable."

The elegant and powerful bits are pretty easy to grasp once you spend some time with vi. You can accomplish a lot with very few keys. It's just important that you remember all those possible combinations of "just a few keys," and prepare to spend weeks training yourself that you can't simply start up vi and start typing. It's a *modal* text editor, which means that you can either be in text-entry mode or command mode. It takes commands to do all those wonderful, powerful, elegant things when it's in command mode, in addition to a few other things, like

The *Joy of Tech*   by Nitrozac and Snaggy

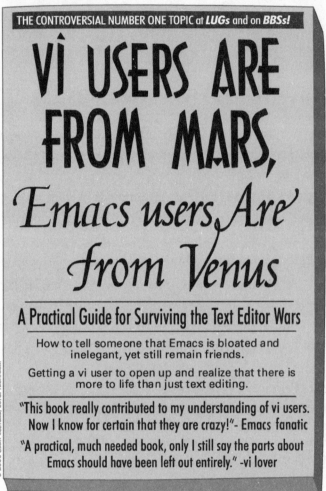

beeping at you repeatedly and making you sorry to be alive if you thought you were in text-entry mode.

In addition to knowing that vi will frustrate you to no end over the course of learning it, you should also know that you must never, ever, pronounce vi's name like it looks. If you call vi, um, vi, you've once again painted "newbie" in Day-Glo colors on your forehead. Vi is to be pronounced like it looks (the other way it looks): as two distinct letters: "vee eye." Practice this.

Vi is held up by its adherents as the only editor a serious Linux hacker will ever want or need. After all, it's elegant, powerful, lightweight, yada yada yada. It's also got a funny name, it's hard to figure out, and it's singularly unhelpful.

Vi fans are proud of their hard-earned knowledge and mastery. You can find Web pages with buttons that read, "Crafted with the vi editor." There are vi coffee cups with the commands you might need to know printed on the sides. Vi people take a ruthless pleasure in telling newbies to use vi. They know what the newbie's getting into, and they aren't about to warn them. If the newbie works in an adjoining cubicle, vi users sit quietly and listen to the newbie's terminal beep over and over and over while the first lesson of vi is pounded into their skulls: You can't "just start typing" with vi. People who want to do that are morally defective.

Emacs: You Could Settle for Just Editing Text...

Emacs is vi's opposite number. Where vi is lightweight, Emacs is crushing. Where vi is elegant, Emacs is elegant—but in a different, alien sort of way. Where vi is powerful in a manner that involves accomplishing much with little, Emacs is powerful in a manner that leaves text files not only successfully edited, but bruised and flattened.

Not content to simply edit files, Emacs can do a lot more, enabling you to manage your calendar, play games, and read mail, in addition to handling IRC chatting, remembering everything you ever wrote and making recommendations on things that might be pertinent to what you're writing about at the moment. Emacs can also remember the e-mail addresses of anyone who's ever written you, insert messages designed to bother the National Security Agency at the end of every mail you send, or even pretend it's vi.

When it comes down to it, you could fire up Emacs and go live in it all day long. It does that much. Some people make very firm decisions about what they will and will not do with Emacs once they discover it's taking over their lives.

> Since we're dealing with efficiency freaks, that's a wasted tenth of a second, and that's unforgiveable.

All this power requires memorizing a lot of commands, and it comes at the expense of your ability to remember to eat or sleep. On the other hand, once you've mastered Emacs, you've probably reached a level where food and sleep are no longer necessary. You have to take the good with the bad, I suppose.

Vi users, for their part, often look at Emacs users as destroyers of the UNIX tradition.

"Emacs," they argue, "is bloated and inelegant."

They buttress this argument with two points. The first is that even on a bad day, vi takes up about a tenth of the memory that Emacs does. The second is that it usually takes more keys to do things with Emacs. Compare:

To save a file with vi, you type the following:

```
:w
```

Sometimes you need to press the Esc key first, but that's nothing compared to the nightmarish complexity of Emacs. To save a file with Emacs, you must execute the following command:

CTRL+X, CTRL+S

See?

That's a tenth of a second off your life. Since we're dealing with efficiency freaks, that's a wasted tenth of a second, and that's unforgiveable.

In addition, vi lovers argue, vi is everywhere. Since it's so small and minimalistic, it will always be found on most computers, it can be stored on a floppy, and it may be all you have available in the event of a real problem with your system.

Emacs users, for their part, consider vi users troglodytes. After all, using an editor that doesn't do much more than, you know, edit text, is as bad as using flint knives and bearskins.

The other item at the heart of the Emacs enthusiasts' love of Emacs is the fact that the editor is programmable using Lisp. Lisp is a venerable language designed for artificial intelligence applications. "Lisp," its adherents will tell you, "is elegant and powerful." (Like vi, now that I think of it.) Like vi, Lisp has driven better people than you or I to madness, which, by extension, evens Emacs and vi up on the insanity-inducement scale.

A final look at this clash of cultures has to involve the text editors' icons as they appear on the Linux desktop. Emacs has a smiling gnu. The gnu is the mascot of the GNU project, of course, and there's something sort of large and shaggy about Emacs, so it's appropriate. Vi, on the other hand, doesn't have an icon. That would be wasteful. Sometimes, though, it is represented by buttons on Web pages. No point in wasting time figuring out the whole GNU/Emacs/large/shaggy thing, though. They always just say "vi."

> Emacs users, for their part, consider vi users troglodytes.

THE DESKTOP WARS: SO MUCH TO FIGHT ABOUT, SO LITTLE TIME

Once upon a time, if you wanted a graphical user interface (GUI) under Linux, you had a limited set of choices, and they were all pretty uncomfortable, especially for someone migrating from Windows or Mac OS.

Some of the early attempts at making Linux "friendlier" were amusing in a half-baked sort of way. One of them made Linux look just enough like Windows 95 (right down to the ugly, teal wallpaper) that you became sort of homesick for it once you realized you'd been tricked and had to deal with something so un-Windows-like underneath that it seemed to be mocking you.

There are also some very good GUIs that are nothing like anything you've ever seen, which is fun. And there are GUIs that look a lot like things you may have seen at some point or another and enjoyed, but that somehow come up lacking for new users. Enter the "desktop environment."

Desktop environments aren't really very new. In the '80s, the UNIX world lined up behind the "Common Desktop Environment," for instance. Users got a set of applications and tools that all looked and acted much the same. CDE was something of a standard in the UNIX world (and still is in some corners), but it had a few things going against it:

First, it was ugly. No one wants an ugly desktop.

> # No one wants an ugly desktop.

Second, as businesses will sometimes do when they smell a potential angle, the politics of cooperating with each other over how to best implement CDE slowed it down. To make a long story short, UNIX never did amount to much on the desktops most of us are familiar with, Microsoft rode to glory, and that was that.

So as it became clear that Linux was being taken more and more seriously as a server operating system, people began to look around for the next thing to improve, and everyone agreed that ease of use for newer and non-technical users had to be addressed.

KDE: Better Flamebait through German Engineering

One group of people decided to address the issue via the K Desktop Environment, more commonly known as "KDE." KDE's designers have made it their mission in life to produce software that

makes Linux (and UNIX in general) more palatable for new users. This is partially in response to charges that Linux will never
amount to anything as an office oper-
ating system without a little more user-
friendly polish. No, in case you're
wondering, speed and reliability are
not factors here. What we're after is
making computers more comfortable
for brighter-than-average chimpanzees.

What we're after is
making computers
more comfortable for
brighter-than-average
chimpanzees.

So the KDE team set about their
work with quiet efficiency, taking bits
and pieces of past interfaces and add-
ing bits of their own, questing after the Holy Grail of "usability,"
which is to say that they wanted to make life easier on any of the
chimpanzees feeling left behind during the whole Windows thing.

KDE turned out quite nice, too. Users who downloaded it
got a "desktop environment" with all sorts of handy little applications: an address book, an e-mail program, and countless other
gimcracks and doo-dads. It even included Solitaire. Admiring
users called it "solid" and "smooth," and even "slick," which is
high praise, indeed.

Unfortunately, according to some (okay, more than "some,"
since the whole thing rates coverage as a quarrel of note), KDE
had some problems, too.

First, there was an issue with the toolkit upon which KDE
was built. Toolkits are a programming thing. They make life easier
on programmers by providing a way to write software that looks
the same and generally acts the same without having to repro-
gram all those looks and behaviors into each and every application a programmer writes. If you open a window on your
computer's desktop and look at the little buttons and scrollbars
and icons the window provides, you're looking at the most vis-
ible manifestation of toolkits: the widgets. Those widgets may

not look like much, but having a toolkit that defines all those widgets just once and then allows them to be included in programs with much less code than it takes to describe the widget in the first place makes life much easier for programmers.

So the good programmers at KDE, out to make life easier on themselves, picked the Qt toolkit by a company from Norway called TrollTech. They reasoned that Qt was the best toolkit going, and they wanted the best for their software. Qt had a problem, though, in the form of its software license.

Licenses, as you'll recall, are what determine how you can use any software you come across. Most licenses you'll encounter in software you want to run on your Windows or Macintosh computer (and Windows and Mac OS themselves) are licensed in such a way that you can't go around sharing their source code with people, don't have any rights to get at the source code even if you could share it, and may have to give up your firstborn if you make the mistake of coming up with too good an approximation of how their software gets put together and tell anybody else.

TrollTech wasn't that nasty about the whole thing, and they had a license that was fairly friendly to Open Source developers. It had some problems, though, where Free Software and the GNU Copyleft were concerned, because some of its restrictions were a bit too, well, restrictive for it to coexist with Free Software. You may be hankering for more detail than that. After all, Qt's license bears about as much historical weight in the Desktop Wars as the assassin who offed Archduke Franz Ferdinand. Someday, someone will write the book it would take to lay it out meaningfully to you.

As it is, whenever someone writes a "guide to licensing," they're doing it to make a point about their favorite one, and they're usually sniping at the other licenses along the way. We could say something nasty about computer-science types who know enough scholarly language to sound reasonable until well after you realize just how far they've stuck the knife, but we won't. They gave us Linux, so we forgive them. When the book is written that doesn't involve sniping and back-stabbing, we'll include it in the appendix. If you can find the authors, they may even buy you a copy if you're a little short that day and really need to know more than two years' worth of near-constant flaming across the Internet, meticulously archived everywhere, can provide.

So, to return to the immediate point, Qt wasn't "free" enough (in that sense of free we talked about earlier that has nothing to do with cost) to satisfy everybody.

There was enough of a problem, in fact, that at one point Red Hat announced it wouldn't include it in their distributions. This has been, as the Desktop Wars have played out, attributed to all sorts of sinister motives on Red Hat's part, including a desire to cripple SuSE (which supports KDE by making it their default desktop), nationalism (many of KDE's principal developers are German), and monopolistic intent (which we'll get to).

> As it is, whenever someone writes a "guide to licensing," they're doing it to make a point about their favorite one, and they're usually sniping at the other licenses along the way.

The second problem, which takes us into yet another battle that predates Linux, and will probably outlive it, was the programming language upon which KDE was to be built: C++. The problem with C++, as any perfectly reasonable person who hates it in favor of say, C, will tell you, is that it isn't C.

"C," a perfectly reasonable person who hates C++ will tell you, "is the language upon which UNIX was built. C is the language of the Linux kernel itself. C is elegant and simple. C is not encumbered by the notions high-foreheaded academicians have about programming languages. C++, on the other hand, is the language of ninnies and eggheads with too much time on their hands. C++ is a trainwreck waiting to happen. C++ does not rule."

At this point, you'll be asked to perform a simple programming task in C++, presumably because you can't. The perfectly reasonable person who hates C++ will sit back smugly and laugh. Then your friend who knows more than you will explain how this is actually quite trivial, which will require a disclaimer that there's something wrong with that approach from your interrogator, which will provoke a nasty jab from your more knowledgeable friend about how C is for Neanderthals. And on and on.

In shorter form: KDE was built on C++. Strike two.

Strike three requires no explanatory text: Some people thought KDE was ugly. These same people are typically quiet during C/C++ wars, and don't have very complex opinions about licensing. They're just very, very concerned that their desktop not look ugly, and they had their say.

> C++, on the other hand, is the language of ninnies and eggheads with too much time on their hands.

Now, these problems with KDE would be non-issues if Linux existed in some sort of locked-in state the way Windows does. We all know that the net result of hating anything about Windows is more of the same the following year, only with a better selection of wallpaper and a new set of things to learn to never do if you don't want to crash your computer daily. It's not that the folks at Microsoft heard your complaints and decided to make you suffer for complaining. They'll make you suffer whether you complain or not.

As we were saying, though, Linux is free in all sorts of ways, including the fact that if you don't like something, you're likely to have the same tools at your disposal as the person who did whatever it is you didn't like.

Enter the GNOME project.

GNOME: Handcrafted With C to Burn out the KDE Heretics

There are several ways to read the beginning of the GNOME project. Some claim it was never motivated by anything other than personal animosity toward KDE's developers. Others buy the "party line," which was that a desktop environment with no licensing problems was required if Linux was to make it as a desktop operating system with its principles intact. Still others just smile and allow that part of the fun of Free Software is the occasional duplication of effort.

There's no denying that GNOME's founder, Miguel de Icaza, had some unpleasant run-ins with KDE developers before deciding to start his own desktop project. There's also no denying that KDE's licensing problems didn't satisfy the strictest members of the Free Software community. And there's no denying that KDE's use of C++ drove some people into a blind rage.

The GNOME desktop environment was announced as an effort to build a "completely free" desktop for Linux. By that, its developers meant that they wouldn't use any toolkits with questionable licenses, or write any software that wasn't completely Free. As a result, they decided to use the GTK toolkit, originally developed for the popular, PhotoShop-like program known as the GIMP.

They also planned to build GNOME on C, which won much applause from everyone bent out of shape over KDE's use of C++. There were some other, more obvious differences to the casual user, as well. Where KDE preferred a somewhat staid look (reviled by a few as "too Windows-like"), GNOME affected a different appearance (reviled by a few as "too cartoonish").

GNOME was widely praised throughout the community as a legitimate effort, and widely scorned as a shabby attempt on the part of Miguel to get even with the KDE community for not listening to him. Whatever the motivations, the hackers surrounding GNOME began to hack, and the project slowly took shape.

Red Hat chipped into the effort by housing several GNOME hackers out of the Red Hat Advanced Development Labs, and announced their intent to push GNOME as the de facto Linux desktop, which fanned the flames of those who claimed the distribution makers were out to corner the desktop market by leveraging their considerable name recognition and market share.

As I sit writing this, over two years later, there's no end in sight to the Desktop Wars.

A few months ago, the GNOME project announced that they were founding the GNOME Foundation. Several major companies like Sun and Compaq got behind the effort, declaring that as far as they were concerned, GNOME was the new standard desktop for not only Linux, but UNIX. Howls went up, as they do whenever companies rear their heads in the Linux world and declare that they've seen the light. There was a little irony involved here, too, since the same companies declaring GNOME the Once and Future Desktop had once said the same thing about CDE, and look where it got them.

Not long after the GNOME Foundation was announced, though, TrollTech, the company that makes Qt, the toolkit that caused so many aspersions to be directed against KDE's licensing purity, decided they'd had enough of the issues their licensing had caused and released their product under the GNU General Public License. This prompted some of the more ardent defenders of KDE to suggest that the GNOME project no longer had any reason to

exist, and ought to just stop all development and call it a day.

Hero of the Free Software Revolution Richard Stallman had something to say about TrollTech's change
of license, too, and although he
praised them for it, he pointed out a
bit of legal esoterica that needed to
be dealt with by some of KDE's developers: There were still a few bits

> Howls went up, as they do whenever companies rear their heads in the Linux world and declare that they've seen the light.

of code floating around here and there that had their licenses
infringed during the years KDE was using a less-than-totally free
toolkit. These infringements, he pointed out, needed to be forgiven. Worried that the Desktop Wars might almost be over, more
howls went up as the word "forgiven" was taken to mean "Apolo-
gize for being naughty and defying my will" instead of the more
commonly understood "Grant an exception to the license to prevent weakening it if it ever had to be enforced."

You could argue that Mr. Stallman could have chosen his
words more carefully, and that he'd shown up at a treaty-signing
in a Kaiser Willhelm helmet brandishing a gun; or you could
argue that the Linux community enjoys a good fight and hated
the thought of letting one as good as the Desktop Wars go.

DISTRIBUTION WARS: NO, JUST SAYING YOU RUN LINUX ISN'T ENOUGH

So, if you're a religious user of the best editor around and you've
got an ethically pure, conceptually superior, attractive desktop,
you're still not out of the woods. If you're running Linux, you're
running a distribution. Distributions are a way of dealing with
what would be a very difficult and messy proposition if there
weren't distributions: getting Linux up and running on your own.

Most of the time, we don't think about what happens when we turn on the computer and wait for it to boot. Linux, of course, isn't the sort of OS to hide behind an attractive screen of clouds on a blue sky—it tells you exactly what it's doing. From loading the kernel to starting up the GUI, you get to read a message about each and every step Linux is taking as it pulls itself up by its bootstraps.

When you send e-mail in Linux, play a CD, compile a program, surf the Web, edit a file (using Emacs, I hope—see how easy it is to pick a fight with just the few tools I've given you already?) or print a picture, you're doing so with one of many, many possible choices and configurations. You could gather up all the software to do these things on your own, and compile it from its source code, and write the configuration files for it, and hope you got all those hundreds of little programs just so. Or you can just go out and buy, borrow, or download a distribution.

> Linux, of course, isn't the sort of OS to hide behind an attractive screen of clouds on a blue sky—it tells you exactly what it's doing.

Distributions take the work out of much of running Linux. Their maintainers preselect a collection of applications, do most of the configuration you need to at least boot up and start using your system, and sometimes offer you support for installing and running Linux on your computer. Some distributions don't cost a dime, others can range up to over $100.

Because there are so many of them, and because they all have such distinct approaches to presenting the end user with a workable Linux installation, they are naturals for all sorts of good fights.

Here's a quick look at the beef with all of them.

Red Hat: Easy Installation for the Masses
(and That's the Whole Problem...)

Red Hat is probably the best known of all the distributions, thanks to fairly agressive marketing and what used to be one of the easiest installations going.

That ease of installation, of course, is what earned it early enemies among the angrier elements of the Linux community, many of whom bemoaned the "dumbing down" of Linux because "just anybody" could have a working installation out of the box. Adding insult to injury, Red Hat even had the gall to provide a way to make installing software really, really, easy.

RPM, which stands for "Red Hat Package Manager," was widely viewed by purists as the worst sort of mollycoddling. Instead of having to build a program from source (which isn't that hard most of the time), users can type a single command to add or remove a program from their computer. RPM isn't the only package manager on the block, but it's the most popular among the more common distributions, and it was a big selling point for Red Hat. People interested in "just running Linux" could be spared one more little chore to try out the newest software.

Some muddleheaded types will try to tell you that RPM, because it seems to work smoothly and allows programs to be packaged pre-compiled, is a "proprietary" program, which raises the ugly specter of a license war, since it would be bad karma indeed if a major Linux distribution were to rely on a closed-source program too much. A quick look at the RPM source code (a tip-off that maybe it isn't that proprietary after all) reveals, though, that it's happily licensed under the GNU General Public License.

Others, who we'll grant their inalienable right to paranoia, insist that Red Hat is out to monopolize Linux and become the next Microsoft. It's hard to disagree with the sentiment that a

> Others, who we'll grant their inalienable right to paranoia, insist that Red Hat is out to monopolize Linux and become the next Microsoft.

business's first priority is to make money and grow, but it's even harder to credit the notion that a community of hackers and free-thinkers who all managed to walk away from Microsoft in the first place would quietly line up behind a new monopolist.

Red Hat's popularity, of course, sets them up for all sorts of other problems. With a relatively huge base of new users out and about with their shiny new Red Hat installations and no sense about how to secure their machines from even rudimentary attacks from the neighborhood script kiddies, there's a lot of squawking about Red Hat (sometimes called "Root Hat" because it's supposedly so easy to "get root" or take control of) and how poor its security is.

Is it that bad? Linux isn't always the most forgiving, no matter which brand name it's being boxed under.

Debian: Live Free or Die, or At Least Don't Run Linux

The Debian Project is another distribution with a distinguished history in the Linux world. Its primary distinction as a community is its insistence on keeping software that isn't free out of its distribution. Many other distributions are happy to include software that isn't free, the Netscape browser being the most notable. Debian, on the other hand, won't. They hedge their bets a little by making Netscape available, of course, but it isn't an "official" part of their distribution, which includes thousands and thousands of programs under the GPL.

Remember the KDE/GNOME flap a section ago? Debian was the last distribution to cave in on that one when it finally admitted

KDE into its distribution after Qt was relicensed. That didn't stop some of Debian's loonier detractors (who hate them for coming off as too consistent with their stated ethics) from accusing them of a nefarious attempt to do a poor packaging job on their release of KDE so as to discredit the project.

And therein lies the source of Debian's special place among Linux distributions: They know what they think is right (free software), and they do what they can to stick to that. So well, in fact, it's hard for some people to deal with rationally.

Debian's other distinction is its nearly glacial production cycle, which is born out of the most meticulous quality-control process going among the major distributions. Where other distributions go through two or three releases, Debian's developers prepare one. The upside to this is that when you install Debian, you're guaranteed a meticulously tested distribution with little that will likely bite you later on. The downside is that you'll celebrate a birthday or two waiting for a new release. Debian's developers are fairly intractable on this point, though, and argue that it's better to have the trailing edge working reliably than the bleeding edge, well, bleeding all over the place.

Debian's other secret weapon is how it manages to get packages of software onto your computer. Through a fairly ingenious tool called "apt-get," Debian's able to download not only a piece of software you want, but every piece of software it might need to work correctly with a single command. The same sort of simplicity is involved with

> This appeals to the cardinal virtue all good hackers share: profound laziness.

updating any software that may have been changed since you installed it. This appeals to the cardinal virtue all good hackers share: profound laziness. Why painstakingly download package after package when one command does it all?

Periodically a Red Hat or Mandrake or SuSE enthusiast will, in the interests of striking a blow for her favorite distribution, announce a remarkably convoluted Perl script to handle the difficulties RPM presents to anyone with a reasonable splash of laziness. The problem is, no one who wants the ease and simplicity of a packaging system wants to put up with Perl scripts. At this point, I'm supposed to say something very prescient about how if someone doesn't work something out soon, there's going to be a terrible problem. Sadly, having just returned from a convention where no fewer than four companies have announced solutions to take care of this very shortcoming in RPM, I'm reduced to shouting "I told you so!" at the walls.

Slackware: On the Internet, Nobody Knows You're Borrowing Big Sis' Computer

The first distribution I ever kept on a machine for more than a week was Slackware. Because it doesn't exactly have a package-management system like Red Hat or Debian, Slackware is often thought of as the "hard distribution." The fact that I managed to make it work with little more than a book and no connection to the Internet during my extensive period as the most rank of Linux newbies suggests that this reputation isn't deserved.

> For some people, the level of difficulty they induce on themselves is a bragging point.

Slackware advocates can be pared down into two general categories: good ones and bad ones. Slackware is well-loved by the more "do-it-yerself" element of the Linux community in large part because its maintainers haven't made an attempt to hold anybody's hand during the configuration of a freshly installed system. People who like having to do things by hand in the name of finer control over every element of their system are usually too busy to contribute to flame wars, and they're the salt-of-the-earth types, anyhow. When you think "Good Slackware Advocate," think, "too busy working to yammer."

As a result of the difficulties it sometimes poses, Slackware also enjoys an unfortunately sterling reputation among the sort of people who talk about "their boxes" as if they run server farms for Fortune 500 companies when what they really mean is the dual-booting Windows machine their parents let them use when their big sister's away at college. For some people, the level of difficulty they induce on themselves is a bragging point. The "bad" Slackware advocate turns up in any flame fest over distributions convinced that mere mention of his favorite distribution will silence the combatants once they realize how indescribably lame they must be in comparison to our intrepid masochist. When you think "Bad Slackware Advocate," think, "too busy yammering to work." Or think of the kid next door with really baggy pants who makes every word that ends with "s" sound like it's ending with "z," as in "Slackware rulez."

Mandrake: Taking It from Both Sides

At the other end of the spectrum from Slackware is Mandrake. Mandrake was, once upon a time, not much more than a finely tuned version of Red Hat with more goodies, nicer default configurations, and the nifty fact that it was built to accomodate Pentium-based computers specifically. Over the years, Mandrake has slowly grown out of its reputation as a Red Hat taillight-chaser and become its own distribution, and it has a very loyal following.

For the most part, Mandrake users aren't the ones starting fights. They just like being able to buy the latest copy down at the local Wal*Mart (Mandrake is very agressively marketed where many other distributions fear to tread) and knowing they'll be getting a fairly well-tuned product out of the box. Lots of people, however, like to start fights with Mandrake users:

"How good can it be if it's based on Root Hat?" they ask.

"How good can it be if you can buy it at Wal*Mart?!" they jeer.

"Pentium optimizations introduce only marginal gains in performance that most users will experience only as figments of their overactive imaginations!" they charge.

> "How good can it be if you can buy it at Wal*Mart?!" they jeer.

The average Mandrake user will point out that it really isn't based on Red Hat so much anymore, and that just because Wal*Mart sells a lot of copies of "Big Bass Fishin'" alongside "Linux Mandrake Deluxe," it doesn't make everything they sell bad, and that they used to think the same thing about Pentium optimizations until they tried them out.

So who's right?

On the one hand, you have the Red Hat users who enjoy the luxury of being right if you put it to a vote. On the other, you have the Debian users who know that every element of their favorite distribution probably *has* been put to a vote. Then you've got the Slackware fans who argue that, like Samurai of old, they've forged their installation in the furnace of their own misery, and the Mandrake fans who argue that it's sheerest lunacy to install something that isn't pretty good out of the box.

Well, they're all right. And therein lies another bit of the Joy of Linux: Like some bizarre amalgam of Disneyland and Las Vegas, it has a little something for every taste. The only people who aren't right, and this goes for just about everything you've read about in this chapter, are the people who don't, in the end, admit that the best judge of which tool is best for you is you.

Chix Who Don't Fake It

IN TOUCH WITH MY FEMININE SIDE

Despite the fact that I possess a Y chromosome, I would like to think that I am among the type of male labeled "sensitive."

I have some solid reasoning to back up this statement. Having been raised by a single mother as an only child, I had to figure women out in a hurry if I had any hope of emerging from my adolescence alive. My mother is not the most tolerant of testosterone displays.

I get the feeling that my upbringing raised some concerns among those members of my extended family. I got taken to a lot of ball games and fishing expeditions by my uncles and grandfather, most likely in the hopes of ensuring my turning out as a heterosexual. There was a collective sigh of relief when I announced in high school that I was dating...a girl.

Still, despite all my empathy and emotional stability, there are some instances when my being a man comes through loud and clear. For instance, I tend to equate success with the number of things I have (the old "who has the most toys" syndrome). I am very competitive, particularly in an argument where all I want to do is win. I don't understand Oprah at all.

In the lab with me was another first-year grad student, who was quietly typing away on her terminal.

Another area where my sense of manhood used to get in the way was the area of tech. Women, I once believed, did not *get* computers.

It took a seriously embarrassing incident to reveal the truth.

Briefly, I was a doctoral student in astrophysics at a major Midwestern university. Really. And as I scrambled to come to grips with this reality, I was exposed to a whole new set of computer interfaces, particularly this new Windows thing.

One day, I was sitting in the computer lab trying to figure out how to print a file on a network printer just across the room. In the lab with me was another first-year grad student, who was quietly typing away on her terminal. No one else was around, which was slowly driving me crazy, because according to the lab schedule, there was supposed to be a lab assistant with the initials AS on duty.

After about 15 minutes of frustration, my fellow student, who must have been getting tired of my mutters and grunts, leaned away from her computer and asked me what was wrong. So, I told her, politely (so I thought) leaving the technical details out of the situation:

"I can't print this file!"

She automatically looked across the room to see if the printer was online, and it was. That should have been my first clue.

"Well," she asked, "what's it telling you?"

"It's not telling me anything," I whined. "I hit Print, the little printer icon appears, but then nothing happens."

Determined to figure this out, I kept looking at the screen in hopes of finding the answer there.

"Are you sending it to the right printer?"

What? Was she on drugs? What was *she* talking about!?

"Huh?" I said, in typical lost fashion.

"I said," she repeated, "are you sending it to the right printer?"

"Ummm...I think so..."

But my answer was too hesitant to satisfy her. She stood up, waved me aside, then proceeded to perform an arcane ritual (she checked the Printer properties, but I was too new to know this) on the screen. Afraid my file was going to disappear, I muttered something rather stupid.

"Er...hey, that's okay, I can wait for the lab assistant..."

She ignored me and said, "You've been sending your files to the wrong printer. Someone set this to print to one of the printers on the third floor of the Engineering building." A few mouse clicks. "There, now it's set to print here."

Then she turned and smiled in a way that could be very charming...

"And by the way, I *am* the lab assistant," said my classmate, Annette Sanders.

...or very cold.

I tried to tell myself later that the reason I did not pick up on the fact that she was the lab assistant was because she was a first-year student like me. But I knew, deep in my sexist little soul, what assumption I had really made.

> **B**ut I knew, deep in my sexist little soul, what assumption I had really made.

The Joy of Tech   by Nitrozac and Snaggy

This is a lesson that I kept with me for a long time, especially after I became the father of two girls. If I wasn't aware of sexism before, it smacked me in the face pretty hard then.

The most telling incident happened with my oldest daughter in her first-grade class. I was visiting the school one day, helping out the teacher like I did once a week. This week, the class was going to their computer lab, to learn (mostly) how to use the keyboard. The computer lab included a collection of about 20 Windows PCs, all equipped with an educational word processor designed to let the students create rudimentary documents.

For the purposes of getting their little six-year-old fingers to learn how to type, it did the job.

My daughter, who knows her way around Windows (that's the machine she uses at home), popped open Word instead of the kids' program, and began to hunt-and-peck the assignment phrase onto the screen. When the lab teacher walked by, she went ballistic. I was on the other side of the lab, helping another student, so I could not see what the concern was. All I heard was "you are NOT following the assignment!"

I walked over; once I saw the screen, I knew what had happened. Still, I did not think this was a big deal. After all, they weren't saving these files, and the output would print just as well to the printer. The lab teacher, however, was unmollified, and proceeded to tell my daughter to scrap the sentences she had already typed and to start over. Not wanting to stomp on a teacher's authority, but really wanting to defend my daughter, I suggested that my daughter cut and paste the text into the kids' program. This sort of worked, but the teacher began to grumble that she did not have time to spend on fixing these mistakes, when the boys in the class were more likely to experiment anyway.

> **W**hen the lab teacher walked by, she went ballistic.

My eyes goggled. I nearly lost it. "Excuse me, but are you saying that because she's a girl, my daughter is somehow technically deficient?" I was trying to speak in a low tone, but, predictably, all chatter in the room ceased when the kids heard the anger resonating through my voice.

The teacher didn't back down. "I have found in my experience that the boys are more likely to try something more advanced on the computer."

> This sort of worked, but the teacher began to grumble that she did not have time to spend on fixing these mistakes, when the boys in the class were more likely to experiment anyway.

I saw jail time and/or a large civil lawsuit in my immediate future.

Calmly, and without pointing at anything on the screen, I told my daughter to select the text, click Edit, click Copy, start the kids' program, then click Edit, Paste. I knew she could not type well yet, but she *could* work the mouse and the menus. My daughter followed the quick instructions, much to the chagrin of the teacher, who clearly did not think her capable. Not only that, my lovely daughter punctuated the action by formally exiting Word—without my instructing her to do so.

Nothing came of this incident, save my daughter knowing how to cut and paste text. I hope, however, that the teacher learned something—but then again, people set in their ways tend to be hard nuts to crack.

At least, that's what Annette Sanders would say.

WOMEN IN IT

Quick: Think of a geek, right now.

Ninety percent of you just had a picture in your head of a bespectacled, skinny little person with some sort of skin condition and an apparent aversion to bathing. And this geek was a male.

We are all guilty of associating geekhood with men. The statistics are with us, after all. Nearly eighty percent of IT staffs in the United States are comprised of men. Unfortunately, because of this overly masculine environment, women in the IT field tend not to be recognized for their abilities.

One tale tells of a high-ranking female engineer who bumped into a male colleague from her company at the airport while waiting for a flight for a business trip. When asked where she was off to, she replied, "San Francisco." To which the man replied "Oh, off to do some shopping?"

This is the kind of thing that women get to contend with almost every day. Research has shown that in a business environment:

- Women are interrupted more often than men.
- People make more eye contact with male employees than female employees in meetings.
- Women are asked fewer or easier questions than men.

> And this geek was a male.

Because IT is a male-dominated environment, it is more difficult for female workers to socially bond with their male colleagues, because non–work related topics tend to be about things that interest men, such as sports or cars, which many women care little about.

These are just the subtle types of bias that occur. Far more overt forms of discrimination and harassment happen, unfortunately, all the time.

Imagine, then, how women hackers who love to work with Linux, which is an even more male-dominated area than most in IT, must feel!

There is hope, however, thanks to the efforts of Deb Richardson, a Canadian Information Architect, who started LinuxChix in 1999. LinuxChix would not only become a site for women to meet and discuss Linux; it would also become a haven for all Linux newbies.

The Joy of Tech — by Nitrozac and Snaggy

PUTTING UP WITH MORONS

It is a sad truth that many new users feel intimidated when requesting help for Linux thanks to the Linux community's insular and territorial nature. Questions posed in perfectly legitimate forums are sometimes answered with "This is not the help desk," or "RTFM" ("Read the f—ing manual"), or some other snide comment.

The people who fire off such statements are typically insecure types who don't want the world to know as much as they *think* they do—otherwise, they wouldn't be quite as special.

Sadly, there are enough of these losers out there that new users, women and men alike, feel insecure when raising a question that might help them understand some nuance of Linux.

Deb Richardson certainly understood this phenomenon, having witnessed it regularly while working as an Ottawa-based tech writer. She also noted an alarming tendency of many tech-oriented Web sites, such as Slashdot, to have little more than a locker-room mentality about women in general, and certainly about women in IT.

Richardson believed most of these loud-mouthed statements came from a minority in the Linux community, but because it was such a vocal minority, new users and people outside the Linux world thought the entire Linux population consisted of unhelpful, territorial, pea-brained geeks.

> She also noted an alarming tendency of many tech-oriented Web sites, such as Slashdot, to have little more than a locker-room mentality about women in general, and certainly about women in IT.

In an attempt to reverse this perception, Richardson founded LinuxChix, an international group that would—hopefully—let new users feel more accepted, and enable them to get more help than the traditional online Linux sites. Although Richardson was targeting women, she has made it clear that LinuxChix is open to all who wish to participate.

LinuxChix members resist the notion that the group is out to promote women over men. "Equalism" is their primary watchword, describing a world where anyone can do any job for which they are qualified, regardless of race, gender, challenge, or location. If a woman wants to be a CEO, that's great; the same goes for the man who wants to be a Kindergarten teacher.

Gender roles do not hold a lot of stock for LinuxChix, but nor does political correctness. To them, equalism is not about quotas or token females. The members of LinuxChix wish to be judged on their individual merits, not given any kind of special treatment.

> **If** a woman wants to be a CEO, that's great; the same goes for the man who wants to be a Kindergarten teacher.

Any visitor to the site can see that it is a thoughtful source of technical information as well as social discussions; it's the social discussions part that detractors (and there are many on Slashdot) criticize. They argue that LinuxChix is not about Linux at all, that it spends too much time dealing with non-technical issues. Although no one could accurately declare LinuxChix to be 100-percent technical, it should be readily apparent that even the most hardened geek has to come up for air some time.

LinuxChix is not the only organization for women in IT, either. Other organizations exist to lend assistance to this underrepresented section of the geek community, which we'll cover in the next section.

THE GIRLS OF THE INTERNET

In the spring of 1995, six women gathered in the @Café in Manhattan to form an organization that, in just a few years, would reach international status. Webgrrls International became one of the premier women's IT organizations, providing training and networking for its members around the world.

Webgrrls is first and foremost a group dedicated to getting women a better footing in the technology industry, by providing mentoring opportunities and job leads to its members.

Webgrrls' founder, Aliza Sherman, was president of her own Internet consulting company, Cybergrrl, Inc., and was interested in meeting other women in her industry. Through her Cybergrrl Web site, she began to regularly correspond by e-mail with her contemporaries, and then organized the first meeting in April, 1995. By November, the membership rolls had grown to over 200 in New York alone.

Webgrrls is still an active organization, though activities have seemed to slow on the international level. Filling this gap, though, is a new women's IT organization: DigitalEve.

DigitalEve began in June, 2000, the brainchild of three women who wanted to start a technology networking organization. In just five months, the membership numbers grew to nearly 7,000. Many DigitalEve members come from Webgrrls chapters; the two organizations have similar goals and ideals.

In Canada, a very strong organization is Women In Trades and Technology (WITT). WITT describes itself as an "education and advocacy group dedicated to promoting and assisting in the recruitment, training, and retention of women in trades, technology, operations, and blue-collar work across Canada." Though not specifically involved with IT, WITT does sponsor the Women in Information Technology group, which targets specific IT issues.

> **W**ebgrrls is first and foremost a group dedicated to getting women a better footing in the technology industry, by providing mentoring opportunities and job leads to its members.

As technology jobs continue to open across the world, it is clear that women in IT will no longer be such a small minority and that all members of the IT community, Linux or otherwise, will soon face the challenges of learning to work together in more productive ways.

HOPE FOR THE FUTURE

Not every professional experience of women in the technology workplace is a tale of woe and injustice. As we enter the 21st Century, some progress has been made in the business relationships between women and men. The personal relationships are still a mess, but one out of two isn't bad.

One positive experience is that of Anna Dirks, a twenty-something User Interface Engineer working with Helix Code, one of the newest commercial Linux organizations. Helix Code is taking the GNOME interface and going beyond its initial programming and creating a polished and powerful version for commercial resale. As the company's sole UI Engineer, Dirks is the person who gets the interface programmers and the back-end programmers to talk nicely to each other long enough to come up with a consistent and branded interface that matches the Helix Code style.

> One positive experience is that of Anna Dirks, a twenty-something User Interface Engineer working with Helix Code, one of the newest commercial Linux organizations.

Helix Code is a brand-new company, and like most start-ups in the technology industry, the work is intense and takes up long hours. The younger staff at Helix Code have better stamina for this kind of work, and Dirks is clearly excited to be working in this environment, if not a little tired.

Dirks' entrance to the technology field came a little late in life, having grown up in Iowa and not being exposed to a com-

puter of any kind until the last year of high school. That all
changed when she attended MIT, where computers are as ubiquitous as air.

At first, Dirks was in the physics
program, but found the "sadistic ten-
dencies of [that] department were beyond anything I could imagine," Dirks
said. So, she switched to the Electrical Engineering program and began
to use UNIX computers on a daily
basis to complete her work there.

In the Electrical Engineering Department, Dirks was part of a population of women that made up just 10
percent of the entire department. She
described instances where being a minority in this male-dominated environment was a legitimate obstacle.

> So, she switched to
> the Electrical
> Engineering program
> and began to use
> UNIX computers on a
> daily basis to complete
> her work there.

One such incident involved one of her professors lecturing
to a group of women in the department and informing them that
in a business environment, it was unforgivable for them to cry.
The men in the department received no such lecture.

Dirks certainly rose above this geek macho environment and
definitely capitalized on her time at MIT, picking up degrees in
creative writing and women's studies to go along with her electrical engineering degree. After graduating from MIT, she traveled for a time, started an Internet business in San Francisco,
and eventually ended up at Helix Code in mid-2000.

While Dirks' experience at Helix Code has largely been positive, being the only woman engineer at the company has raised
some awkward moments. Dirks cites large differences in how
she approaches conflict compared to her male colleagues.

"I'm learning how to use constructive conflict here," she
explained.

After graduating from MIT, she traveled for a time, started an Internet business in San Francisco, and eventually ended up at Helix Code in mid-2000.

Dirks could not think of an incident where her professional opinion was challenged because of her gender. Actually, the nature of her particular job places her in more conflicts than male-female issues. Conflict resolution is an integral part of what she does, and Dirks does not sense she has any disadvantage in this area.

Dirks' experiences seem fairly indicative of what goes on at technology start-ups, where the younger and less traditional staffs tend to be less concerned with gender roles and more concerned about getting the work done fast and right. This is good news for everyone entering the technology workplace, as people become judged more on their merits than their chromosomes.

MOVING ON TO SOMETHING NEW

Now that we've concluded our look at some of the culture behind Linux, it's time to delve into the stuff that really makes a geek's heart beat pitter-pat. It's time to talk tech.

In Part II, "Doin' It," we'll start looking at why Linux is cool from a techie's point of view, without getting too technical and making you nod off. Chapter 6 will launch the discussion with a topic near and dear to the minds of many computer users: security. You'll find out why security for Linux is more than just an afterthought, and why Linux users chuckle a lot when the latest e-mail virus makes the rounds.

The Joy of Tech   by Nitrozac and Snaggy

PART TWO

Doin' It

I'm Clean!
I Swear!

Fortunately for me, I've spent the majority of my computer life virus free. When the Melissa virus raged its way through the Windows computers of the world, not a single viral message appeared in my office machine's Outlook, and the only person telling me "I Love You" when that infamous little bug spread its cheer was my wife.

Once, though, an evil little package was dropped on my hard drive and caused all manner of trouble. It was, of course, on a Windows machine, in the days before I began to use Linux. The tale is a classic one; even so, the strife of the young hero can still bring a tear to the eye.

OUR HERO'S TALE OF VIRAL WOE

With firm resolution, our hero jabbed his finger into the power button, to be rewarded by the pleasant hum of the fans inside his PC. Suddenly, a beep bleated from the speakers, when no beep

The Joy of Tech

by Nitrozac and Snaggy

was ever heard before. The hero riveted his eyes to see these cold letters burning on the screen:

```
Can't find system disk.
```

With a nervous chuckle, the young user resolutely pressed the Enter key.

```
Can't find system disk.
```

He pressed the Enter key again.

```
Can't find system disk.
```

Puzzled, our intrepid hero squarely set his jaw and performed the next logical step when dealing with a Windows PC—pressing Ctrl+Alt+Delete to restart the system—only to have his jaw drop when the message came up again:

```
Can't find system disk.
```

Denial yielded to anger, which became grief as attempt after attempt was made to start the machine. Finally, hours later, the dejected user broke open the PC case and removed the hard drive. A short trip to a friend's house later, he connected the hard drive to another PC in the hopes of salvaging the data from the errant drive.

The hero's friend, at that time a far more skilled wizard in the dark arts of the PC, took one look at his screen and muttered four arcane words:

"Dude, boot sector virus."

"Say again?" our hero asked.

"Your drive, man," the wizard said between sips of cola, "it got hit by a boot sector virus. It's toast until you put a new master boot record on there, but to be sure, you need to reformat the drive."

And the world came crashing down. The end.

Embellishments aside, this is a familiar tale to many Windows users. One way or another, viruses of all shapes and sizes seem to creep into the memory and hard drives of PCs around the world every day. My story had a semi-happy ending: Although I lost about a day of work while reinstalling all my software, the vital data I needed was backed up, so I really lost nothing important, save a bit of ego.

> **P**uzzled, our intrepid hero squarely set his jaw and performed the next logical step when dealing with a Windows PC— pressing Ctrl+Alt+Delete

"I FEEL SO *VIOLATED!*"

The feeling you get upon realizing that your PC has been violated is like none other. It's a sickening feeling, yet you find you can't look away, like staring at a train wreck. And while viruses are perhaps the most common form of this violation, they are just one way your machine can be compromised. The real danger is from the intelligent cracker-warrior who is actively trying to enter your PC.

A couple years ago, when I worked in the IT department of a big real estate management company, I witnessed just such an attack. I had ducked into the server room to escape the demands of my users and was swapping stories with the ultra-geeks, who lovingly maintained the swarm of Windows NT machines. As I extolled the virtues of Linux for the umpteenth time, one of the keepers shushed me as he focused on his screen. I looked over his shoulder and watched an activity log scroll by.

"What is it?" I asked, less annoyed at his interruption than by the fact that I could not read as quickly as he could.

> The simple truth is, if someone really wants at your PC, they will eventually find a way in.

"Someone's trying to break in," he muttered, his voice nearly obscured by the white noise of the servers and the air conditioning.

And so they were. I watched an attempted crack by someone using a valid user ID but not, it seemed, a valid password. I asked my colleague how he knew this wasn't just some user forgetting his or her password.

"See that IP address? That's not our network," he said. "And that ID is for John Smith."

"Is he logging in remotely?" I asked, already suspecting the answer.

"That would be a neat trick, seeing as how I just saw him in his office 10 minutes ago."

And so the attack went. Luckily, Mr. Smith (names have been changed to appease the litigious) had a decent password and the cracker was unable to guess it before the keeper of the servers locked the attack out.

In all, a rather anti-climatic event, until I asked how many times this had happened.

"Oh, we get something like this about every day."

Something to think about.

YOU CAN HAVE IT ONLINE OR REAL-WORLD

Although the Linux community has a bit of a superiority complex (it gets a bit smug whenever a new virus makes its rounds through the Windows PCs of the world), Linux is not, nor has it ever been, invulnerable to attacks. That said, Linux is, code for code, a more security-minded operating system than any of the Windows family. But even a cop on the street can get mugged; so, too, can a Linux system be compromised by mischief makers and evil doers, should they put their minds to it.

The simple truth is, if someone really wants at your PC, they will eventually find a way in. The trick is to make it hard enough for them that they will get discouraged and go away, or increase the likelihood that they will be busted on their way in.

Linux, by its very nature, makes setting up such obstacles pretty easy to do. The attributes that some critics contend make Linux clunky and difficult to use are the very attributes that make it hard for intruders to do a number on your Linux machine.

Before examining these mystical attributes, let's review the ways that a Linux machine (or any other PC for that matter) can be boarded and plundered. Then it will be easier to see how Linux can repel these different types of intruders.

Getting Physical

Physical access is the most straightforward way someone can get to your machine and its data. One way this is done is with the use of rappel lines from the ceiling. Usually, however, it simply involves someone, maybe even someone you know, casually sauntering up to your PC and reading what's on the screen.

Access is often not that difficult to obtain, particularly in an office environment. If you work for a medium-sized or large company, you probably don't know everyone personally, which makes it easy for a cracker to bluff his or her way onto your machine. He may say he is a new consultant for the IT department, coming to check on a problem with the network, and could you, like, please log him in? You might fuss a bit about being interrupted, but chances are you'd slide out of your chair and let the newcomer do his work on your PC.

While all of this seems to be heavily into the cloak-and-dagger realm, the simple truth is that letting people have access to your PC is always a risky proposition.

Brown-Paper Packages

If physical-access security does not get a lot of press, the opposite is certainly true for the distribution of PC viruses. Like a badge of honor, people simultaneously bemoan and brag about the fact they've been hit with a really nasty strain.

This attitude is a holdover from when *we* get sick. After being out from work for a few days, we stagger back into the office and boast about how many times we worshipped the porcelain god. Likewise, when our computer is laid flat by a bug, we find ourselves saying things like "That worm really did a number on my system! I must have infected over a couple dozen people with it."

Even if our entire hard drive gets whacked, the eventual reaction will typically be like this one. But as with the stages of dealing with death, one experiences five stages before reaching this state of equanimity:

- **Stage One: Denial.** "No way, man. Not *me*. I *know* that virus didn't hit *my* machine!"
- **Stage Two: Anger.** "That rat-$#@!*&! SOB virus programmer better not cross the street in front of me!"

- **Stage Three: Bargaining.** "Oh, c'mon, just let me get these files! You can have the rest, just let me open these, please!"
- **Stage Four: Depression.** "My life is ruined. I can't even play Solitaire…"
- **Stage Five: Acceptance.** This is when we rebuild the mess the virus left and move on with our lives. This includes broadcasting the aftermath to all who will listen. After all, misery loves company.

At the risk of being repetitive, since the topic of viruses is examined *ad nauseum* in popular media, here's the quick definition of a computer virus: A *virus* is a computer program, sometimes embedded within another file or application, that runs on an infected computer against the user's wishes.

Viruses are classified by how they are spread, and there are two basic types:

- Straightforward, run-of-the-mill viruses
- Worms

There is a third type of evil program that does damage like a virus, but is not really a virus at all. Even though Trojan horses have the same end result as many viruses, what makes these programs so different is the fact that they cannot self-replicate; worms and viruses can.

> Like a badge of honor, people simultaneously bemoan and brag about the fact they've been hit with a really nasty strain.

Regular viruses can cling to executable files, or even the boot sector of a floppy disc, ready to infect the next PC they come to. A plain-old "ordinary" virus always reproduces a copy of itself at some point in its life span. Sometimes it is the very act of replication that does the harm to the PC, since an endless replication cycle of even the slightest bit of code will eventually fill up the memory and ultimately stall the system. Other viruses simply create a nuisance, like displaying "Windows SUX!" on the top of your screen or causing your computer to forget what printers are connected to it. And some act as doomsday weapons and destroy any file they can sink their electronic claws into.

The Trojan Horses are so named because, like the ploy used by Odysseus and his fellow Greeks when they took on the city of Troy with the big wooden horse, Trojan Horses can hide in files that appear to be innocent, such as documents, images, or executables. If the Trojan Horse is hidden within an executable file, often the executable does what it is expected to do—while also doing something sneaky to your PC. Trojan Horses don't replicate themselves; they are a one-time only kind of weapon.

Worms are special forms of viruses that spread themselves over a network connection to infect other computers. Worms typically exploit some kind of network security flaw to get into other PCs. The infamous ILOVEYOU virus is a good example of a worm, since it used e-mail connections to spread the love.

Although viruses are the best-known form of attack to PCs, they usually do little damage, other than replicate themselves. Even so, the sheer number of viruses out there (50,000 at last count) tends to scare the pants off of even the most reckless PC user.

> So far, only three viruses out of 50,000 have been aimed at Linux users.

Actually, it scares the *Windows* users. So far, only three viruses out of 50,000 have been aimed at Linux users. Little wonder Linux users don't tense up when an attached file shows up in their e-mail inboxes! Little wonder they laugh themselves silly whenever an anti-virus company like McAfee tries to peddle its wares to the Linux community! It's like an atheist asking a priest if he needs Bible help. Of course, Linux users' tendency

toward cockiness about viruses could lead to trouble later on. Although bullets don't harm the Man of Steel, sooner or later someone finds out about kryptonite.

1-900-HACKERS

Few people in the world are as hard to pin down as the cracker, the law-breaking version of a hacker. Views on these outlaws differ depending on whom you ask. For example, if you ask an experienced corporate business person or a member of an IT staff how they feel about crackers, the answer would most likely be "burn 'em." This less-than-friendly response is due to the hundreds of thousands of dollars of damage crackers manage to create in the U.S. every year—for which corporations end up picking up the tab. (Of course, once you find out your own 13-year-old is holed up in his room doing a lot more than downloading porn from the Internet, the idea of jail time for crackers loses a lot of its appeal.)

On the other hand, if you poll the younger, more creative computer crowd, they might speak certain names in hushed, awed tones—names such as Mitnick, Hackweiser, and Hackah Jak, crackers who are the elite of the elite. To a young geek, these are the Joe DiMaggios and Willie Mays of their generation.

To you, the average intrepid PC user, they are at worst criminals to be feared and at best someone who hopefully won't find

your system an attractive target. In any case, they deserve some respect, and you should prepare your system to handle an attack by them.

Crackers make up the third level of security breaches: completely remote attacks on your system. To get at your system, all they need to see is your box on a network, even if that network is on the Internet. Having a dial-up connection is no guarantee of protection, either. To them, a door is a door. The question is, have you locked the door well enough to keep them out?

> Crackers use a variety of tools to break down the defenses of your system, the most dangerous being their brains.

Crackers use a variety of tools to break down the defenses of your system, the most dangerous being their brains. Besides this rather scary and obsessed bit of equipment, they can use a full rack of ammunition to pick the locks, including Trojan Horses and scripts designed to ferret out the secrets of your PC before you even realize what's happening.

Some crackers borrow their techniques from the FBI and DEA, who typically announce their presence in full body armor and brandishing semi-automatic weapons, and screaming at everyone to get down on the floor, giving no one a chance to react. A smash-and-grab attack from a cracker has a similar disorienting effect for PC users.

The truly dangerous cracker attacks are the quiet ones—the ones you don't see until hours, perhaps days, after the fact. These attacks are masterful in their stealth and patience, leaving few clues behind.

Then there is the script kiddie, a new breed of cracker who probes for vulnerable systems at random out on the Internet. Script kiddies aren't looking for specific information or targeting a specific computer; they want to get root access on any computer they can. They usually do this by focusing on a small number of known security holes in Linux. By searching the Internet for machines with just these holes, eventually they find a machine they can get into. Script kiddies, contrary to their own beliefs, are not necessarily as smart as crackers; often they don't understand the scripts they are using to batter victim machines.

> There may be no method of profit here, just the rush of finding out someone's dirty little secrets.

What do these crackers usually want? That's a tough one, since lots of times, their goals are as diverse as their methods. Many attacks are aimed at Web sites, where crackers and script kiddies take inordinate pleasure in replacing the contents of a Web page with their own versions. On the surface, this doesn't sound like a big deal, unless the Web site in question is something like CNN or Amazon, where revenue is dependent on the faultless running of the site.

Other crackers don't want to deface Web sites so much as take them down. Using a technique known as DDoS (*Distributed Denial of Service*) attacks, they break into some poor unsuspecting person's computer and instruct it to do nothing but send requests to the target Web site. Once a cracker has broken into a significant number of PCs, which are now called *zombies*, the zombies will aim a massive number of requests at the Web site. Web sites send information out to any PC requesting it, so when a bunch of zombie PCs launch a hundred million requests for pages in a few measly minutes, the effect is akin to putting a pea into a microwave and turning it on high for 10 minutes. The pea implodes into a shriveled black piece of carbon.

Some crackers are simply nosy; they access a system and then monitor the activity on the PC to see what they can learn about the person or company who owns the machine. There may be no method of profit here, just the rush of finding out someone's dirty little secrets. Others, however, operate with a more capitalistic frame of mind. These are the people who jump into a PC to see what kind of data they can get in order to sell it for their own profit. Like the pirates of the seven seas, they pillage and plunder computers from the relative safety of their own havens. Fortunately, however, not too many crackers fall into this particular mindset, which, as Martha Stewart says, is a good thing.

The simple truth is that when software developers create their applications, security is not the first thing on their minds—getting the program to work is. In many cases, security is not even third or fourth on the list of priorities when an application is coded. Many of the programs standing as gatekeepers of information on the Internet and private networks may look tough, but are the electronic equivalent of Barney Fife in actuality. That's why it's a good thing most crackers perceive themselves not as criminals, but as knights errant, protectors of the Internet world they fiercely call their own. Unfortunately, they resort to methods that shatter privacy and damage content.

This attitude is seen throughout the cracker community and it is summed up well in this passage from the hacked Web site of the NAACP, which was briefly taken over by a cracker or crackers known as the United Loan Gunmen on September 19, 1999:

> ...The internet is our play ground, its (sic) our side of the tracks. When you step into it, claim your own corner of cyberspace, and put up your house...dont (sic) expect not to arouse our curiosity. With thousands of large organizations, instituations (sic), and companys (sic) who already have their spot on the net...(sic) and the thousands on their way...this is a message to you, and a message to the people that you trust to run and protect your data.

```
    Be carefull (sic). As hackers we are not out to
destroy you…(sic) we are here to watch, wait, and
learn. As i (sic) have said before, we are the
knights of the internet. We see and hear things that
you think you only hear and see, we are places only
you think you can go. We watch what you do.
    Call this what you will…we call it work.
```

Spelling errors aside, this statement generates a lot of speculation about the cracker community's motivations. Speculating, however, is like standing inside the Alamo and wondering what all those Mexicans are doing on the horizon. It's better to prepare for their arrival, so you have a fighting chance to survive.

WHY LINUX IS (ALMOST) VIRUS-FREE

So what's Linux's big secret? Why does it have to contend with only a handful of viruses, while Windows battles tens of thousands?

> A cynical observer might point out that the dearth of Linux viruses exists because Linux is the favored OS of the virus maker and only an idiot would make a virus that could come back and bite him on the, er, PC.

A cynical observer might point out that the dearth of Linux viruses exists because Linux is the favored OS of the virus maker and only an idiot would make a virus that could come back and bite him on the, er, PC. You might be able to make a case for this, but this argument involves a lot of supposition. For all we know, crackers might be using Microsoft Bob to incubate their viruses. After all, Bob had to be good for something. Still, given the ease with which viruses can infect the Windows operating system, it does make some sense that virus makers would shift to a safer playing field to craft their wares.

Is Linux safer because of abstinence? Would it fall down just as hard as Windows if a virus slid its way into a Linux box? The ambiguous answer is yes...and no. Let me explain: The Linux environment is not conducive to a virus attack—unless some knucklehead fails to set it up properly. Then it can be open season.

Here is the secret to Linux's success with viruses: multi-user configuration. In English: A properly configured Linux PC, even just a stand-alone home computer, should have the superuser account known as root, and then at least one additional "regular" user account to be used on a daily basis.

Most viruses infect existing executable files; the only way infection can occur is if the virus can write over the executable file. On most Linux systems, only the root account can write over executables. So if Joe Average is logged on to a machine as javerage and lets a virus get on the hard drive, nothing will happen, because the javerage account cannot write over executable files; it can only read them. The virus, unable to latch onto anything, will instantly die.

Now, if javerage happens to own an executable file or two, the virus still won't be able to do much damage; at most, Joe loses the ability to run a few apps on his system. He will likely just reinstall or recompile the application files to get the apps running again, thus killing the virus.

Linux is also an unhealthy environment for viruses because it does not let viruses perform certain tricks that work under other operating systems. No regular user account is able to lock out services or privileges from another user by crashing the PC or eating up system resources—two popular tricks in the Windows virus pantheon.

> After all, behind every triple-shielded titanium hard drive PC is a potential dumb mistake by a user that could make all that protection seem like so much tissue paper.

Another reason a Linux virus epidemic has not yet occurred is because of a weakness in the Windows operating system that Linux simply does not have. Microsoft, for good or ill, decided long ago to increase the ease with which files could be shared across a network, even if the network was the Internet. So, in products such as Outlook or Outlook Express, executables of any size and shape can be pulled in with a message and (to make things even easier for the user) run by clicking the attachment within the message!

The ability to run an application that is not saved to your system without any kind of security blocks created a heaven and hell for Outlook users. Sure, it was cool to run the little frog in the blender executable, unless it turned out to be something else with the same file name and a far more sinister purpose than watching a little animated frog get puréed. (And that's saying something there, don't you think?) If such an application were e-mailed to a Linux user, it would have to first be saved to the file system before being run. Again, even if it were infected, the virus likely would not be able to do much damage.

This method of e-mail infection does raise one possible way of introducing a virus that could wreak some havoc on a Linux PC, whether it was well-shielded or not. After all, behind every triple-shielded titanium hard drive PC is a potential dumb mistake by a user that could make all that protection seem like so much tissue paper.

Thus far, it sounds like Linux is pretty much secure, as long as some bozo doesn't leave his system running the root account 24/7. This certainly applies to viruses, which do not have a lot of intelligence and therefore give up and die whenever they reach an obstacle. But remember, people write viruses, and people can make for a devious and very effective delivery system.

WHEN ROOT IS A BAD THING

When a cracker or a virus is trying to manipulate your system, they would like nothing better than to have root access to your machine. With root powers, a cracker or script kiddie can play with your system and its defenses like Silly Putty. A virus could replicate itself through a Linux box with ease. Still, despite countless warnings from the Linux community, users habitually use root when running their PCs.

Root, it cannot be stressed enough, should be used only when you have to perform administrative tasks on your PC. Using root on a daily basis is nothing short of madness.

Here is one scenario that could cause some major damage for users:

One day, a new application shows up on Freshmeat that allows you to view real-time satellite imagery on the background of your computer. It's nothing too complicated, but it's kind of nifty in a geeky sort of way. Some users download it and install it on their machines. When they install it, they install it as root, since that's what the README file says to do (this is by no means an unusual request). Nor is the request to run the application as root, though this should make any user wary. Now the application is installed, and the user happily has real-time visuals of his hometown (and the rest of his continent) popping up on his desktop. All is well.

Except...

The author of this application has included a few surprises in the source code that have nothing to do with satellites. One of these surprises includes commands to e-mail the author various information about the system's accounts (including root) and network information. Another surprise might append some access information to the PC's /etc/password file. Now the author/cracker has a whole slew of root accounts sitting in his mailbox, ready to use at his leisure, with perhaps none the wiser.

The reason for this is simple: A lot of people in the Linux community tend to trust the things they download and install on their machines, especially if they have gotten the original source code and compiled it themselves.

Although it is true that hiding a viral piece of code in the source code is difficult, it is by no means impossible. Besides, viruses can hide in plain sight within an application's source code because very few people actually look at the code before they run Makefile to compile the code into an executable.

This is a potential Achilles heel for Linux security, because too often users point to open source as a barrier for viruses. The fact is, only the most sophisticated Linux user actually examines the source code before installing it, and even then, that's only to make needed modifications—not read it line by line. Most of us just get the code and run make, which is really no different from downloading a binary file and installing that.

> A lot of people in the Linux community tend to trust the things they download and install on their machines, especially if they have gotten the original source code and compiled it themselves.

Open source is a potential stumbling block for the virus maker, but like other forms of viral attack, the defense is only as good as the user who set up the Linux box.

EXPLOITATION OF THE LINUX BOX

This next statement sounds like snobbery, but it is true of all users, not just the new ones: People are the weakest security layer for any computer system. Cracker Kevin Mitnick coined the phrase "social engineering," which was what he called the business of bluffing his way to getting information about a computer. Mitnick, and now other crackers, social engineer users by identifying themselves as system administrators and asking for a user's password. Users, not realizing that there is never a reason the sysadmin would need their password, give out the information almost immediately. Anything to help the IT guys, right?

Again, this is not to criticize new or inexperienced users, the way IT staffers do over beers on Friday night when they laugh about the latest "luser" mistake. This applies to those staffers, too. Anyone can get conned. In fact, IT employees are often the primary targets for social engineering, because they have the most knowledge to reveal.

To give users some credit, though, they are not the only way into a PC. There are many ways a cracker can get root access on your machine without any help from you.

Linux, like anything else made by human beings, is not perfect. There are flaws and imperfections within the Linux kernel and the other components. Sometimes these bugs are just a pain in the butt. Every once in a while, though, someone discovers that with the right bit of tweaking and prying, the bug is an actual security hole that might allow crackers more access to the system than they should have.

This kind of security hole is called an *exploit*. Exploits are often hard to find; the sheer amount of code in a Linux distribution makes it possible to predict how the OS will react in all situations. Once an exploit is found, however (and one is found in some distribution nearly every day) a fix is created and distributed to all who want it—often before a script kiddie is even aware of it. Nearly every major distribution has some sort of e-mail announcement system as well as a Web site where all security exploits are posted, so even the more apathetic users can check in once in a while to get the latest patches to fix the problem.

Exploits are *the* number-one target for the script kiddies out there. They are counting on you not keeping your system up to date, leaving it open for attack (once again, the user proves to be the weak link in the security barriers). Suppose, for example, that our kiddie has a tool that can exploit ld.so on Linux systems. This tool is often just a refined script designed to force the bug to break the code in a way Linux's designers did not intend. The script kiddie will first sit down at her PC and obtain a list of targets. She does this by sending bad packets of data to each machine in a list of Internet addresses (known as IP addresses) to determine which ones are Linux boxes. Of course, this process is completely automated, allowing the script kiddie to accomplish a great deal with just a few typed commands. After locating Linux machines, the kiddie runs another scan to determine which Linux systems are running the right version of ld.so. The one that has the security hole that the user hasn't gotten plugged yet. Now the targets are in the crosshairs, and the kiddie goes to work.

In fact, IT employees are often the primary targets for social engineering, because they have the most knowledge to reveal.

All of this scanning should be noticed by the systems getting visited by the script kiddies, but all too often the users of these PCs don't check their system logs, which is where records of all of these scans are made. Of course, even if a scan or intrusion is found, the script kiddie is often using another system as a zombie to do her dirty work. If her attacks are caught and traced, it's the zombie system that gets busted, not her own. Another camouflaging factor is the fact that script kiddies often share their databases of vulnerable machines with each other, making it possible for your system to get cracked long after any scans are made. And the really good script kiddies often add viral applications to a targeted computer, which allow them to create back doors to the victimized PC. Once a back door is made, visitors can enter and inflict changes without any logs made of their presence.

It's getting better of course. As more exploits get found, fewer avenues of opportunity are available for someone to take advantage of. Updating your PC for exploits should not be the end of your security procedures, however. There's a lot more the owner of a Linux PC can and should do.

PUTTING ON PROTECTION

When things are going well during a date, men often make sure that the special packet is safely tucked away in their wallets. The contents of this packet are there to provide one thing: security in an often insecure world. It's a very simple device that when used right has a lot of potential to keep things where they need to be.

> The really cool thing about Linux is that it does not take a Herculean amount of effort to set up these kinds of road blocks.

Such an approach cannot work for any computer system, and anyone who tries to sell you such a system should be smacked upside the head. There is no such thing as blanket, universal protection from attacks on a PC, because, as you just read, your system can be breached in myriad ways. Nor is any combination of shields going to keep everything out, either. When you put a computer up against the intelligence of a cracker, the computer will lose every time—provided the cracker has enough time to accomplish what he wants to do.

And there is the key: time. Security measures will never keep out everyone. Computers are too stupid to dance their way around a talented cracker, no matter what operating system is in use. That's why you never see computers with legs on them: They would walk off a cliff if you told them to. That said, a security system can succeed if it first blocks the copy-cat script kiddies out there who try to exploit systems almost by rote (as is the case with most script kiddies), and then manages to trip up the truly talented hackers long enough that you can discover the attack and (hopefully) do something about it.

The really cool thing about Linux is that it does not take a Herculean amount of effort to set up these kinds of road blocks. The operating system, as indicated before, is already pre-disposed to being secure. All you have to do is beef it up.

Before reviewing some of the simple ways you can better lock down a Linux system, let's get one thing straight: This is not a Linux security manual, nor does it pretend to be. If you have Linux, or are planning to use it in the near future, be sure to research security procedures thoroughly before implementing them. The solutions presented in the remainder of this chapter are intended as a guide only. For resources on Linux security, see Chapter 13, "The Linux Sutra: Resources."

Access Is Denied

If someone can get to your machine and has the talent and the time, then eventually he or she will be able to break into it. This is simply inevitable. What you, the user, need to do is tweak your machine to the point where the amount of time and energy spent on breaking into your PC's data stores is not worth it to the casual thief, and maybe even the professional one. Following are some ways you can make a cracker's life a little harder.

First, you need to get rid of a serious security flaw that shows up right after you boot some versions of Linux. During the boot process, a program called the Linux Loader (LILO) starts up and (barring any new input) automatically starts the Linux OS for you. When LILO first starts, it typically pauses for a few seconds to see if the user has some other instructions. If a sneaky person types `linux single` during this pause, the system automatically boots to the root account, without asking for a password! This may seem really stupid on the part of the LILO designers, but it actually is an emergency entrance into your system for cases when something seriously wrong has happened to it and you need to perform maintenance in a really bad way.

To fix this problem, you need to open the /etc/inittab file and add this line right after the `initdefault` line:

```
~:S:wait:/sbin/sulogin
```

This forces the user to enter the root password before getting to the single-user mode in Linux.

This isn't the only trick a cracker can perform at the LILO prompt; other commands will get them root access. You need to eliminate their access to the LILO prompt altogether. To do this, edit the /etc/lilo.conf file and add the line `delay=1` to the contents. This trick will give a user one tenth of a second to type instructions at the LILO prompt, something that no amount of Jolt cola will enable them to do.

If the user needs to get to the LILO prompt for a legitimate reason, they can always use a boot disk that has a copy of LILO on it.

Locking out the LILO prompt is just the start. If your PC is like most, then it will initially look to the floppy or CD-ROM drives to boot before the hard drive. If someone stuck a Linux system floppy disk into your drive and rebooted the machine, he would get root access to your system. All he would have to do is mount your hard drive and start scoping it out. The best way around this is to configure the PC's BIOS so that it will boot only from the hard drive. For extra security, add a password to the system BIOS so only you can edit it.

By this point, someone's going to need to crack your PC's case open and start monkeying with the insides before they can get to your data. So, if you get a good lock for the case, you will have likely eliminated 99 percent of the crackers trying to get inside your machine via physical access.

Earlier Is Better

The best time to start securing your PC is during the installation of Linux on your computer. If you start with a fresh install, you will know exactly what is on your system, which will reduce the chance of a nasty surprise.

A classic error that many users make is taking up a Linux installer on its offer to install pre-determined sets of software packages. Red Hat, for example, has setups for a workstation and a server. These settings, if chosen, will install everything Red Hat thinks you need to run your machine in these capacities. Other distributions do this too, trying to save time for the user.

This is very sweet, but the amount of time you will spend fixing up a trashed system is a whole lot greater than the time you'd spend up front during installation. Specifically, if your distribution has some sort of Custom install option, use that. Sure, you'll have to choose all the packages you want, but in the end you will get two major benefits from this.

For starters, your system will be running fewer applications, which translates into fewer security holes to exploit. Second, your hard drive will be less crammed with unnecessary apps, leaving you more room to download MP3s from the RIAA...or whomever. Besides, if you find out you need something that wasn't installed, Linux installs are frighteningly easy to do.

When you partition your system, you can give some thought to security. It is recommended that you place the /var mount point on a separate partition. /var is usually where your e-mail is saved upon receipt. If you were, perchance, e-mail bombed, /var could fill up very quickly. If the /var directory was in the same drive partition as the root (/) directory, that would be bad; if the / partition fills up, your system will likely grind to a halt. Sticking /var on its own partition will avoid this calamity.

You might also consider making partitions for individual users, just in case they get cute and try to fill up the / partition to crash the system.

And after you install your system, make sure you know exactly where to find updates for your distribution of Linux, and check this update location often, so your system is as up to date as possible.

Less Is More

Installing less software is a good security procedure for your Linux box. But even a minimalist installation of Linux may leave you with some applications running without your knowledge. These applications are known as *services*, which Linux runs because it is, at heart, a server OS. Three well-known services that may be running on your system now are ftp, telnet, and sendmail, but a lot more may have started running when you booted Linux. Quite a few of these services present security exploits to the outside world if they are not configured properly.

Tomes of material deal with the topic of configuring these services so they are resistant to attack. For now, just turn the things off. Running services you don't need is like using a GPS unit to get to the corner grocery store. Not only does it pose a huge security risk, it also eats up processor time.

Consult your distribution's manuals to see if there are any specialized tools for managing services; if not, you basically need to edit the /etc/initd.conf and /etc/rc.d/rc5.d files to stop services from running. This is definitely something you should research first, but you'll find the payoff well worth the while.

> **R**unning services you don't need is like using a GPS unit to get to the corner grocery store.

MOVING ON TO A NEW THING

There is no perfect hardware or software solution to keeping people out of your PC. At best, you can simply hope to deter them. This strategy has worked for a long time throughout many civilizations.

The ancient Egyptians, for instance, clued into deterrence when they decided to stop burying their kings inside mammoth pyramids, which were essentially big billboards that said "Steal Me" to any thieves hanging around the Nile. In 1504 B.C., they started burying their kings in hidden tombs within the Valley of the Kings.

Most of the tombs did, eventually, get looted. But one tomb survived relatively intact until 1922: that of the young pharaoh Tutankhamun.

But the ancient grave robbers did have one thing on their side: time. Time to search, time to dig, and time to rob.

Even with the lightening speed of the Internet, today's modern plunderers do not have that luxury anymore. They have got to be fast and quiet, before someone catches them with their hand in the cookie jar.

Steal time from them and they may not be able to steal data from you.

You will meet all kinds in the Linux community, and certainly not all of them will be surly crackers and hackers. Many of these people fit well within the inclusive Linux community, no matter how odd they act. But there are some users that even we look at askance. They're the switch hitters, the users of Linux *and* the dread Windows.

Switch Hitters

At the first Linux users' meeting I ever went to, there was a kid in black vinyl pants. This was in the late '90s, mind you, so Billy Idol and Depeche Mode were way more than 15 minutes ago.

I tend to react badly to odd fashion choices, which is pretty hypocritical considering I would be comfortable in jeans and a sweatshirt at any time day or night, regardless of the social situation. My reaction to seeing this kid was typical for me—I picked a seat on the other side of the room.

This kind of judgmental behavior is typical in all of us. We take one look at someone and make an opinion. It's hard-wired into our systems, from the days when we were monkeys hanging out in the African savanna. In those happy times, we needed to make the call based on what we saw, because we often had little time to do anything else.

Snake? Run.

Saber-toothed tiger? Book.

Beautiful girl monkey? Saunter on over and act like a big dope.

The very same principle holds true today.

IRS agent? Run.

The Joy of Tech   by Nitrozac and Snaggy

Raging horde of Backstreet Boys fans? Book.

Incredibly beautiful woman? Saunter on over and act like a big dope.

For good or ill, we are a judgmental species, walking around labeling everything. When we encounter something or someone we don't understand, instead of just trying to figure it out, we tend to label it a Bad Thing and then keep that opinion until proven otherwise. People who really excel at this kind of labeling are often avid watchers or even participants of *The Jerry Springer Show*. Androgynous people, for instance, are mocked and called "she-males," held up for all the world (the producers hope) to see. Some of us, thankfully, resist this tendency more than others. Even so, it constantly gets us into trouble.

Once an opinion is formed, whether it was well-considered or not, it is often very, very difficult to change someone's mind. Saber-toothed tigers, the monkeys figured out, wreak all kinds of havoc. And Linux users, the Windows crowd has decided, are nothing but trouble. It's not just the weird operating system with the penguin that gets lambasted, its those freaky people who run Linux boxes that need a stern talking to as well.

Of course, Windows users are misguided corporate zombies who need to be liberated from their electronic shackles. At least, so sayeth the Penguinistas.

> And Linux users, the Windows crowd has decided, are nothing but trouble.

Linux users, even at our most vitriolic, hold a deep-seated belief that any user from any operating system can be saved and brought into the brotherhood of the penguin.

"Your *(insert operating system here)* sucks," the typical statement from a Penguinista might go, "you need to use Linux because it can do *(insert three to four positive characteristics of Linux here)* for you."

And then there are the folk who both sides look at with a mixture of revulsion and admiration, and maybe a touch of

The Joy of Tech   by Nitrozac and Snaggy

© 2000 GEEK CULTURE, JOYOFTECH.COM

bemusement. These are the people who, for reasons all their own, straddle the operating system fence and choose to use Linux *and* another operating system. Once reviled as misfits and outcasts by all sides of the argument, multi-OS users are an increasing faction within the computing world. I, too, am a member of this dual-user faction, switching between Linux and Windows whenever the need arises.

That's right. You heard me. My name is Brian Proffitt, and I use Windows.

So far, acceptance of my choice since coming out of the case has been mixed. My Windows-using friends think I'm wasting my time. My Linux compadres tease me (my co-author once called me a "quisling bastard".) But in general, they support my lifestyle decision, patiently waiting for me to see the light and be delivered into salvation. I, on the other hand, merrily continue my heretical ways, living in peaceful co-existence with the Penguin and the Borg.

MAKING THE LIFESTYLE CHOICE

Linux users take great pride in the flexibility of the operating system they use. It can run on almost anything that has a silicon chip, and performs admirably when doing so. Pride, however, is one of

The Joy of Tech by Nitrozac and Snaggy

© 2000 GEEK CULTURE, JOYOFTECH.COM

the seven deadly sins—a fact never more evident than when you approach a Linux user and ask us about specific software.

"You guys have Outlook?" you might ask, checking to see if Linux can run Microsoft's flagship personal information manager application.

To which we reply, "No, but Linux has a variety of powerful e-mail clients that will allow you to manage your messages."

It is a known phenomenon that Linux users, particularly the hard-core geeks, can never answer a technical question without showing off a bit. In the end, we end up sounding like a nerdy game show host.

Undaunted, you might try again.

"Do these e-mail clients come with an address-book feature?"

> It is a known phenomenon that Linux users, particularly the hard-core geeks, can never answer a technical question without showing off a bit.

Slightly flustered now, we might twitch in exasperation and give you this answer: "Not many have that. The Gnome people are working on an Outlook-killer called Evolution, though."

By the time this statement is finished, we feel confident again, having delivered the requested information and perhaps started you on your way so we can get back to recompiling something.

"Outlook-killer?"

Unfortunately, we have lapsed into geek-speak and must now not-so-patiently explain what we mean in everyday English. Mentally, we start stroking the cute little penguin as a calming mantra. Tux will show us the way. Then, we explain that by "Outlook-killer," we mean an application that performs in much the same way as Outlook on the Linux platform.

You brighten. "Great! When can I get it?"

In our minds, we begin to clutch at Tux a bit.

"Errr...," we answer, "it's not quite ready yet."

"Oh," you say, a bit crestfallen.

We may be disappointed that you did not get a satisfactory answer, but we really need to get to this compilation now, so if you'll—

"Well, do you guys have Quicken?"

And suddenly the mental image of Tux is getting choked. Hard.

Not all conversations about applications in the Linux sphere go like this, but a lot still do, because of a big misconception about Linux that burns us every time it comes up: Linux has no good applications. We get very, very defensive about this, because in truth, there are hundreds of wonderfully written stable applications available for the Linux platform. They just aren't all gussied-up for the graphic user interface like all Window applications are.

At this point, any Windows user is going to go apoplectic. To them, using a command-line application is akin to trying to walk naked down the street while blindfolded. It's just that daunting. We, however, just take it in stride, which gives you a dark glimpse into our collective mindset.

This is the crux of the application argument, and the reason why Linux users get so hyper-defensive. Because the Windows community does not want to recognize the existence of any application that doesn't have a window, menu, or mouse pointer, there is a strong belief that there are hardly any Linux applications to be found.

Another factor contributing to this is the near-total lack of retail presence for Linux applications. If someone goes into the average computer store, the odds of him finding a boxed Linux application are higher than winning the lottery. Since most Linux apps are downloaded to the user's PC, boxed sets of a Linux application are rare. This seems to lower Linux apps' status in the eyes of the rest of the world. Apparently, an app is not that good unless you kill a few hundred trees to wrap it up and ship it.

A third, and perhaps the most galling, factor is that computer users seem to put a lot of stock into buying software that they have to, well, buy. An application that is not commercially sold is beneath a Windows user's notice (unless of course, they can lay their hands on a pirated copy). This mindset is shocking to Linux users,

Apparently, an app is not that good unless you kill a few hundred trees to wrap it up and ship it.

because here we are, offering the world really good software at either a low price or for free, and it's getting tsked at because it doesn't cost a fortune! Is it any wonder that the Linux operating system itself gained the general PC users' attention only when it showed up in shrink-wrapped boxes in computer stores?

There are, of course, gaps in the equation. Because Windows was initially targeted for the home and business workstation market, there is a preponderance of personal entertainment and productivity applications for the Windows platform. That's why (for now) you can't get a Quicken-like product for Linux, or very many children's educational games. Pretty soon, however, Linux will close this gap. As more and more Linux users come into being, software companies will start seeing a potential market for their wares. And the Linux developers who are already working with the platform will start working more with the graphic interfaces available in Linux, and thus will create more user-friendly apps.

In the meantime, many are in a limbo state, hanging between the two operating systems, unable to choose between them. But now the secret's coming out. You don't have to choose one or the other. Now, my friends, you can have both.

You Can Have It Both Ways

There are several pros and cons for using multiple operating systems on one computer. The cons include the headaches of installing two or more operating systems on a machine, resulting in more limited memory available for each of the operating systems. But the benefits of using multiple operating systems are huge. For instance, you can run all the programs available for each of the operating systems. You will also be able to use all the hardware your PC has. Finally, you'll save money by not needing to buy another PC.

While we may not run out into the street shouting this, many Linux users think dual booting is a good way to go—especially for new users just learning how to get around in Linux. This option gives you the benefits of using Linux without a lot of investment in time or money.

Curiously Exploring a New Lifestyle

If you decide to include Linux in addition to Windows on your PC, you will need to make room for it on your hard drive. Making room on your hard drive for Linux is far different from making room for the latest computer game; you must create a brand new *partition* from which Linux will operate.

Now you get a crash course in disk partitions and why you can't write data to a disk without them, so hang on to your collective hats.

The Birds and the Bees

Imagine the bee, buzzing around your garden. If you were to follow this bee back to its home, you would find a seemingly chaotic mass of buzzing insects, each looking as if it aimlessly wanders about with nothing better to do than hang out and buzz. As we all know, however, bees all have a specific purpose, working together for the collective benefit of the hive. One group of bees has the job of taking care of all the cute little baby bees after the queen lays her eggs. Now, think back to your science classes:

Where are the baby bees raised? If you said the honeycomb, you're right. If you're wondering what the heck this has to do with partitions, just bee patient.

The honeycomb is an ingenious device composed of hexagonal cells made of beeswax, where honey and bee larvae are stored for safekeeping. Now, ponder this: How would the bees get by if they did not have honeycombs? The answer is they wouldn't.

Keeping the honeycombs in mind, consider how data is stored on a disk drive. Data, you see, cannot be stored on a drive without some sort of structure already in place for the data to be organized. When data is placed on a drive, it is written into this structure, called a *file system* in the Linux community. A file system is the format in which data is stored—a honeycomb of cells if you will, where each little piece of data gets placed.

Computers being computers, it's a little more complicated than that. Data for a single file, for example, does not get stored in data blocks that sit right next to each other. The data may be stored in data blocks 456, 457, and 458, and then block 6,134, then block 7,111, and so on. (This is an oversimplification, but you get the idea.) It's the job of the file system to track the location of every part of a file. When you send a command to work with a file, the file system knows all the separate blocks where the file is stored.

While we may not run out into the street shouting this, many Linux users think dual booting is a good way to go—especially for new users just learning how to get around in Linux.

Because of all this file tracking and retrieving, computer engineers came up with idea of keeping the file systems small, even on large hard drives. In this way, the idea of partitions came into play. Basically, the *partition* is a virtual barrier that tells the file system: "You used to be able to write to blocks 1–25,000 all over the disk, but now you're only allowed to write to blocks 1–17,500. A second file system will write to blocks 17,501–25,000, so hands off!"

Thus, you have partitions, and each partition can use a different file system. As an analogy, honeycombs created by honeybees are different from those created by wasps—similar structure but different outcomes.

There are six major types of file systems used on Intel-compatible PCs today:

- **FAT.** Used by the DOS (including Windows 3.1 and Windows 95) and Windows NT operating systems.
- **FAT32.** Used by the DOS (including Windows 95b and Windows 98), Windows NT, and Windows 2000 operating systems.
- **NTFS.** Used by Windows NT and Windows 2000.
- **ext2.** Used by Linux.
- **HPFS.** Used by OS/2.
- **swap.** All operating systems use this type of format, which is used by the PC as auxiliary RAM. Linux, however, puts this space on a separate partition. When a program or process uses more memory than RAM exists on the computer, the swap partition provides additional memory for the process to use.

Different types of partitions typically do not work with other operating systems. Thus, in order to install Linux on your PC, you will need to create an ext2 partition on your hard drive. Unfortunately, if your PC contains a typical installation of Windows, your Windows file system is contained within one big partition that covers your entire hard drive. This leaves no room for a partition and a new file system. Remember, even if you have gigabytes of empty space on your drive, this space, like files and directories, may be scattered throughout the drive.

The easiest way to add a partition to your existing hard drive file system is to use a third-party application. This shoves all your data into a single collection of data blocks, leaving truly contiguous empty and unstructured (unformatted) space elsewhere in the drive where you can create a partition.

Getting Down to Business

Of all of the partitioning software out on the market today, PartitionMagic is arguably the easiest for Windows users to handle. PartitionMagic enables you to create partitions on your hard drives with ease. It even comes with BootMagic, a multi–operating system boot utility.

What makes PartitionMagic so great to use is that it actually creates a Linux ext2 partition without potential loss of data. Using PartitionMagic to create a native Linux partition saves you a lot of steps in installation. For more information on PartitionMagic, surf to http://www.powerquest.com/partitionmagic.

There you will find detailed product information. We heartily recommend this product for your use if you're going to be coming from the Windows platform.

If you do not want to plunk down the cash for PartitionMagic, never fear. Many Linux distributions thoughtfully provide fips, a utility that can resize and create FAT (either FAT16 or FAT32) partitions in Windows systems. The fips utility reduces the size of your current FAT partition and creates a new FAT partition. Because Linux will only sit inside an ext2 file system, created only from unformatted space during the installation process, you'll need to run the DOS fdisk utility to remove the new FAT partition.

You may have heard in computer legend and lore that eventually you will have to use the DOS utility fdisk on your PC. This utility is used when you have to completely wipe the data from your hard drive.

When you install Linux, there are really two instances where you will need to use fdisk. The first instance is if you plan to install Linux by itself on the PC. The fdisk utility may be the preferred method should you want to completely wipe the slate clean and create new partitions to install Linux. The second instance is to eliminate any partitions a third-party partitioning utility (such as fips) might have created for you. The fdisk utility can wipe these non-ext2 partitions from the hard drive.

Now that you have an idea of the tools you can use to make room for a Linux partition, it's time to examine just how Linux partitions work. That's right: partitions—plural.

Breaking up Is Not Hard to Do

The world of partitions is a strange one to the average Windows user, but its something we eat, sleep, and breathe with in Linux.

On most Windows machines, there is typically one partition on a hard drive. This is often true whether the hard drive is 6 or 60GB in size. You say you have multiple hard drives listed in Explorer when you know the system just has one physical hard drive? That's because when Windows sees a new partition, it automatically assigns a drive letter to the drive. This is a pretty simple system.

This is not what happens in Linux, however. A good Linux installation needs several partitions to work well. But if you were to open the File Manager in Linux, you would see the appearance of a single drive's directory tree. So what gives?

Linux manages its files in a completely different way than Windows does. Rather than using drive letters to refer to a partition and its corresponding file system, Linux separates the files and directories needed to compose its single file directory. In truth, this "single" file system is really composed of separate directory trees that are seamlessly connected across partitions. Where these sub-trees connect or break from the main directory tree are called *mount points*.

Rather than using drive letters to denote partitions, Linux uses a different naming convention:

```
/dev/[Drive Type][Device Where Partition⏎
Resides][Partition Number]
```

This naming convention isn't too tricky, once you get the hang of it:

- **/dev/.** All devices in Linux are managed in the /dev/ directory, including hard drives and their partitions.

- [Drive Type]. This is a two-letter indicator of the hard drive type. Possible values are hd (IDE disk) and sd (SCSI disk).
- [Device Where Partition Resides]. This is the device the partition is on. Possible values are /dev/sda (first SCSI disk) and /dev/hdc (third IDE disk).
- [Partition Number]. This denotes the partition. Possible values are 1–4 (primary or extended partitions), and 5+ (logical partitions).

Within Linux, this division of directories among partitions will be seamless. But when installing Linux with another operating system, you'll need to think through what partitions you want, what the mount points will be, and how much memory you'll allot to each partition, making sure to leave room for the other OS you'll be using. After all, it will not just be a case of having one Linux partition and one Windows partition.

Since you are curious on how to use more than one operating system on your Linux PC, you will need to understand the Linux Loader (LILO) application. This small but very useful app is the reason why having an alternative operating system is so easy, as you'll see in the next section.

Coming out

There is nothing hard-wired into a PC that prefers one operating system over another. It is simply string of software commands that starts with the application known as the BIOS on an Intel PC that chooses what OS should be run.

The BIOS is the application that tells the computer how to wake up when it is first turned on. Here's how it works: When a system with a single operating system boots, the BIOS looks at a special section of the hard drive called the MBR (*Master Boot Record* or boot sector) to see what operating system will be loaded. Any application in the boot sector is then activated. In the case of

Windows, it's the application that shakes Windows out and gets it moving. In Linux, it's the LILO application that springs to life. When a system has two or more operating systems, a special multi-boot application must reside in the boot sector that temporarily halts the boot process and allows the user to choose which operating system to load. LILO is just such a program.

To configure LILO to run Linux and another operating system, all you really need to do is install your Linux distribution on a machine with a clear partition available.

That's it, that's the big secret.

LILO is smart enough to see any and every partition file type and operating system start files on your PC, be it Linux, Windows, or even UNIX. It is a very flexible application. Only one operating system is resistant to sharing booting rights with Linux, and that's Mr. Big itself: Windows NT.

> Only one operating system is resistant to sharing booting rights with Linux, and that's Mr. Big itself: Windows NT.

Windows NT has issues with booting with Linux. Our side of the fence has accused Microsoft of once again locking out the competition. Whether you believe the motivation is sinister or not, the problem is still there.

Basically, the problem is this: The Windows NT OS Loader, the counterpart to Linux's LILO, does not recognize Linux as a valid operating system (imagine that!) because Linux does not produce the type of file the NT OS Loader needs to read before starting an operating system. In addition, the NT OS Loader will not function from anywhere other than the boot sector. Since only one boot loader can be in the boot sector at a time, NT could have a problem if LILO sits in the MBR—so Microsoft claims.

Quite simply, the easiest way to get Linux and Windows NT to work together is to install NT first on your machine.

Then, when you install Linux, just overwrite the NT OS Loader by making LILO boot to the Master Boot Record (MBR). Finally, edit your /etc/lilo.conf file and add an "nt" option that points to the device NT resides on (for example, /dev/hda1). This works because unlike the NT OS Loader, LILO is smart enough to figure out how to work with NT—another example of Linux's open nature.

If you want to run Linux with Windows NT or Windows 2000 installed later, and don't want to completely erase your Linux partitions to start all over again, you will need to take some special steps before installing NT. Of primary importance is that you *must* install LILO in the first sector of the Linux boot partition instead of the MBR. If you do this, there will be no conflict between LILO and the NT OS Loader. Unfortunately, the NT OS Loader will still not see Linux and it won't present Linux as a boot choice. Now comes the chicanery.

There is a way to create a file in Linux that the NT OS Loader *can* use to boot Linux. But since creating it takes a bit of time, we recommend that you obtain a little third-party program called Bootpart, available at http://www.winimage.com/bootpart.htm. This program will quickly create the Linux boot file for NT OS Loader and place it where NT OS Loader can use it. We highly recommend this application if you plan to use either Windows NT or Windows 2000 with Linux.

Now that you have managed to finagle your computer into handling more than one operating system, you will find it easy to hop back and forth between partitions to use the specialized applications you need. You can even share data between the partitions—without having to reboot your computer.

MOUNTING THE NEW OS

If you have set up your PC for dual-booting Linux and Windows, or Linux and anything else, then you can access all the other OS's directories with ease. All you need to do is mount the drive, just like a floppy or CD-ROM drive.

Mounting is another concept that seems really weird to Windows users. When Microsofties access a drive, it opens up, plain and simple. The only trouble they run into is if they forgot to stick in the floppy or CD-ROM disk to the appropriate drive. In Linux, which prefers not to waste processor time and memory keeping an eye on every single drive and partition on the machine, you have to tell Linux about a new floppy in the floppy drive, and tell it how to read it. This is called *mounting*.

This seems really backwards to Windows users, but it makes a lot of sense when you ponder it for a bit. Aside from the savings in processor usage, it's an excellent way to maintain security on your system. Still, in an effort to be nice to the New Kids on the Block, the Linux developers have incorporated the concept known as automount into many distributions. Automount does just what you would think: It lets Linux access any new disk inserted into a peripheral drive, just like Windows.

Automounting does not work right off the bat when accessing another partition on your hard drive. To get to another partition that uses another operating system, you have to mount the alternative partition by hand. The first thing to do is to find out what your Windows partition is named—and it won't be something easy like Butch, either. A few easy steps will set this up for you after you have made your computer a multi-boot system.

In your Linux system, open the file /var/log/dmesg, which is a log of the messages sent to the Linux kernel at boot time. We like to use the Emacs text editor, so just type:

```
emacs /var/log/dmesg
```

In the file, look for a set of lines that list your system's drives.

```
hda: WDC AC36400L, ATA DISK drive
hdc: ATAPI CDROM, ATAPI CDROM drive
```

From this set of values, you can see that your hard drive is named hda (most hard drives are, but you should check anyway). Go ahead and exit Emacs.

Now you know the name of your hard drive. But what is the name of your Windows *partition* on that drive? Remember, Linux does not use such silly notations as C:\ or D:\ drive. Luckily, there's an easy answer to this question.

In your terminal window (as the root user), type

```
fdisk -l /dev/hda
```

Hey now, don't get excited; we're not going to use fdisk to change partitions, just to check them out. This prompt will appear first:

```
Command (m for help):
```

Type p at this prompt to see a list of the partitions located on your hard drive, like this example:

```
    Device Boot   Start    End   Blocks   Id System
/dev/hda1     *       1    827  6642846    c Win95↵
FAT32 (LBA)
/dev/hda2           828    830    24097+  83 Linux
/dev/hda3           831   1655  6626812+   5 Extended
/dev/hda5           831   1646  6554488+  83 Linux
/dev/hda6          1647   1655    77261   82 Linux swap
```

And right there, in black and white, is the specific name of the Windows partition: hda1.

You're almost there. The first thing you need to do is make a directory on your Linux file system to mount the Windows partition. This kind of a directory is called a *mount point*, which is a fancy name for a directory the Linux file system can use to give the file system in the new partition a commonly labeled starting point. We usually do something like:

```
mkdir /mnt/win
```

Now, if you are the root user, you could enter the `mount` command to access the Windows partition. The syntax of this command is always:

```
mount    device name    mount directory
```

So, in this instance, you might type:

```
mount /dev/hda1 /mnt/win
```

But this would not quite be right. After all, the file system format on your Linux partition is ext2, while Windows uses FAT32. So to get these two systems to work together, you just need to add the `-t` parameter and specify the file system of the Windows partition so Linux knows how to work with it. The file system notation for FAT32 is `vfat`, so the complete command line would be:

```
mount -t vfat /dev/hda1 /mnt/win
```

Now you can access the files on the Windows partition to your heart's content. But if you want to use the partition as a regular user instead of root, which is a darned good idea, this command won't fly. And, even if you were logged in as root, why retype the mount command every time? What you need to do is edit the /etc/fstab file so the partition is—you guessed it—automounted.

When you open the /etc/fstab file, you might see something along these lines:

```
LABEL=/                  /                       ext2↵
defaults         1 1
LABEL=/boot          /boot                   ext2↵
defaults         1 2
/dev/cdrom           /mnt/cdrom              iso9660↵
noauto,owner,ro 0 0
/dev/cdrom1          /mnt/cdrom1             iso966↵
noauto,owner,ro 0 0
```

```
/dev/fd0              /mnt/floppy           auto⏎
noauto,owner   0 0
none                  /proc                 proc⏎
defaults       0 0
none                  /dev/pts              devpts⏎
gid=5,mode=620 0 0
/dev/hda6             swap                  swap⏎
defaults       0 0
```

So, if you add a line for your Windows partition, you'll be all set. The format of the line is similar to that of the `mount` command. If you add something similar to this line to the file, your Windows partition will be automounted every time Linux starts:

```
/dev/hda1             /mnt/win              vfat⏎
defaults       1 3
```

If you want to mount other types of partitions, you are certainly able to do so with the `mount` command or the /etc/fstab file. All you need to know is the partition name and the file system type. For a complete list of file system types, refer to the Samba section in Chapter 13, "The Linux Sutra: Resources."

LET'S ALL DO THE SAMBA!

Using the Samba server is another excellent way of connecting to Windows PCs that your Linux might be networked to. Going through the configuration of Samba is a bit much for this book. We strongly recommend you read the Samba series of help files listed in Chapter 13.

After you get done setting up Samba, we have one further suggestion: Make a copy of these six files in the /etc directory:

- inetd.conf
- hosts
- lmhosts

- host.deny
- host.allow
- smb.conf

Save these files on a floppy, or on another partition or machine. That way, if you ever install another version of Linux on your machine, all you need to do is reinstall the Samba server, create the smb group, the smbuser, and the public and data directories. Then you can just copy over these six files to your /etc directory and you're all set! Trust us, it saves quite a bit of typing, especially in the smb.conf file!

> As you can see, the process of sharing your computer with something other than Linux is not unlike a lot of relationships: a little pain here and there, but in the end, a huge reward.

MOVING ON TO SOMETHING NEW

The information in this chapter is just the tip of the proverbial iceberg when it comes to working with alternative operating systems. As you can see, the process of sharing your computer with something other than Linux is not unlike a lot of relationships: a little pain here and there, but in the end, a huge reward.

In Chapter 8, "The Joy of Toys," we abandon all pretense at civility and start getting into what (regrettably) gets the Y chromosome all geared up and ready to go: the hardware and the toys for your Linux PC.

CHAPTER 8

The Joy of Toys

When my then-fiancée and I went to graduate school, we lived in a large apartment complex along a river bank, down the hill from campus. To get to the university, you could hike straight up the hill on the steepest slope through a residential neighborhood, or you could go down along the river and go up the hill on a less-steep slope through a business district.

Money was tight then, so driving was a luxury we used only to go to places really far away. Otherwise, we walked or rode bikes. Because I was (and still am) not athletically inclined, I would ride my bike up the less-steep path in the mornings, despite the increased distance. (You can safely assume I barreled down the really steep hill in the afternoon.)

Along the river road were all manner of strip malls and restaurants, and one establishment that always caught my eye: a long white building with no windows and a big parking lot. There was little signage at this business, only one of those portable signs with the blinking arrow on top and plastic letters on both sides. It read as follows:

ADULT BOOKSTORE COME ON IN! 20% OFF ALL MERCH WHEN PROTESTED

You had to appreciate the inventiveness of the owners, especially because once a week or so, some church group or other organization would picket the adult bookstore. Whenever this happened, the braver clientele would duck through the lines to get their discount.

Because both my wife to be and I were raised in small to mid-sized Midwestern towns, neither of us had a strong sense of what types of wares were sold in an adult bookstore. So one day, I got the bright idea to go in and check it out.I was the only one in the relationship that would be willing to go through with it, since I was the one with the Y chromosome and could tap into the primitive male long enough to chuck my social upbringing and saunter in there. I confirmed this with my fiancée first, of course. I was being primitive, not stupid. The first thing I noticed about the inside of the place was that it was really dark. Ever the naïf, my first thought was, "How the heck can anyone read a book in here?"

Boy, did I find out why it was dark. There were no books, *per se*, just lots of magazines proclaiming Big This, That, and the Other Thing. And let's just say there was lots of hardware of the type to which no geek should ever be exposed. After a couple minutes of discomfiture upon discovering some coin-operated live viewing booths along the back wall, I quickly beat a blushing path to the door and walked out into the sun a more educated person.

Upon my exit, I blinked my eyes to adjust to the bright sunlight, and there, on the edge of the parking lot, was a bunch of (apparently late) protestors, who immediately started haranguing me with cries of "Sinner!" and "Exploiter!" and the like.

So much for social exploration. I got really good at riding up that steep part on the hill by the end of the semester, because there was no way I was *ever* going down to the easy part of the hill again.

We all have really embarrassing moments that we normally don't share with others, or a guilty pleasure or two that we keep to ourselves. For some it's chocolate. For others, it's watching NASCAR. One of my guilty pleasures used to be the palpable sense of, well, joy I got when I bought a piece of PC hardware and saw the "Microsoft compatible" label on it. My heart went all aflutter as I took it to the cashier, knowing this brand new toy would work in my Windows machine.

That was before I firmly embraced Linux and its philosophy. Even though I have a Windows partition running at home, all my hardware purchases are now dictated by the abilities of Linux. No longer does "Microsoft compatible" hold any meaning for me.

> **I**nstead of lazily depending on the corporate flunkies of the world to configure my computer for me, I get to learn how all of the parts work together myself.

I am consigned to the shadowy world of hardware compatibility lists and compilation of kernel modules to get my toys running on my Linux box.

This kind of effort has its own rewards, of course. Instead of lazily depending on the corporate flunkies of the world to configure my computer for me, I get to learn how all of the parts work together myself. Like that bookstore of days gone by, it's an education.

Things are, as the song goes, getting better all the time. As Linux strengthens its position in the IT community and in the marketplace, efforts are made to facilitate all the different kinds of hardware out there.

But it's a long, hard hill to climb.

WELCOME TO THE WORLD OF MEGA-HARDWARE STORES

Let's come right out and say it: Windows offers more hardware compatibility than Linux.

Windows has won this tussle because Microsoft has copped a serious attitude of "your hardware needs to be good enough to work with our software" to the computer hardware manufacturers. And as everyone knows, attitude is nearly everything.

Here's how the attitude works. Since the inception of Windows 95, PC users have become accustomed to relying on those ubiquitous device drivers, which automatically install a computer's new components. Drivers are designed to match the appropriate files with the new component, and place those files in the proper locations on your computer (you hope). In doing all this, it has set up the configuration of your new piece of hardware to behave nicely with the rest of the PC.

Windows users can get away with this simply because Microsoft, with its very pervasiveness, has managed to keep hardware systems within a certain "compatibility window." Of course, each PC manufacturer attempts to make improvements over its competitors, changing and enhancing various components and then aggressively marketing those enhancements. However, if each wants to include Windows with its products, thus taking advantage of the (thus far) huge Microsoft following, then each will adhere to Microsoft's specs despite fierce competition. That way, any enhancements will, in theory, work with Windows thanks to the drivers that come with the product.

Critics of Linux have said that it is rigid and inflexible, and thus is too difficult to use. Although Linux does indeed have its problems, inflexibility is certainly not one of them. Windows only appears to be more flexible—but that's because the installation path of hardware on a given PC has already been paved by hardware manufacturers whose components conform to Windows' suggested standards. It's sort of like claiming a victory in an election when you were the one doing all of the vote counting.

Linux, on the other hand, does not have cooperative agreements with PC and hardware manufacturers (although some have come into existence very recently). So, like Scarlett O'Hara, Linux must depend on the kindness of strangers to get software support for all the different pieces of hardware in the world. It is partly

> **A**lthough Linux does indeed have its problems, inflexibility is certainly not one of them.

through the efforts of talented and dedicated volunteers that hardware support is accomplished.

These volunteers think nothing of spending hours or even days picking apart a piece of hardware, rummaging through its

electronic guts to see what signals go where to which component. Then, with brilliant displays of reverse engineering, they
write a program that will manage that hardware for Linux.

Of course, some hardware manufacturers, being rather prig-
gish by nature, take exception to having the internal workings of
their products figured out for the entire world to see. Corporate
cries of "intellectual theft" occasionally sound out to this hacker
community, punctuated with cease-and-desist orders from some
of the more stringent manufacturers. The manufacturers who
put up the most protest are usually the ones, for whatever reason, who are not inclined to produce their own drivers and modules for Linux. Maybe they don't have the internal resources to
devote to Linux work or, more sadly, their executive/marketing
staff has been blinded by the great Microsoft marketing blitz-
krieg. The ultimate irony of this is, of course, that by withhold-
ing their hardware stats from the Linux community, manufacturers are depriving themselves of a tremendous revenue base,
not the potential for patent violations.

Control freaks notwithstanding, as Linux gets more popular,
the strength of its signal to the public and corporate audience will
overpower the noise coming from other sources, and hardware
manufacturers will start seeing Linux as an attainable revenue resource. In fact, this is already happening. As Linux flowers into
more of a commercial enterprise, the manufacturer bees are buzzing around looking for a way to start tapping into its nectar.

This is all well and good for the future, but those of us using
Linux today have some real obstacles to overcome.

CHOOSING THE RIGHT TOYS

You may have the impression that installing a new toy on your
Linux PC is as difficult as climbing Mt. Everest in a bathing suit.
Nothing could be farther from the truth. But for users who are

used to taking advantage of the mutual embrace Microsoft and hardware manufacturers have had for each other over the years, it may seem pretty difficult. Let's see how the typical hardware customer can shed this addiction to the Windows chokehold and get on with the business of getting hardware for their Linux box.

First, when users buy hardware for their PCs, they usually fall into one of two categories. One is the careful buyer, who researches all the different statistics of all the different hardware types before meticulously deciding which to purchase. You know the type—they're really wound up, but they always seem to have really nice stuff. Then there is the kind of buyer who just likes their hardware fast and powerful. They may hear about some new piece of machinery through the grapevine and decide it's time for a change. You know the type—they're really relaxed, but they always seem to have really nice stuff.

These two personality types—and everyone in between—can operate in the world of Linux hardware. They just have to take some precautions first. Enter the HCLs (*Linux Hardware Compatibility Lists*). These are Linux's answer to those little "Microsoft compatible" labels.

> So, like Scarlett O'Hara, Linux must depend on the kindness of strangers to get software support for all the different pieces of hardware in the world.

The Linux Hardware Compatibility HOWTO is the mother of all HCLs, maintained by the Linux Documentation Project. This document lists all the hardware that is known to work with the central Linux kernel. It doesn't get updated very often, because in these modern times, the individual Linux distributions themselves keep their own HCLs.

Checking the HCL for your distribution is the most important thing you can do before installing new hardware, no matter what your buying tactics are. If the hardware you desire is on the list, you're all set. If it isn't, you may find yourself having hardware performance problems.

HCLs are often used as ammunition by outside sources to tear down Linux. "You have to check a list before you can install anything? How stupid is that?" This kind of criticism usually stops when the critics are reminded that the use of HCLs in an operating system is not something unique to Linux. Microsoft's own Windows NT line of operating systems, up to and including Windows 2000, also makes use of some form of HCL. Microsoft's Web site will even probe your current hardware setup for you to see if there are any potential conflicts with Windows—which is all any of us need: a big-time corporation peeking into and possibly recording what hardware we have on our PCs. That's like asking the IRS to check our bank accounts whenever they feel like it.

Even though HCLs are not a Linux-only artifact, the Linux community tends to wear them as a badge of honor. "Look at how many new devices are on the list this month," we say, throwing a mocking laugh at the efforts of those who would stymie us. But a hardware compatibility list does more than point out to the world Linux's lack of resources and corporate partnerships. The HCL also serves another purpose: to make sure that the Linux operating system remains as pure as it possibly can. The current dearth of corporate support for Linux actually works for the platform, because device support can only be created by a few dedicated programmer-hackers. Unlike with Windows, not just any device can join the club. It has to be something fairly reliable; otherwise no one would bother building a driver module for it. And because of the "home brew" nature of these drivers, they are crafted with less focus on the bottom line and more focus on quality.

The total result of this situation is a smaller, but much more reliable set of hardware for the Linux OS. Device conflicts rarely occur, because so much care and crafting went into the creation of our device drivers. Oh sure, a mistake is made every once in a while and some piece of hardware hiccups because of an error in the module. Developers and hackers are, after all, human.

When such an event happens in the Windows community, and yes, it happens a lot, users are forced to jump through hoops to get some kind of software fix. When Linux users face a problem like this, however, we have two options, and none includes a lot of waiting. We can either dig into the source code and try to fix it ourselves, or we can contact the developer of the driver and ask them to fix it. And because of our strong sense of community, often the developer will oblige us

" **L**ook at how many new devices are on the list this month," we say, throwing a mocking laugh at the efforts of those who would stymie us.

as soon as they can, or put us in touch with some other user who can fix it for us. No strings, no fuss. Maybe they'll need a favor from us someday, and we will happily lend a hand if we can.

Here's an example of the community spirit in action. During a recent Linux convention in New York City, many of the booths needed a PC or two to display their wares or provide an online connection to the home office. Imagine the participants' shock when they discovered that many of the PCs were (gasp) loaded with Windows. Suddenly hundreds of PCs turned into very large paperweights.

Because at any given Linux convention there are literally hundreds of Linux distributions to choose from, everyone whipped out their favorite Linux CDs and started installing Linux before any of the convention-goers showed up. Fickle Fate had one more trick to play that day, however, as the convention center's PCs all used an obscure display card that Linux

> ...and thus Linux quietly grew stronger and closer on the same day.

did not like. The slow creep of fear began to trickle across the convention floor as hundreds of attendees began lining up outside the doors.

Luckily, some developers had seen this particular glitch before and, without fanfare or compensation, quickly hacked a specific driver for the errant display card and made several copies for all to use. All was well at the convention. That hack later ended up being a part of several distributions' arsenals of drivers, and thus Linux quietly grew stronger and closer on the same day.

ASK THE TOUGH QUESTION: IN OR OUT?

Myriad hardware components can be attached to or installed in a Linux box. You've got your modems, video cards, sound cards, hard drives, floppy drives, CD-ROM drives, DVD drives, printers, scanners, cameras, hand-held PDAs, and even a ham radio or two. Linux basically defines anything connected to the processor via a bus as some sort of hardware peripheral. What it really boils down to for this discussion are external and internal devices.

External devices are the easiest to add because you simply plug them in. Because nothing important is on the outside of your Linux box, you don't risk corrupting your machine. You can install an external device even if you are still new to computers. For example, to add a printer, you simply connect the printer cable to both the printer and the back of the computer, and then plug in the power supply.

There are many types of external devices. Specific devices exist for each of the ports on the back of your system, and, because they all have different socket sizes, you really can't connect the wrong device to the wrong port. For example, a standard parallel printer port is a female connection with 25 holes, and a mouse or modem serial port is a male connection containing either 9 or 25 pins. It's really just a matter of figuring out which socket plugs in where.

External devices are sometimes directly controlled by Linux, such as in the case of a printer, and sometimes indirectly controlled, as in the case of a monitor. Linux actually does not control the monitor, but instead sends a signal to your PC's video card and tells it what kind of picture to send to the monitor.

And then there are the internal devices, which are always managed directly by Linux. Internal devices are more difficult to install only because they require you to work inside your box. Few things are more nerve-wracking than cracking open the case of your PC and messing around with its guts.

The most common internal devices are sound cards, network cards, and hard drives. In most systems, you can also add memory, change the motherboard, or even upgrade the CPU, although we would advise you against doing so unless you know exactly what you are doing. There are factors to consider when changing a CPU and memory such as bus speed, clock multiplier, and memory timing.

There are hardware books out there that can guide you through the arduous task of physically adding a new component inside your box, and we strongly urge you to read them first before diving into the case of the PC.

TURN ONS AND POWER UPS

After you've managed to install a new hardware component, you'll need to do quite a bit more in order to get it working. Once the system is turned back on, your PC and then Linux start the process of detecting and configuring new devices.

The first thing that happens when a PC starts is that the bootstrap code is run. The bootstrap is a small program located in static memory (ROM) inside your computer's BIOS chip.

The Joy of Tech   by Nitrozac and Snaggy

You remember the BIOS is the hardware/software that controls the start-up processes. The bootstrap is part of the BIOS and it's always there, locked into permanent memory. The bootstrap quickly checks the internal system parts of your box to see if any major failure can be detected, such as memory corruption.

When finished, the bootstrap passes control to the rest of the BIOS, which is the heart of your input/output (I/O) subsystem. The BIOS' job is to detect the system components at start time and to work with the operating system to handle device calls.

Every device connected to your computer has a unique signal that allows the processor to distinguish one device from another. That signal is sometimes referred to a *device call* or *interrupt*. The BIOS sorts out all these devices and the software on your PC and starts figuring out how one set will work with the other.

To make this all a little clearer, imagine an old-style telephone switchboard, where an operator would have to physically patch connections between two phones in the network. It's the same process, really, just sorting out connections. Only the BIOS does it in milliseconds and doesn't say "one-ringy-dingy…"

You usually see the BIOS output on the screen every time you turn your computer on. The BIOS is the application that counts up all the memory you have in RAM on your PC, for example. You may also see a list of hard disks and then an information screen about your main system components. The BIOS is responsible for first detecting your hard disks, determining which one contains the kernel you want to boot, and optionally configuring any plug-and-play devices.

Once the BIOS completes its various jobs, control is passed to the first sector of your bootable hard disk (known as the *Master Boot Record*, or *MBR* for short). If you'll recall from the last chapter, the MBR contains LILO, the Linux boot loader, which simply tells the processor to load your Linux kernel or any other operating system you have configured on your PC.

This is not the end of the hardware tale. Once the BIOS and LILO have finished running, the really complex part begins. Try not to groan.

The Linux kernel itself then takes over and must detect, configure, and manage all the internal and external devices so that *Linux* (and all Linux applications) can use them. It does this using complicated data structures, device drivers, and kernel processes. The gobbledy-gook of text that appears onscreen before you see the first Linux prompt or graphical login screen explains what hardware is being found by the kernel and various device drivers.

When the kernel has finished setting up the main hardware, it passes control to device drivers, which are separate little programs designed to control a particular device. For example, to handle a SoundBlaster card, you need a SoundBlaster-compatible sound driver. There are also less-specific drivers that deal with things such as networking and your serial devices. All these drivers are loaded at start time after the kernel is finished linking up devices it can handle itself and looking for new devices connected to your computer. If it helps, think of the kernel as Santa Claus and the device drivers as all the little helper elves who do the grunt work without getting union wages.

Device drivers have to find the hardware they work with before they can start working. You might think the BIOS would handle this, but remember, the device drivers get started at the *end* of the boot process, long after the BIOS has finished its work and turned itself off. The solution is rather simple: Make the drivers themselves figure out where the devices they are supposed to control might be connected. For example, a network card driver knows that a network card will most likely be located at one of just a few input-output addresses on a PC, so it probes these addresses to see if a card can be found. If found, the driver then links the card with the right software to start the network connection.

Interestingly, this happens every time you start your computer. Worse than goldfish with a five-second memory, the drivers don't "remember" where the device was the last time and only look there—someone could have physically moved the card or removed it. Or maybe the card malfunctioned and no signal is getting sent from it. By making drivers look everywhere, it decreases the chances of a driver locking up the computer just because it can't find a device in one certain place.

If your card happens to be at an address that isn't on the driver's list of likely suspects, the driver may not find it; in that case, you must tell the driver where to look. Your hardware manual should give you an idea of how to change this setting on your component.

Aside from physically installing the hardware device, dealing with drivers is the foremost issue you face when contending with hardware installations. Lucky for you, though, drivers are far more user-accessible and flexible than the bootstrap and the BIOS code.

If a driver is available for your new hardware, then great. You're all set. You may have some touch-up work to do later on, but a lot of that can be done in the user interface. If, however, a device is not detected during all this booting rigmarole, then you need to determine whether the driver for that component was loaded to begin with—but first you need to find out whether the problem is a missing driver or a broken device.

> **I**f it helps, think of the kernel as Santa Claus and the device drivers as all the little helper elves who do the grunt work without getting union wages.

Nothing's ever easy in the land of computers, is it?

To help you determine whether a device has actually been detected, Linux provides a command (`cat /proc/devices`) that lists all devices detected by your Linux system at startup. If your device is not on that list and you are sure the device is connected properly, then you need a driver for it.

A driver can be used in two ways; the first and more common way is as a module. A *module* is a separate piece of code that works with the Linux kernel to run your device. This idea is familiar to most computer users, as Microsoft and Apple operating systems both utilize a separate driver code for device management. You get a device, you get the module set up, and bada bing bada boom, you're good to go.

While many drivers in non-Linux systems are wrapped up in little automatic installation scripts, modules for Linux and other UNIX-based systems need to be brought to the attention of the kernel manually. They just don't sit there and say, "Hello, here I am, use me!"

Several Linux distributions provide a set of tools specifically designed to help users get modules officially recognized by the kernel so the latter can start making use of the former. They all work on this premise: Tell the kernel where the module is, and the next time the kernel is started, it will use the module and (ideally) the hardware device itself.

We say ideally because sometimes some more configuration is needed to finish the job. For instance, sound cards may be installed and their modules all in place, but may still not utter a peep. Depending on your distribution of Linux, you may have to turn on some more settings before your PC's speakers will emit melodious tones. Typically this is not complicated and every distribution worth its salt has extensive documentation on sound-card configuration. After all, although the PC was never intended to be a stereo system, that's what a lot of people want to use it for, and Linux programmers know it.

Modules are all well and good, but we truly maniacal Linux users usually go one step further to maximize our hardware's performance: We'll modify the actual Linux source code to include the drivers directly, and then recompile the code to form what essentially becomes our own custom distribution of Linux.

Crazy? Like a fox!

PLUNGING INTO THE KERNEL

The whole act of modifying the source code of an application and then turning that source code into an actual executable program is described in Linux shorthand as *compiling code*. Technically, you should use this term to describe only the last step in the process, but either way, everyone in the Linux community knows what you're talking about. Here is a quick lesson from Programming 101 to get you up to speed with compilation.

Whenever a programmer makes a new program or modifies an existing one, she will use a programming language to describe what she wants the application to do when certain situations arise. "If this button is clicked," the code might say, "then open this dialog box."

Of course, the code does not spell this all out in English, though many programming languages approximate English in verbiage, syntax, and basic vocabulary. Instead, instructions are broken down into nice, neat logical argument statements that make the average person's head explode if they contemplate them too long. Luckily, programmers are anything but average.

If you recall all those beginning computer lessons you took in high school, computers do not understand English or any other language on Earth, spoken or written. All they really understand are 0s and 1s—binary numbers. And, as confusing as a program

The Joy of Tech   by Nitrozac and Snaggy

may seem to you and me, it is still unintelligible to computer processors because the code is still written for humans to read, not a computer. It can't even try to interpret the letters in the code, because the code file is usually just a simple text file, not an actual program. This is what compiling does: It converts the text files the programmer writes into an application that can be understood by a computer.

Because of the open-source nature of Linux, we have access to the source code files of almost every application used on Linux platforms. We can open the files and modify them to our own needs, provided, of course, that we have (A) the time and (B) the skill. And the thing that really gets us wound up, the thing that brings us true glee, is the fact that we also have source code access to the kernel of Linux itself. This is something few other operating systems would dare to do, but Linux programmers do it as a matter of course.

This kind of open-source mentality is completely alien to the Microsofts of the world. To open the source code of Windows would blaspheme the very core of Bill Gates' assertion that code written by a programmer belongs to the programmer only and no one else. Gates takes a very corporate stance on this topic, which one might expect from a man whose personal wealth exceeds that of the nation of Peru: We made it, we own it, we make money off of it.

Opening the kernel up to the masses demonstrate not a reversal of this thinking, but rather a broadening of what ownership implies. In the Linux community, the stance is more along the lines of we made it, you own it, we make money by helping you work with it. Note that there isn't a complete absence of capitalism here, nor should there ever be. Believe it or not, programmers have kids to feed, and there's no shame in getting financially rewarded for being good at something.

This is a win-win situation that engenders a lot of loyalty among our happy little community. Linux distributors, for the most part, have great customer loyalty, because we (the customers) feel that we're being treated like real customers and that once we buy a product, it's ours to change as we please.

On a more practical level, an open kernel provides Linux users with some real, everyday benefits. A kernel you compile yourself will almost always be faster than the kernel you originally installed, for three reasons.

> **B**elieve it or not, programmers have kids to feed, and there's no shame in getting financially rewarded for being good at something.

For starters, if you support only the hardware on your machine, you will significantly cut down the size of the kernel on your machine. This leaves more memory for programs, so your machine will swap a little less. This will be most noticeable on machines with little RAM.

Secondly, when you use new compilers to compile your kernel, you may get the benefit of better optimization techniques in the compiler that can slightly speed up your kernel.

Additionally, you can compile your kernel to take direct advantage of your particular processor's features. Most generic kernels cannot do this, because they must be able to boot a wide range of machines when initially installed. Once you have the kernel on a unique system, you can skim off all the extra support you don't need and beef up the processor configuration you do need.

Besides an increase in speed, being able to manipulate the kernel will also get you a more stable machine. This may come as a shock to some of the penguinistas out there, but no software is perfect, not even the Linux kernel. Some bugs do creep into the OS every so often. But, because these are fixed over time, getting the latest, most stable kernel may eliminate problems.

Furthermore, compiling your own kernel lets you pick and choose what parts of it you want to include. We have already indicated that this will increase the speed of the kernel, but it also helps its reliability. The less code in your kernel, the less chance there is for conflicts. Also, with each new compilation of the kernel, you should get the added benefit of new features that did not exist or were not well supported in earlier versions. This kernel evolution is unique to Linux systems, as it is a slow, gradual increase of capabilities rather than the sudden quantum leap of features you get every year or so when a new Windows-based product is released.

Finally, kernel compilation will help businesses in an area just now taking hold in the corporate world today: *configuration management*. Configuration management (CM) allows owners of large amounts of computer hardware and software to track and maintain every piece of hardware they own and every application installed. The advantages of CM for a business are great when it's properly implemented. If all types of computer hardware are inventoried, it becomes that much easier to start unifying and consolidating the hardware base. Instead of 25 different kinds of CD-ROM drives in the company, CM techniques will get the number of types down to two or three.

Linux has an advantage in CM because of the uniquely personalized way kernels can be installed. If all the machines in an organization are made to be alike, then the Linux kernel optimized for one of the machines will work well for all the others.

YOU ALWAYS REMEMBER YOUR FIRST TIME

The prospect of compiling a new kernel is pretty daunting for most new Linux users, which is why newbies tend to stick close to the automated installation packages for their Linux apps and configurations. After a while, though, the scare wears off and the sheer brilliance of this methodology turns them into kernel-heads. Still, this is not always the best option for everyone to take. Don't use a sledgehammer to get at a problem when a nutcracker will do just fine.

The first obstacle that many people face is that they are not programmers, so they could never even *think* about changing code in the kernel. This seemingly major obstacle is actually one of the easiest to overcome. The nice thing about changing the kernel source code is that you don't have to type a line of code if

> Don't use a sledgehammer to get at a problem when a nutcracker will do just fine.

you don't want to. Many tools out there, such as kernelcfg, xconfig, and menuconfig, provide menu-driven interfaces to change the kernel. Want to drop SCSI support on your box because you don't have a SCSI bus in your PC? Just follow the menus and turn the support off.

Whatever tool you end up using to change the kernel, you can't just save your changes when you finish and call it a day. The changes you made altered the code of the kernel, and now you need to get that code into a binary form for the computer to digest. The exact methodology varies from computer to computer, but here's the really short version of the story.

Once the changes are made to the kernel, you, the user, enter commands to compile the code into an image file. An *image file* is what sits in the /boot directory of your Linux box and actually loads Linux when the LILO application points to it and says "you're on."

Once the new Linux image file is created, you copy it to the /boot directory and then configure the LILO application via lilo.conf to accept the new Linux image. If, during all of this, you configured part of your kernel to act as modules, then you will need to take some additional steps to compile the modules separately and get them into the /lib/modules directory. Keep in mind this is a very cursory view of the steps involved in kernel compilation. You should always make a backup of your current system—in particular the current Linux image and lilo.conf files—in case something goes amiss. For more information, see Chapter 13, "The Linux Sutra: Resources."

Once your kernel is recompiled, you will have actually created your very own operating system, which is almost as good as getting a vanity plate for your car. And the satisfaction you'll get from running all your new hardware is very pleasing indeed.

MOVING ON TO SOMETHING NEW

You should now have a good idea of what's involved in getting hardware up and running on your Linux box. Despite rumors to the contrary, the number of hardware components getting supported by Linux is growing at a phenomenal rate and soon hardware installs will not be such a big deal.

In the meantime, methods such as module and kernel compilation may seem out of your reach but they are typically not difficult to accomplish with some research and forethought.

This extreme adaptability of the Linux kernel not only helps it get customized for your PC, it also makes it very flexible for use on other machines as well. From watches, to handheld PCs, to large mainframe computers, Linux is starting to show up in the most unusual places. In Chapter 9, "You Want to Put That Where?," you'll learn about all the different platforms Linux is running on these days.

You Want to Put That Where?

IN WHICH POOH GIVES THE AUTHOR THE HEEBIE JEEBIES

"Hello, friend!"

A yellow, fuzzy, creature, about a foot high, looked around the room from where it's perch in my three-year-old's arms. Our cat bolted from the room. I bit down an expletive, because expletives are not the sort of thing a three-year-old should hear, unless Daddy's driving on the highway.

"Well," I drawled, "That's a neat toy, honey. Did Mommy buy that for you?"

"Yes, Daddy!" she giggled, "Pooh talks! He's mine!"

"Mine" is a word my little one uses quite a bit these days, mostly in response to my oldest's firm territorialism about Her Stuff in Her Room.

Cautiously, I continued the conversation. "And what does he say?"

So she brought Pooh over to me, threw her coat down, and climbed up onto my lap. Pooh, it turned out, played a pretty nice set of games with her. Nothing too long, of course; after all, he was designed to play with a three-year-old.

Sure enough, in the middle of one of Pooh's riddles, my daughter took off for her quarter-hourly Bug the Big Sister appointment and left this thing on my lap. Being a guy, I immediately put him off to the side on the couch, for fear someone would see me with it. Being a husband, I lurched off the couch and went to help my wife bring in the rest of the stuff from the store.

Four bags of clothes later, I went back into the family room and stopped cold. Pooh was no longer looking straight ahead. Pooh was now looking at the television, which was displaying the antics of Emeril Lagasse in his studio kitchen.

Slowly, I looked back over my shoulder to see my wife puttering around in our kitchen. "Honey, what does—"

And Pooh moved his head to look at me.

"Holy !@#$%!" I yelped.

"What?" my long-suffering wife asked.

"That Pooh is looking at me!" I said.

I was concentrating on the doll, but I could hear my wife's eyes rolling behind me. "It's a talking doll, didn't she show it to you? It's supposed to move," my wife explained. Now Pooh was looking at her.

"Yes, but is it supposed to follow you around the room like that? Where are the instructions?"

After a quick read, I soon discovered that this behavior was not the result of some sort of demonic possession, but an actual programmed response to sound. This little anthropomorphized bear was supposed to try to maintain eye contact with its playmates. I settled down eventually, but I still move the bear whenever my daughter leaves it in my office.

How many embedded systems can you spy?

This bear of very little brain, it seems, was actually nothing of the sort. This Pooh had a computer on board, a computer known as an *embedded system.*

Simply defined, embedded systems are processor-based systems that handle computing functions in devices other than computers. Embedded systems are showing up where you least expect them, and although they can sometimes be pretty frightening, they are usually pretty useful. If you look around the room in which you are sitting right now, you will likely spot at least six devices that have some kind of processor in them, happily working away like little gnomes, making the world a better place with automatic drip coffee and altitude-sensing wristwatches. In fact, the average household in the United States has dozens of pieces of electronic hardware with computer processors in them. Beyond the obvious devices like the television and the microwave, there are furnace controls, stereo speakers, refrigerators, cars, and even irons that have some kind of thinking ability.

These aren't Cray supercomputers, mind you. Many of these devices don't do much more than keep the time and monitor a very limited set of input to keep the device working in just a certain way. But they are there nonetheless. The fact that only 15 percent of all manufactured computer chips actually get installed into a computer should tell you something.

> The fact that only 15 percent of all manufactured computer chips actually get installed into a computer should tell you something.

Embedded systems are usually invisible to the general public, since they are usually asked to manage just a few things at any given time, often in devices not usually associated with a computer. Take, for instance, the modern elevator. You wouldn't think an elevator would need a sophisticated processor to operate, but in truth most elevators these days have more to do than just go up and down. Elevators are programmed to pay attention to the time of day. If it's the morning, they all place themselves at the ground floor of the building. Once a passenger is dropped off at an upper floor, the elevator will send itself right back down again. Conversely, during the afternoon rush out of the building, elevators space themselves throughout the building to catch outgoing passengers. Once those passengers are dropped off at the ground floor, the elevators will rise up once more to an upper floor to meet the demands of the happy workforce trying to get the hell out of the workplace.

Elevators are often smart enough to know when it's the weekend, when they can just sit at rest for the whole day, lollygagging and catching up with the other elevators. The really smart systems even track the calendar and know when office holidays are. When you're eating turkey on Thanksgiving Thursday, you can rest easy in the knowledge that your office's elevators are not running about willy-nilly looking for passengers that aren't there. More important, these smart elevators should run more efficiently, thus saving the owners of the office building a fair chunk of change in energy and maintenance costs.

Moonshine Software and Caffeine Gods

All these chips running in all these devices need some kind of software to make them run. As you would expect, almost none of these devices has a CD-ROM drive that you can use to install a new program. Toasters and little plastic discs do not mix.

In the early days of embedded systems, programmers used their own home-grown code for these chipsets, which worked for awhile. But two things started happening that really screwed this plan up.

First, whenever device A had to talk to device B, there was often a communications conflict on the order of a drunken Welshman trying to explain quantum mechanics to an equally inebriated citizen of Taiwan. To solve this problem, the makers of device A might change their code to accommodate device B, build a copy of device B for themselves to use (damn the lawsuits for copyright infringement), or just buy the company that makes device B and make the workers there change

> When you're eating turkey on Thanksgiving Thursday, you can rest easy in the knowledge that your office's elevators are not running about willy-nilly looking for passengers that aren't there.

their device to comply. All these scenarios are equally likely when proprietary software is used in the real world.

> # Moore's Law is generally seen as a huge driving force in the IT hardware world, and a bit of a pain in the ass for the software community.

The second problem affected everyone in the embedded community, not just the companies trying to cooperate or assimilate each other. This is the occurrence of Moore's Law. The Moore in Moore's Law is Gordon Moore, former Chairman of Intel, who first stated this idea succinctly: Current technology development will allow the doubling of processor power every 18 months (Moore's Law). This is the reason we all get to slavishly debate upgrading our PCs every couple of years.

Moore's Law is generally seen as a huge driving force in the IT hardware world, and a bit of a pain in the ass for the software community. After all, what good is it to run the latest hyperprocessor with all the coolest functions if the software is unable to take full advantage of it? So, thanks to the hardware group, the software group has to completely revamp its code on a regular basis. Which chucks all the trips to Tahiti.

This was especially true in the early stages of embedded systems. The processors using homemade code would become obsolete after only a year and a half at most. The makers of devices A and B could, of course, stand pat and keep the processors they had. Doing so, however, risked the makers of device C (with the new faster processor) coming along, kicking some serious butt, and thumbing the makers of devices A and B into the ground like puny ants.

In order to maintain some semblance of sanity in this mercurial development platform, embedded software engineers got the idea to embed a miniature operating system into the device with the code written specifically to handle the device. Though it would add some overhead in the device's memory, the benefits would be significant.

Having an operating system on the processor solves a lot of the communications issues devices might have. If devices A and B are both using an operating system of some sort, the OS on each device could manage the communications tasks, letting the original code go about its business unmolested. In addition, operating systems bring other advantages to the table, such as device management. If the operating system is managing the device, then the embedded programmer doesn't really need to worry about the latest advances in chipset technology. It's the OS's job, after all. Operating systems can also carry libraries of code around, which is a big help.

Code libraries are something you may have heard some tech-geeks around the office blathering about in the coffee room

Linux programmers are powered by their *faith.*

during their great prayer to the caffeine god. The ritual goes something like this: They stand around the coffee urn, muttering about their work and how hard it is to contend with recalcitrant code and hardware. These are offerings to the caffeine god: "See how hard we work! Please allow us the benefit of your liquid nectar!" In addition to appeasing a minor deity, these offerings erect a sonic screen of techno-babble that renders non-techies insensate, and thus unable to stay in the coffee room for one second longer than is necessary. This gives the tech-geeks a social camouflage until they can get back to the relative safety of their cubicles. The best counter to this is to leap into the coffee room and scream "BOO!" With the amount of caffeine in their systems, it will take some time for them to wrench their heads from the ceiling tiles, giving you plenty to time to find enough creamer and sugar for your own cup of coffee.

> **I**f the programmer has access to a library that oh, say, will automatically grab e-mail messages off a mail server, then the programmer does not have to write the code herself.

Anyway, if you were paying attention to the geek jabber when you first came upon them, you may have heard the programmers among themselves chanting about those code libraries. Libraries of code are very important to programmers because they give them more time to converse among themselves or to various coffee urns.

The short version is this: When an application is written, it contains many lines of code. The more sophisticated the application, the more code there is, until logic statement after logic statement piles up into a full-fledged application (or so the coder hopes). There are several problems to writing an entire application from scratch, not the least of which is the potential for making a mistake buried so deep in the code that the error is never found. But a problem that is sure to occur is the sheer amount of time it would take to type all of that code in. Incredibly, even programmers get a date now and then, so this situation would soon become intolerable.

Enter libraries, which are compact groups of code that contain a lot of generic functions for the programmer to tap into. If the programmer has access to a library that oh, say, will automatically grab e-mail messages off a mail server, then the programmer does not have to write the code herself. She just writes the code in her program that points to the proper function in the proper library, and she's done. Her application will call the library at the right place and time, the library will do the job for the application, and everyone's tickled pink.

Besides savings in time, there is also a large savings in the amount of memory an application that uses code libraries takes up. An application that can tap into the power of different libraries is a smaller application—and a smaller application often means a faster application.

To summarize: Operating systems good, stand-alone applications bad. Glib commentary aside, the question then becomes: which operating system?

ENTER THE PENGUIN

Several thousand years ago, over in southern Mesopotamia, the whole population of the planet still spoke the same language. Or so the story goes.

One day, a bunch of people nomadically hanging out in this region got together and decided the nomadic life was just not for them. They decided that instead of running around the wilderness chasing goats, they would transform their agrarian society into an urban trade society, announce their new city to everyone all around, and start living the high life.

Pretty darn clever, those southern Mesopotamians. Their architects got to work designing and building the city, the PR and marketing people went to work flashing the concept to all of the other hovels in that part of the world, and generally all was well.

Then one day someone got the bright idea of building a huge tower in the center of the growing city, a tower that would celebrate how hip and cosmopolitan these newly-urbanized Mesopotamians really were. The plans were drawn up and construction got underway.

Meanwhile, God, in typical Old Testament fashion, had some issues with these people. First off, by abandoning their nomadic ways and staying put, they were ignoring a rule He had set up quite some time before: "Go forth and multiply." Sure, they were multiplying; the Mesopotamians had built too many nightclubs and motels for that *not* to happen. But the "go forth" part was being cheerfully ignored.

Then came this tower—a tower that was being built not to celebrate Him, but rather the sun, the moon, the stars...every thing in heaven *but* Him. Stepping on Superman's cape? No, this was much worse. These were smiting-level offenses, and God wasted no time in smiting these folks big time. And when he was done smiting, everyone in the city below could not understand a word anyone else was saying. With the birth of different languages, the tower and city were abandoned, and the invention of Starbucks was pushed back several thousand years.

This is a good story, full of the usual dramatic elements: sex, pathos, and tragedy. Whether you buy into it or not, we still

> And thus, like languages, we are left with a big mess of proprietary operating systems to deal with on our PCs and in embedded systems, too.

have lots of different languages coming out of lots of different mouths. It may seem rather strange to a child learning the ways of the world that language is still a barrier to communication. After all, they wonder, we've had phones for almost 100 years, and widespread e-mail communication for 10 years or so. Why can't we all just start talking with the same language? Which is when we pat little Johnny on the head for being such a clever lad and begin to point out the vagaries of operating systems, which are a microcosm of language development in human history.

"The evolution of the various operating systems is directly due to human creativity," we tell Johnny, "because different developers came up with different ways of doing the same things. And it is human pride and stubbornness that keeps the divergence growing."

And thus, like languages, we are left with a big mess of proprietary operating systems to deal with on our PCs and in embedded systems, too. This is currently the big challenge for embedded programmers: Given that they should use an operating system on their chipsets, which one should they use?

The choices are as varied as human language, but they can be boiled down to five groups:

- Windows and Windows-related operating systems
- DOS and other command-line operating systems
- UNIX
- Real-time operating systems
- Kernel-based operating systems, such as Linux or homemade kernels, which are just an OS wrapped with additional tools.

Honey, I Shrunk the Operating System

Microsoft has made significant inroads into the embedded system market in recent months by peddling its Windows CE OS to the chipset programmers. Citing operational familiarity, Microsoft has shamelessly touted WinCE, its handheld PDA operating system, as an embedded operating system. Manufacturers who have bought into the Microsoft mythos have begun using WinCE, only to find an operating system that's extremely large even in its most scaled-down form, which is not very small.

The ancient Greeks figured out that if you divide up a hunk of gold repeatedly, eventually you would get to the smallest possible piece of gold: the atom. This was an oversimplification, granted, since we now know an atom of gold does not so much resemble a glittery metallic substance as a cloud of subatomic particles. Still, not bad for a culture that hadn't yet gotten the knack of indoor plumbing.

> Microsoft's assumption seems to be if you divide Windows enough times, you get a smaller version of Windows.

Microsoft may have the plumbing problem licked, but it missed the Tidy-Bowl boat on the atomic metaphor. Microsoft's assumption seems to be if you divide Windows enough times, you get a smaller version of Windows. What you really get, however, is lots of pieces of busted code that have to be logically stitched together to make some perverse Mini Me version of Windows.

WinCE, like its big brother Windows 98, also has an unfortunate tendency to snarl itself up on its own operations and crash. Not something you want to see in a chipset in a heart bypass machine.

WinCE is also a proprietary solution, which means that it will function most efficiently only with other WinCE chipsets. Now you're back to the communications problem you started with. Proprietary also means licensing is going to come into play and that means royalty fees.

Who Do You Want to Swindle Today?

DOS is also a proprietary operating system, thanks to Bill Gates and company's purchase of the QDOS operating system from Tim Patterson of Seattle Computer Products for a mere $50,000. This was more of a bargain than people realize, because Microsoft was pitching IBM a concept to start writing applications in BASIC for a new entry into the fledgling microcomputer market, the IBM PC. An operating system was needed for this new device and at the time no one at Microsoft knew how to write one (some wags maintain this is still the case.)

Gates recommended that IBM contact Gary Kildall, who had developed the CP/M operating system. At that time, CP/M was the hot new OS. Unfortunately, IBM was repeatedly unable to meet with Kildall, and eventually went back to Microsoft and said they could do the operating system, too.

Once they had the operating system ball, Microsoft approached Patterson and Seattle Computer Products and negotiated the purchase of Patterson's QDOS (*Quick and Dirty Operating System*), which was based on CP/M. In fact, Patterson used a CP/M manual to write the whole thing in six weeks. No copyright violation here, because Patterson modified QDOS enough from the original CP/M. After some quick edits, QDOS became MS-DOS (*Microsoft Disk Operating System*) and was sold to IBM. Microsoft conveniently did not mention to Seattle Computer Products the upcoming IBM deal. Gates also managed to negotiate the rights to market MS-DOS separately from the IBM PC project and made millions selling the new operating system to other hardware vendors.

> Despite its rather shady origins, DOS is still a fairly efficient operating system, and it's rather small, which makes it a fair candidate for inclusion on embedded systems

Despite its rather shady origins, DOS is still a fairly efficient operating system, and it's rather small, which makes it a fair candidate for inclusion on embedded systems. The only problem is that this OS was originally written for a 1981 chipset and never progressed very far in its evolution—especially after Windows was slapped on top of it and the GUI began handling many functions that DOS would normally be required to do. In the strange symbiotic relationship between DOS and Windows, DOS has atrophied into a less-than-current OS.

UNIX: The Grandfather of Linux

Any discussion of embedded system architecture is going to include UNIX, the operating system that begat Minix, which begat Linux.

It seems at first glance that UNIX is a good fit for embedded systems, because it is scalable and much more stable than its Microsoft competitors. Unfortunately, UNIX's history reads like that of a young basketball star who goes pro for the love of the game and ends up addicted to fame, money, and who knows what else in two or three seasons. Like Snoopy's Christmas, UNIX went commercial.

UNIX was born in AT&T Bell Labs in 1969, as a derivative of the old Multic system. The parents of this little OS, Ken Thompson and Dennis Ritchie, named it UNICS (*UNiplexed Information and Computing System*), which eventually got corrupted to UNIX. AT&T, being AT&T, owned UNIX lock, stock, and barrel, and it ended up becoming the operating system of choice for networked systems, including telephone switching systems and the new academic network ARPANet. Because the OS was so good, it managed to find its way out of AT&T's purview, where other well intentioned folks started to play around with the code.

By 1975, the first commercial release of UNIX outside of AT&T was showing up in universities, created by developers at the University of California at Berkeley. This was the first UNIX fork, and unlike the cooperative distribution arrangement Linux enjoys today, it was a true evolutionary split.

The distinction is subtle, but important. All the different distributions of Linux, no matter how varied, stem from the one central kernel. So, users of Red Hat or Slackware or Yellow Dog know that down under the hood of their OS is the same kernel developed by Linus Torvalds and his cadre of kernel developers. UNIX flavors have no such kernel sharing, and are as different from each other as dogs and cats.

> **U**nfortunately, UNIX's history reads like that of a young basketball star who goes pro for the love of the game and ends up addicted to fame, money, and who knows what else in two or three seasons.

This forking of UNIX represents yet another example of the proprietary mentality creeping into a perfectly good operating system and therefore counts strongly against using UNIX as an embedded OS.

Forking, by the way, is something that Linux users fear greatly. If Linux were to ever break up, it would represent not only a division of the OS, but also the dismantling of the ideals behind Linux. When we hear about rumblings of dissention in Linus'

The Joy of Tech   by Nitrozac and Snaggy

"I INSTALLED THOSE PARTS MYSELF, NOT ONLY THAT, I HACKED THE
KERNEL SPECIFICALLY FOR THE DRIVER! YEP, THIS BABY RUNS
SMOOTH AS SILK! IT'S A SPEEDSTER TOO, I TELL YA!"

core kernel development group, we mentally clutch our Linux
boxes and start praying like a bunch of teeny-boppers worrying
that Paul is *really* dead. If you want to make a Linux user really
edgy, just go up to them and say "fork you."

Tricked-Up Kernels

The next two classifications of operating systems for the embedded system can be discussed at the same time, because they present
the same pros and cons for embedded use.

The first class of OS is the real-time system. Real-time systems are the OS equivalent of running nitrous oxide through the engine of an old Chevy Nova. Instead of providing support for running applications, real-time operating systems do everything they can to let the application run as fast as it can. Essentially, a real-time OS sets everything up for the app and then gets out of the way.

Some of these real-time OSs are derived from Linux—scaled down versions that are souped up to handle demanding real-time needs. But all of them to date, regardless of their origins, are proprietary in nature, which leads to standards problems and licensing fees. Real-time operating systems are also very specialized pieces of software that not many people know how to program for, so companies who use them are plagued with staffing problems and a large amount of dependence on the operating system.

The same issues also hold true for those hardy adventurers who decide to just make their own operating system to run on the chipset. This may seem like the perfect solution, since the OS should ideally be the most optimum OS for that particular chipset. But once again, the proprietary bull rears it ugly head to create headaches for all involved.

> Real-time systems are the OS equivalent of running nitrous oxide through the engine of an old Chevy Nova.

You Knew This Was Coming

Which leads us to our favorite operating system for the embedded platform, plain ordinary Linux. If you have read this far, you can likely guess why Linux is such a strong candidate for embedded system work.

First off, after having beat this horse into the ground, Linux is *not* proprietary. It's open, so anyone can grab it, whip it, and beat it into whatever shape or function they desire. Because Linux is an open platform, the learning curve is much smaller, because programmers new to Linux won't find anything they can't handle. Even if they run into something they don't recognize, the nature of the Linux community lends itself to support via discussion groups and mailing lists. Many is the time that a programmer posts a specific question and gets the answer in minutes. All they have to do is ask nicely. The openness of Linux means there are no proprietary standards to get in the way, either, nor are there any pesky royalty fees.

> It's open, so anyone can grab it, whip it, and beat it into whatever shape or function they desire.

The very architecture of Linux is perfect for embedded systems. The central kernel surrounded by modules can easily be adapted to the smallest of systems; just drop all the modules and recompile the kernel with just the drivers and libraries needed to run on the system in question. This newly compiled kernel may be just a mere shadow of the Linux running on your desktop, but it can do the job it needs to do. Because the kennel is custom-built for each processor it's sitting on, the stability of the OS is very strong, suitable for mission-critical chipsets, like the ones in heart monitors.

Linux as an embedded operating system has exploded like wildfire in the last few years, quickly replacing proprietary systems out on the market, for just these reasons. When surveyed, manufacturers' favorite feature about Linux is the fact that it's free. Money still talks, after all.

Regardless of why industries are starting to use Linux, they are using it with ever-increasing frequency. Many industry analysts are pointing to chipset installations as one reason companies are starting to seriously look at Linux for the desktop. After all, they reason, if Linux is good enough for the chips, it should be good enough for our PCs.

Linux may be backing into the house, but it's still coming inside.

Size Doesn't Matter...Really

The superior scalability of Linux means that it will fit on almost any platform you put it on, as long as you modify the kernel for that device. That's why we're starting to see Linux showing up on hand-held PDAs and watches, along with massive mainframe devices. This is one case where one size fits all. All is not sunshine and roses, though. It sometimes takes quite a bit of effort to mold Linux into oddball systems—especially the larger ones.

Linux was designed to run on a personal computer platform. Because of its modular nature, it can be trimmed down fairly easily. Building it up is easy too, but the more code added to the kernel, either directly or within modules, the slower the system becomes.

Linux isn't perfect, either, and the more modules or code that get added to the kernel, the more chance there is for even Linux to trip itself up. The challenge to developers is to optimize Linux to the platform of choice without overloading it with functions it doesn't need. Otherwise, speed and simplicity get sacrificed and Linux becomes just another bloated operating system.

> The challenge to developers is to optimize Linux to the platform of choice without overloading it with functions it doesn't need.

Right now, Linux developers are in a voyeuristic state of mind, trying to fit Linux on any kind of platform just to see if it can be done. Ultimately, a state of equilibrium will be found, and Linux will mature on the platforms that really need it. Linux won't try to take over all the platforms in the world, like some operating systems we know. But it may end up in that position anyway.

You may even end up wearing it on your body.

STRAP-ON LINUX

Professor Steve Mann of the University of Toronto is a man on a holy quest: to deliver portable computing to the masses. Not just any portable computing—this is the kind of computer you wear.

Mann's early efforts may be known to some of you already. He was the man who walked around MIT with a big video camera on his head that put images of what he was seeing on the Web. This was a rather disconcerting sight, as the camera covered half of his face and broadcast its signal on what looked to be big rabbit ear antennas. It was a TV news director's dream piece (look at what those kooky MIT guys are doing now!) Today, people still look askance at wearable computers, but no one's laughing that hard now. More and more developers are looking seriously at the concepts Mann and his fellow WearComp users are proposing.

Wearable computers are slowly emerging in the workplace, as more and more employees with jobs that are characterized as "hands-free" find themselves needing some kind of intelligent support. But you can't use a laptop when you're hanging on the side of a telephone pole. If the computer were strapped to your belt, the keyboard to your arm, and the display appeared in a heads-up next to your eye, however, you would have a pretty efficient helper. Even better if the system were voice activated. Wearable computers would provide instant information for everyone when they needed it. No more delays like the ones you get in the office everyday: "Hang on, I left that file back in my PC. I'll e-mail it to you later."

An on-board camera could record everything you do during the day, allowing you to keep a personal diary of your life. More practically, it could recognize that person who just came up to you and started yammering, and you have no idea who they are. A surreptitious name would pop up on your display, and you would not blow off "JOE DRAYSON, Father-in-law's business partner."

This is the kind of future Mann wants to bring us, and he's using Linux to do it. Linux fits well into what Mann describes as his COSHER (Completely Open Source, Headers, Engineering, and Research) ideal. To be truly scientific, he maintains, tools need to have all their working parts available for modification and discovery.

"Imagine a clock designed so that when the cover was lifted off, all the gears would fly out in different directions, such that a young child could not open up his or her parents' clock and determine how it works," Mann wrote in an article earlier this year for Linux Journal. "Devices made in this manner would not be good for society, in particular for the growth and development of young engineers and scientists with a natural curiosity about the world around them."

> Wearable computers would provide instant information for everyone when they needed it.

Software that is closed and proprietary is software Mann has no truck with. Discoveries in science are often founded on the work of others. Even if Mann could perfectly fit closed-source software on his various devices, he wouldn't want to, because no one else seeking to make discoveries after him would be able to build on that part of his work.

In the pursuit of science, open source must always be the way to go.

MOVING ON TO SOMETHING NEW

Linux in the workplace. Linux in the home. Linux in your TV remote. Linux on your head. Where will it all end?

You need to relax, take some time off. Chill out and fool around. And what better way than to fire up the old Linux box for maximum gaming pleasure?

Scoff if you will, but after being trapped in a video dark age, Linux is slowly becoming a true gamers' platform. It's not Nintendo yet, but with the collective energy of thousands of hormone-crazed hackers fixing their attention on the problem, can a haven for Lara Croft be long in coming? Find out in Chapter 10.

CHAPTER

10

Messing around: The Penguin Plays Games

For Courage and Valor above and beyond

"Where is she?" John hissed into my ear. Not knowing, I shrugged reflexively, then stopped, realizing it would express little in the near-pitch blackness. That I'd heard John at all was a miracle, given the incredible din blasting through the air around us: running feet, screams of dismay, and, like a bad soundtrack, very, very loud thrasher music.

With sweaty palms, I clutched the gun in my hands, holding it close to my chest. I jerked my head around, trying to pick up some sort of movement. We had seen the woman we were trying to find duck behind the set of boxes in front of us, but in the dark, we weren't sure where she was now. This was bad, because all around us was the enemy, and punching our way out with three weapons would be a lot easier than trying to do it with two.

The Joy of Tech   by Nitrozac and Snaggy

The floor was hard and would betray no footprints, even if we could see anything. I kept my back to my companion's as we slowly approached the boxes. Behind us I saw and heard the furtive movements of another firefight in progress. It was far enough away to not involve us directly, but I knew that if anyone ran off from that melee trying to get clear—

There! Someone running right at us! I sighted my weapon, looked for the color of the uniform...not ours. I squinted and pulled the trigger, watching in a semi-detached manner the way red splashed from the person's chest. They were no longer my concern.

I turned around and found that my partner had rounded a corner while I had been covering our backs. Cursing under my breath, I followed; to my relief, I saw my companion was not hit. Beyond him was a rare light in this building, silhouetting his upper body in its pale yellow glow. Just in front of him was a stack of boxes. I hissed at him to slow down, but John didn't hear me.

Too late!

In horror, I watched the outline of his forehead explode in a spray of liquid!

Then I heard the gloating words of his attacker:

"Oh! Oh my God! I'm sorry! I'm sorry! Are you okay?"

Well, not quite gloating.

It was our friend Kate, who, after hiding, had mistakenly thought we were the enemy and had shot John in the head. Friendly fire at its worst.

John, for his part, staggered slightly under the onslaught, then calmly wiped the paint from his head and helmet, chuckling at Kate's reaction instead of being angry for the illegal paintball shot to the head.

The reality of the moment had reasserted itself once more, reminding us that this was, after all, just a game, played in the basement of an old warehouse—our publishing imprint against our corporate rivals, playing a game of capture the flag with paintball guns, and with heavy metal music thrumming in our ears.

But others had heard Kate's frantic apologies, and we heard the footfalls of our foes racing towards us.

"Go, go, go!" John yelled, firing past me into the dark beyond.

And the game began again.

IN WHICH TWO GEEKS CALCULATE WIND SPEED

Human beings are obsessed with games. Given the opportunity, everyone on the planet will play a game of something. All they need is the time, and many times not even that.

Sociologists typically point to this behavior as a natural outcome from early humans' sense of competition. Only the strong survive, the faster primate wins the mammoth, yada yada. After delivering this theory, by the way, the sociologists break out the mitts and bats and go play a killer game of softball.

Games are played anywhere and everywhere. From elaborate mock combats in warehouses to equally savage street chess matches in the parks of Brooklyn, we will meet the challenge of our foes anywhere and anytime.

It only make sense that the computer would become another arena for games, since the malleability of its interface is a perfect platform to launch any game we can think of—from 3D dog-fights in space, to solving mysteries in worlds other than our own, to grandmaster chess, to strip poker. (Though this last is a bit less exciting from the computer's point of view.)

All computer games require a lot of programming in order to work just so, because the game has to anticipate the actions of the most unpredictable element in the world: the human player. All game developers have to contend with this, even, once upon a time, myself.

> All computer games require a lot of programming in order to work just so, because the game has to anticipate the actions of the most unpredictable element in the world: the human player.

It was 1984, and I was a geeky little junior in high school. I was very interested in girls at this stage in life, but alas, they were not too interested in me. Thus my energies were channeled into other pursuits, just to keep my head from exploding whenever a cheerleader walked by. Computer class was one such outlet, and I threw myself into the Apple IIc—then the hottest PC ever with a whopping 512Kb of hard drive—with wild abandon.

One of our assignments in class was to learn how to program a game for this raging platform with the green cathode-ray screen. To save time, the instructor gave us partly finished templates of programs to use, which we would then complete and build the next Pac Man. Or so we thought.

The game my lab partner and I chose was a simple little artillery-style game that faced off two large guns across the screen from each other. Taking into account ballistic movements, wind, and the angle of the guns, players would fire over a mountain in hopes of striking the opposing gun.

Like I said, geeky.

The graphics of the program, such as they were, were already completed, as were the controls for the guns. All my friend and I had to do was calculate the formula needed to track a shell across the screen in a ballistic fashion and then adjust the motion of the shell for launch force of the shot and wind.

The first part was pretty easy: just a parabolic arc formula and a simple force/mass equation to compute the shell's trajectory and speed. But the wind! The wind was killing us! For days we hammered at that code, trying to get the wind correction figured in.

Oh yes, I needed a date. Badly.

Then, on the last day of the assignment, our math teacher gave us the clue we needed to get the correction formula. We ran to the computer class, typed in the BASIC line of code, and voilá! Our first game!

> For days we hammered at that code, trying to get the wind correction figured in.

Two things happened right after that that kept me from the extravagant life of a game programmer. First, I decided that programming in general was just too stressful for me. Second, I started going steady with a beautiful girl.

Computer? What computer?

GAMES PEOPLE PLAY

The first video game was invented in 1958. It was an interactive video tennis game you could play on an oscilloscope, invented fourteen years before Atari's Pong.

You have to start somewhere, after all.

Like a virgin's first awkward kiss, this exciting monochrome game was at once gawky and addicting: Despite its cumbersome nature, once people played it, they wanted more. At the time, the people playing the thing were mostly scientists themselves, which better served the drive to create the world's first computer game.

Officially, this milestone was reached a mere three years later, when an MIT student named Steve Russell came up with a text-based game for the Digital PDP-1 called "Spacewar." MIT students in those days were frustrated beyond belief, it seems, and they did a *lot* of computer programming.

> Like a virgin's first awkward kiss, this exciting monochrome game was at once gawky and addicting: Despite its cumbersome nature, once people played it, they wanted more.

This wasn't exactly a portable game, either, since the PDP took up roughly the same space as a small house. But it was interactive, and it was on a computer, so it counts for many historians. (Others point to Midway Game's Gunfight as the first real computer game, since it was developed for a microprocessor platform instead of the solid-state circuits of earlier computer models. This is a pretty fine distinction, one that the historians should just wrangle among themselves. We just want to play games.)

What's Your Game Sign?

There are, as usual, a great many misconceptions about the subject of Linux and games. The big one is that there are no games to play on Linux. This one is pretty easy to dispute. There are hundreds of games available for the Linux platform, all ready for salivating users to get their hands on. But if you had inquired about the availability of Linux games just a few years ago, you would have been pretty disappointed. The dearth of arcade-style action games was overwhelming.

How did Linux start off so poorly in the games arena? That actually depends on what kind of games we're talking about, since in some areas, Linux was (and still is) practically overloaded with things to play with. Most mainstream distributions of Linux come with scads of little diversionary games, such as Mahjongg, Reversi, and the ubiquitous Solitaire. These are the games people play while hiding away in their little cubicles, waiting for five o'clock to roll around.

These games are based on the classic non-electronic games of yore, when playing poker involved plastic chips, cigars, and green felt-covered tables rather than a beeping computer that couldn't bluff if its life depended on it. Many of the games in this category appeal to older computer users, because they are pleasant reminders of the real games they used to play in their younger days.

Another classification of games available with most Linux distributions includes the more graphics-intensive games that are not quite full-motion, 3D ex-slam-aramas, but are more exciting than Reversi. The games that fall into this category are Asteroids, Space Duel, and Konquest; they're the kind of games people play when they know the boss is going to be out of the office for quite some time.

> **I**t is to the now-older Gen X'ers that these games have the most appeal, though a lot of younger kids play them just to see what their parents were doing when they were young.

A lot of these games look and feel like arcade games of the early Eighties. These are the ones Gen X'ers spent all their time, money, and energy in the arcades playing while their parents sat back contentedly and thought "at least it's not drugs" (and then wondered why little Johnny's grades took some serious dips). Moderation was not a big Eighties fad, it seemed. It is to the now-older Gen X'ers that these games have the most appeal, though a lot of younger kids play them just to see what their parents were doing when they were young.

A third type of amusement available on the Linux platform includes games that are not really games in the classical sense, in that there's not a lot of interactivity between user and computer or user and user. These are the applets designed to soothe the troubled brow of our inner geek; they are usually named, appropriately enough, *toys*.

Toys on Linux are self-contained mini-applications that usually do something sort of neat and sort of useful. For instance, there is Worldwatch, which electronically emulates those big wall displays that show the position of day and night on the face of the Earth at any given time. It's sort of neat, because it's a pretty effect; it's sort of useful if you regularly deal with overseas contacts and are never sure what time of day it is over there.

> Even their names convey a sense of violence: Doom, Quake, Heretic 2, Soldier of Fortune... the timid should not be playing these games, unless it's to let out a lot of inner frustration.

There are quite a few toys for Linux, some more useful than others. The Tea Cooker times how long you should steep your teabag and pops a message up when the tea is ready. Wmsun shows the weather situation—on the surface of the Sun. There are many more like this, made to fit many situations, so their appeal is more compartmentalized to whomever finds these little babies cool.

The Joy of Tech   by Nitrozac and Snaggy

And then there are the Big Games. Like a visit to Helga, Mistress of the Night, these monster applications will grab a user, mangle him quite handily, then spit him out, leaving the user oddly satisfied and smoking a cigarette. These games are typically violent shoot-em-ups that put the gamer up against all manner of demons, mutants, and alien starships. Even their names convey a sense of violence: Doom, Quake, Heretic 2, Soldier of Fortune...the timid should not be playing these games, unless it's to let out a lot of inner frustration. To serious gamers—who buy a PC based on "how many games can it run?" rather than "how much space on the hard drive?"—these are the arenas in which to test their collective mettle.

But games like this are few and far between on the Linux platform, which has kept gamers cheating on the Linux platform they love in favor of the Windows platform where many of their games can be played.

At least in the past.

With each passing day, more games are added to the Linux platform, into the waiting arms of desperate Linux users who are riddled with guilt and want nothing more than to be faithful to the penguin.

Until the next game comes out.

More Than Just a Pretty Face

Newcomers to Linux often ask this question, or a similar variant: "If Linux is so hot, how come there aren't many games made for it?"

Responding to this question, we might get a bit defensive and mutter something along the lines of, "Serious Linux users don't need to play games." Or, "Sure we have games. How about some Asteroid 3D?" These answers reek of rationalization.

The simple truth is that until a couple of years ago, the Microsoft Mistress was easily able to seduce the faithful Linux user into sneaking around behind a partition, fooling around

John had sworn to be faithful to Linux, but somehow he always found himself seduced by his Microsoft Mistress.

with Starfleet Command on the side, while the Linux partition sat up alone.

The Mistress was stunningly attired, wearing flashy applications that cloaked her true nature, and adept at luring good users and bad into her web of deception. "After all," users said, "if it runs Myst, how can it be bad?"

Users may have been easily fooled by this façade, but developers weren't. They knew what the real Mistress was like underneath all of that flash and glitz. For them, the Mistress had another, more powerful lure: cold, hard cash.

> **B**uilding a Linux game as a commercial venture was nothing short of product suicide, or so the theory went.

In the past, a games developer was faced with a choice. They could build a fast, exciting game on Linux and live happily in the knowledge that their game would be loved and adored by Linux gamers everywhere. Alternatively, they could be seduced into building a not-so-fast (but still exciting) game on Windows and live happily in the knowledge that their game would be played by some Windows users, and that their (the games' developers, not the users') bank accounts would grow fat with royalties.

Guess which path they took.

The gaming market on the Windows platform exploded because of its huge customer base, plain and simple. Building a Linux game as a commercial venture was nothing short of product suicide, or so the theory went.

Other factors came into play, too, luring the developers and their corporate masters to the Windows platform. To see how the Mistress worked this particular spell, it's important to understand how this system works.

Running a game on a PC is an interesting proposition on any platform. Games, more than any other application, need a huge amount of video processing and hardware access. PCs were never originally designed to handle this kind of video, and neither were the operating systems that ran on them. After all, who needs massive video computations just to paint a word processor on the screen?

When the first three-dimensional games were written, it was quickly determined that there was no way anyone without the highest level of processor power and RAM was going to be able to run the things. But so large was the consumer desire to play cool games, it actually drove the hardware developers to come up with a solution much faster than they would otherwise.

Enter the video accelerator card: a piece of hardware that was to revolutionize the gaming industry. The video accelerator was created to take the huge processing load of displaying 3D graphics in real time off the virtual hands of the processor, thus saving a lot of time. Accelerator cards have their own processing capability as well as some amount of video RAM (VRAM), which frees up the main RAM within the PC.

For an application to fully use all the accelerator card's capabilities, it needs to be able to control the hardware's functions directly. All applications use modules of code called libraries to control hardware via APIs (*Application Program Interfaces*) by way of the operating system. This overly manipulative method may seem like a bad game of Telephone, but that's what the operating system is really for: the go-between for the application and the computer hardware. APIs are the intermediaries between the application and the operating system.

For a game to work really well, you need an API with a certain *je ne sais quoi*—a graphics API, to be exact. And the best API out there is Silicon Graphic's OpenGL. Almost every game ever made for the PC uses OpenGL in one form or another. The only other significant competitor is Microsoft DirectX 3D API, which not very many outside Redmond think is such a hot property.

Still, the Mistress hedged her bets and early on developed a Windows version of OpenGL, which Silicon Graphics originally developed for its own platform. At the same time, another one of those classic market-driven situations further sealed the bargain with the devil programmers had to make: In order to sell their products to PC manufacturers, accelerator card makers had to make the cards compliant with Windows, because, thanks to the wheeling and dealing of the Mistress, that was the operating system that would be shipped with most PCs.

Compliance with an operating system occurs through drivers, which are the components of the operating system that let it communicate with hardware. Card makers could make drivers that worked with Linux, too, but the additional programming took up too much time and too much money with (the card makers reasoned) little return on the investment.

Early PC game developers were given no choice at all on what platform to make their games for. If they wanted to use the most robust graphics API, they would use OpenGL, which only runs on Silicon Graphics Irix or Microsoft Windows machines. If their games had anything more than a modicum of graphics, then they needed to target machines with accelerator cards, and the only machines that could do that were Windows machines. Which, by the way, were where all the customers were, and therefore, all the money.

Linux didn't stand a chance. The Mistress was in full control. Until...

Somebody noticed that there sure were a lot of folks buying this Linux thingamajig—especially Europeans. There was a big untapped market of Linux users out there, and in the highly competitive gaming world, it was like wolves sniffing out the last sheep in the fold. The trouble was, there was little there could be done to get games on Linux-based machines. OpenGL did not run on Linux, and very few accelerator cards had Linux drivers.

This situation began to change as early as 1993, when a Masters student at the University of Wisconsin named Brian Paul began writing Mesa, an OpenGL clone designed to work on the X Window graphic user interface for UNIX and Linux. Mesa is a free and open-source API, which allows game programmers to crack open the hood and make sure their game works with it with optimal performance. Even so, Mesa was slow to get rolling, because although it functioned exactly like OpenGL on Irix and Windows, Silicon Graphics did not license the product. But in an incredibly generous move in this litigious society, they didn't sue Paul, either. SGI's position is, "It's there, it works, but we didn't make it, so we're not going to support it."

> The trouble was, there was little there could be done to get games on Linux-based machines.

Hackers began to play a key role in this Linux game migration. With permission, and sometimes without, hackers began to reverse-engineer the accelerator cards on their PCs to figure out exactly how they worked. Once that was done, they could build Linux drivers for the cards.

In some cases, the card manufacturers grudgingly accepted the gift of the drivers—then promptly turned around and marketed their cards as Linux compatible. In other situations, the manufacturers got huffy and threatened to sue hackers for monkeying around with the super-secret inner workings of their product. The hackers just laughed and passed the drivers around to their friends, who passed them on to their friends, and so on and so on...

Once some cards got into the Linux game, several other accelerator card makers got into the act too, not willing to let a new market pass them by. When this happened, game developers began to view Linux as a viable market in which to set up shop.

Gamers, especially the two-timers, were tickled pink. The Mistress was slowly but steadily being asked to leave, as fidelity began to reassert itself. Even better, long-time Windows users started seriously looking at Linux as a new partner, because despite having all the glitz and the tools, *their* partner just couldn't perform.

> Hackers began to play a key role in this Linux game migration.

Linux, they reasoned, might not be as pretty, but looks aren't everything.

FANTASY VERSUS REALITY

The reality of games on Linux is simply this: If you are a casual gamer, interested in nice little diversions, then Linux will satisfy your needs in all ways. If you are a hard-core gamer, Linux is improving, but it is going to be a while before the variety of games on Linux approaches that found on Windows.

Once you find a game for Linux, ideally it may be as simple as buying the boxed set of disks and manuals to help you install the game and get you on your way. Sometimes, though, there's more to it than that. Some games require you buy the Windows version of the game, then get the Linux version, too. This may seem redundant, but there really is a good reason for it. Today's games come with huge amounts of graphics, which fill up the bulk of the CDs the games come on. To save production costs, game developers will just ship the parts of the program that will let the game run on Linux and access the graphics from the original game CD.

Linux users put up with this hair shirt as just being one more way to show their devotion to the penguin. New Linux users, however, want no part of this kind of installation hooey. Just gives us games, they decry.

And there are developers who are listening. Loki Entertainment Software got started in 1998 doing nothing but porting games over to the Linux platform. This function serves the gaming industry well, since they don't have to invest in the time and money to build Linux ports of their games themselves. It certainly helps the Linux gamers, who are still hungry for games. Loki doesn't do too badly as the middleman in this exchange, either.

> Linux users put up with this hair shirt as just being one more way to show their devotion to the penguin.

This three-tier arrangement isn't perfect for the Linux community—nothing ever is. In this case, there is a strong reluctance on the part of the original game developers to release the source code for their games. So, the games coming into Linux are closed binaries, unable to be tweaked and manipulated for better performance. Thus far, the community response has just been low grumbles, since playing with games may actually rank as high as coding for many programmers.

It's all a matter of priorities.

Things are getting better in other ways, too. In February 2000, a game software company called Vicarious Visions developed the first high-end 3D action game specifically for the Linux platform. Terminus, a real-time spacer simulator game, was well received by many Linux game critics not just because it was the "first" commercial game made for Linux, but because it was good.

Slowly but surely, game publishers are waking up to the fact that Linux represents not just a New World to exploit, but also a world full of intelligent users who know what they need and what they like, and aren't shy about giving developers some insightful feedback—feedback that doesn't just say "this SUX!," but tells the developers of the game exactly why the game SUX and a suggestion or two on how to fix it.

Linux drivers for accelerator cards still remain behind the curve, sad to say. The conformity chokehold Microsoft placed on the hardware community has loosened, but manufacturers are still light-headed from the lack of oxygen to their corporate brains. This problem should turn around soon, as more card drivers are created for the Linux platform.

When cards are released with Windows and Linux drivers simultaneously, then the game developers should start flooding the Linux gamers with a torrent of new games.

> The conformity chokehold Microsoft placed on the hardware community has loosened, but manufacturers are still light-headed from the lack of oxygen to their corporate brains.

Where there's a gamer, after all, there's money to be had.

MOVING ON TO SOMETHING NEW

Games on Linux have had a rocky start, thanks to the mechanizations of the jezebel operating system who lured users and developers away with promises of excitement and cash.

The siren call has started to wane, though, as game developers are starting to come to their senses and finally getting their games ported to the Linux platform.

The clarion call has gone out: games are coming to Linux, and a lot of cheatin' hearts are glad to hear it.

All Linux users are glad to hear anything coming out of their machines, truth be told. Next to graphics, sound cards are the most important peripheral device a user can have. Graphics have a lot more uses than just games, too. How Linux handles aural and visual tools is the topic of Chapter 11, "Loud and Graphic."

11

Loud and Graphic

SENSORY DEPRIVATION

I knew I was going to have trouble with this Linux thing when I couldn't hear anything coming out of my speakers.

It was early 1999, and I was making my first Linux box. I was not having a good time. I had used Linux before, of course, on professional machines that were all preinstalled and configured long before I came upon them. This would be the first time I actually installed and configured the penguin myself.

The installation itself seemed to go well. The installation routine identified my monitor and configured it correctly, though it was displaying in a God-awful 640×480 resolution which I not-so-lovingly call the "Reader's Digest Large Print" desktop. That I could fix later (or so I thought). Right now, I wanted to hear sounds coming out of my computer.

Within the desktop environments of most Linux distributions are a group of control utilities labeled the Control Panel. This one was no exception, and it was there I clicked to first. There I found the Sound controls. Within Sound was the Enable

Sound Server option, which was checked off for some reason. Happy to have found the solution, I checked the box, clicked OK, and waited to hear something.

Nothing.

Well, maybe after a restart.

Nothing.

I went back to the Sound control. The option I'd checked was still checked. So where was the sound? I still had enough Microsoft expectations in my brain at that time to believe that once something was activated, then it should work. Windows took care of this for me, why couldn't Linux? For one dark moment, I felt betrayed.

> For one dark moment, I felt betrayed.

Then I shook it off and started going through the documentation. The on-board help system did not give me many clues, save one: Check the hardware. This was something that I thought was already taken care of, since the installation screen had specifically displayed the detected sound card, and it was the right one.

I turned to the Holy Grail of Linux help: the alt.os.linux newsgroups. These vast marketplaces of information usually contained the answers I needed, if I had the patience to rummage through the thousands of different messages to find the knowledge I sought.

A half-hour later, I had a better handle on the situation. Even if hardware is detected in Linux, I discovered, it does not automatically mean it's *configured* to work. In other words, Linux knew my sound card was there, but it had to be further instructed exactly how to use it.

This initially seems like a huge pain in the butt to new Linux users, and that was certainly a thought going through my mind that day, among several that are best not put in print. After some more experience with Linux, I came to see why this approach was not necessarily such a bad thing.

Linux is, ultimately, all about putting control in the hands of the user. *Everything* can be configured in Linux, with superuser access, something that is not entirely possible on Windows or Macintosh machines.

For instance, if you go the command line on a Windows machine, you get to use DOS. That's it. In Linux, you can specify exactly which shell will be used in the command line, based on your preferences: bash, tcsh, csh, and so on. I know, try not to get so excited. This is just one (incredibly geeky) example, but it does serve to show just how detailed Linux configuration can get, if you really want to use it.

Which brings me back to the sound card. Linux wants the user to configure a sound card, not because of some laziness on the part of the programmer, but because the Linux programmers don't want to presume how you want that card configured. This is a subtle yet very significant difference between Linux and Windows, which many don't appreciate.

Flush with my new knowledge, I started the sound card configuration utility, stepped through the settings, restarted the computer, and poof! Worf from *Star Trek* was telling me I had "incoming messages."

> Linux is, ultimately, all about putting control in the hands of the user.

When you come right down to it, we all tend to treat our PCs like tricked-out lowriders bouncing down the streets of L.A. Having sound just makes it that much easier to hang the aural equivalent of fuzzy dice. The same theory applies to what's getting displayed on our monitors. Once people find out they can change the colors on their desktops, there is usually an experimentation phase when they go crazy trying to mate mauve and teal or some other bizarre color combination.

First, you have to get the monitor working, though, which is not always the easiest thing to do. I was lucky on this first installation, since Linux was happy enough with my monitor and video card to at least display the X Window interface, albeit in Reader's Digest Large Print.

This time finding the solution to my problem, which was getting that screen resolution to something a bit more manageable, like 1024×768, was not so simple. I tried the hardware tack, only to discover that for the video display, this was one instance where Linux did automate some of the configuration. It has to; otherwise there would be nothing displayed.

In my case, the default configuration was horrendous, and I needed to locate the utility to finish the job. So, like Gay Talese, I began the personal journey to find how to change my screen.

The answer, I soon discovered, was in X.

X is not part of the big *X-Men* craze that swept the nation like so many other summer movies of the past. X is the shorthand name for the X Window System. X will be discussed later in this chapter, but the simple description of it is the graphical user interface for Linux.

Since X manages the display of the windows, menus, and dialog boxes on the Linux desktop, it gets the job of setting the

The **Joy of Tech** by Nitrozac and Snaggy

screen resolution size. Using the xf86config utility, I was able to get the screen to the size I wanted it.

You will have noted, in these two short and rather unexciting examples, a peculiar feature of Linux that comes up a lot when integrating hardware with the operating system—namely, the compartmentalization of the controls. Critics of Linux always jump on this apparent fragmentation of the configuration utilities. "You can't set anything up," they whine, "because it's too hard to find the right utility."

When you come right down to it, we all tend to treat our PCs like tricked-out lowriders bouncing down the streets of L.A.

Windows PCs and Macs do tend to centralize their system controls, or at least appear to by grouping all the start icons in a central Control Panel folder. In truth, however, these operating systems, just like Linux, use separate utilities for sound, video, and networks. It's just that Linux users are supposed to figure out where everything is. This is, I think, my one genuine beef with Linux: the apparent need to memorize a half-dozen or so utility names just to tweak things on your computer.

Things are getting better, however. Red Hat Linux includes Setup, which points the user to several configuration utilities. SuSE Linux has YaST and YaST2, text-based and graphical master configuration utilities. Other Linux distributions are following suit, recognizing the need for a more central control paradigm.

Personal quests are all well and good, but who wants to spend them looking up computer stuff?

Rated X

With only two chapters left in the book, now might be a good time to tell you that when you look at the typical screen on the typical Linux machine, you're not looking at Linux at all. You're looking at X Window, or X for short. It's called *X* not so much to keep it short but to keep Linux users from having to even say the word "window" too often. It makes us a bit jittery.

Non–Linux users are often a bit confused about what X does. On the surface, it looks like it just runs the windows and menus you see on the screen. But there is a lot more going on here than it appears.

In the Microsoft Windows environment, you have the DOS operating system with the Windows operating system interface running on top of it. "Running on top" means that Windows is essentially one big program that runs from the DOS platform, essentially no different from running a program like Doom for DOS. The result of this is that you must have DOS running in order to run Windows.

For Windows NT users, it's a bit more simplified. Windows NT/2000 is a true graphical user interface (GUI) that runs on its own. The advantage here is that you really do get what you see. You can still run DOS when you have to, but in Windows NT, a DOS emulator runs within Windows. An *emulator* is a program that can mimic the look and feel of another operating system. One disadvantage to Windows NT, however, is that a PC must have a lot more memory and speed to run as efficiently as a comparable Windows 98 system. All that pure GUI eats up a lot of system resources.

The Linux operating system is most analogous to the DOS/ Windows system. Like DOS, Linux is a text-based, command-line operating system (albeit a *much* more sophisticated one) and that's *all*. This is an important distinction. Linux was designed to be a command-line OS, not a GUI. The same holds true for DOS. But in both cases, someone has come along and added the frills and functionality of a pretty GUI that runs on top of these command-line OSs.

In the case of Linux, the X interface was ready and waiting for Linux. In 1986, an international consortium of UNIX programmers began putting together a graphical operating system based on the GUI research done by the Xerox Palo Alto Research Center. This is the same place that came up with the GUI interface known in the IT world as WIMP (*Windows Icons Menus Pointing device*), so these guys aren't just sitting around sniffing toner. They're into some serious interface work and most modern GUIs have them to thank.

After Linux was introduced in 1991, X soon found its way to the Linux desktop. When Linux began appearing on Intel-based PCs, a new implementation of X, XFree86, helped make the transition. XFree86 is the heart of most GUIs that run on Linux. It is not the only visual interface available for Linux on an Intel machine, but it easily is the most popular.

I't's called X not so much to keep it short but to keep Linux users from having to even say the word "window" too often.

Also referred to as the *X server*, XFree86 is where video output and PC input is brought together to form one cohesive interface. PC input is obtained from two basic input devices: the keyboard and the mouse. Video output is then sent through the graphics card to the monitor.

Although this sounds like the entirety of the GUI, it's not. In fact, X alone is not a GUI at all.

Here's where things get interesting.

The X server is only one layer of the display system: the layer that provides the "home" for the GUI to operate. X is just a video *tabula rasa*, able to display whatever signals get sent to it. To generate the actual windows and menus that make up what is traditionally considered a GUI, you need a window manager running in this X server display layer. A *window manager* is the application that gives X server its "look" and determines how graphical applications will be displayed. *This* is where the menus and windows are generated and controlled.

Several window managers can be used with Linux: AfterStep, AnotherLevel, Enlightenment, fvwm, fvwm95, KWM, olvm, Sawfish, and tvm, to name a few. Two other interfaces you may have heard of are GNOME and KDE, but they are not truly window managers.

> **X** is just a video *tabula rasa*, able to display whatever signals get sent to it.

As you read in Chapter 4, KDE is the K Desktop Environment, which was created in 1996 by German student Matthias Ettrich. Ettrich, already involved in the LyX development project, yearned to create a straightforward interface for the UNIX platform. In 1996, he came upon the Qt code libraries, which he quickly realized could be the technology to achieve his goal. After quickly assembling a team of volunteer developers, work soon began on KDE 1.0.

Often referred to as a window manager, in fact KDE is not. KDE usually runs over a window manager called KWM (*K Window Manager*). As KWM enhances the look and feel of XFree86, so KDE enhances the look and tool sets of KWM. Because of this, KDE (and GNOME) is referred to as a *desktop environment*.

Around the Linux community, KDE is the one that's referred to as "the one that looks like Windows 95." But that's not where the controversy lies. Until September of 2000, TrollTech, the Norwegian publisher of the Qt libraries upon which KDE is built, did not release the libraries under the GPL open-source license. This caused several prominent members of the Linux community to shun KDE and KDE-related applications. The organizers of the Debian distribution would not officially support the KDE desktop on their desktop, for example, because of the lack of a GPL.

Once the Qt libraries were placed under GPL status, however, things began to change for KDE. Long pressured by users who support the interface, distributions began to pick up the desktop environment and support it, including Debian. KDE is currently enjoying renewed success in the community, as users are devouring the release of KDE2 in November 2000, which already looks to be a strong competitor to any GUI on any platform.

The other major desktop environment for Linux is the GNOME (*GNU Network Object Model Environment*) desktop. GNOME was started a mere nine months after KDE, and may have been created by Miguel de Icaza in direct response to some of the perceived limitations of KDE, as we discussed in Chapter 4.

Icaza's idea took off like a rocket, and soon programmers from all over the world were joining the development project.

Recall that like KDE, GNOME is not a true window manager. GNOME is an enhancement for a window manager running on XFree86. Usually this is the Sawfish window manager, though it does not have to be.

GNOME has enjoyed high success in the Linux community, especially among those purists who insist on only open-source software on their PCs.

A big question that's often asked, though, is what do all these choices mean? What is each of these components responsible for? Here is a list of components, and what each one does, on a typical Linux system running the GNOME environment:

- **Linux.** This is the base on which everything runs. It handles all basic file-system and device tasks, as well as translating commands into the PC's rudimentary machine language.

- **XFree86.** This is the heart of the GUI. It generates a display layer that allows the creation of graphics and then marries those graphics to input from the keyboard and mouse.
- **gtk.** This is responsible for the look of all menus, buttons, and other doodads you play with on the screen.
- **Sawfish.** The window manager is responsible for the look of all windows, dialog boxes, and menus that are generated from the applications being used.
- **GNOME.** This enhances the Sawfish window manager by providing additional interface tools and appearance. Additional controls are provided for input-device configuration. Several applications custom-made for this environment ship with this tool.

Whether you use KDE or GNOME, it should be noted that just because a certain combination of window managers and desktop environments has been installed on a Linux box, it does not mean that the user must be locked into that combination. For example, you can run GNOME on top of fvm95 if you want

The Joy of Tech   by Nitrozac and Snaggy

to. That's one of the great things about Linux's open platform philosophy: You have real choices on how to run your PC.

AIRBRUSHES AND TOUCH-UPS

Graphics in Linux can do more than run the user interface, and anyone who thinks differently can go grab a bucket of popcorn and pop a copy of *Titanic* into the VCR or DVD player. See that big boat in the movie? It's pretty much not real, since even King of the World James Cameron didn't want to tackle building a full-size replica of the ill-fated White Star Lines ship. It's actually a composite of miniature models, computer animation, and some full-size sets, all blended together by 160 Alpha processor computers at the effects company Digital Domain. 105 of these computers were running Red Hat Linux 4.1, and the rest Windows NT.

Alpha processors are different from the Intel processors found in most non-Apple PCs. They are, by a huge degree, much more powerful than Intel chips. Even so, using the wrong operating system would slow the systems down to a painful (and costly) rate. Faced with a choice between Windows NT, Digital UNIX, and Linux, Digital Domain weighed in with Linux for the machines that performed the really heavy graphical work. This was primarily because Linux was flexible, and the open-source availability of the Linux code allowed the workers at Digital Domain to modify the operating system to their exact needs. The stability of Linux paid off as well. Digital Domain ran the machines 24 hours a day for three solid months with no significant downtime.

Of course, if you don't have Kate Winslet or Leonardo DiCaprio hanging about the house ready to make a home movie, there are other ways to use Linux for your graphic needs. The best, and certainly most powerful way for the home user to play with graphics on their Linux box is to make use of the GIMP.

Whenever new users hear about this application, there's usually some sort of reaction, from a snorting laugh to a vague sense of discomfort from the notion that Linux users are making fun of the disabled in some way. It is an odd name, to be sure, but no odder than Coca Cola, which is directly derived from one of the early ingredients of the famous soft drink: cocaine. In this case, the name is derived from the GNU Image Manipulation Program. And that name pretty much says it all. The "the" in "the GIMP" is a sort of a fond affectation that has stuck with the program since its 1997 creation. The ultra-geeks use this to indicate that this is the one and only GIMP. (Some maintain it's a sly reference to a line in the black comedy *Pulp Fiction*: "Bring in the gimp.")

> It is an odd name, to be sure, but no odder than Coca Cola, which is directly derived from one of the early ingredients of the famous soft drink: cocaine.

GNU means the GIMP is in direct compliance with the Free Software Foundation's GPL. Not only does this tend to give most Linux users a warm and fuzzy feeling, it also allows us to modify the guts of the application should we so desire (more on this in a moment). *Image Manipulation Program* means just what it says: If you have an image, then this program will slice, dice, and twist it every which way to make it look exactly the way you want. The onboard tools for the GIMP rival any found in Adobe's PhotoShop. That's not bad, considering PhotoShop 6 sells for about $600. The GIMP, on the other hand, is free.

For the things the GIMP can't do by itself, the ability to get into the code that comprises the GIMP has allowed programmers to create plug-ins for the GIMP that will get these specialized jobs done. There are literally hundreds of plug-ins created for this application, giving users incredible flexibility to do anything they can imagine to an image. Beyond the plug-ins are the script-fus, little script applications that are not quite plug-ins, but still give added functionality to the GIMP.

The GIMP represents more than a pretty face in Linux; it is the very embodiment of the best that Linux can offer when everything works as it should. It is a highly robust application rivaling any commercial software on the market and it is open source, which gives users the ability to customize the GIMP like a cherry '62 Corvette.

> The GIMP represents more than a pretty face in Linux; it is the very embodiment of the best that Linux can offer when everything works as it should.

WHY PAY FOR MILK WHEN YOU CAN GET THE COW FOR FREE?

Unless you have been hiding (or whatever) in bed for the last six months, you have probably heard of this thing called Napster. Napster has been called everything from "the most revolutionary tool on the Internet ever" to a "thief's wet dream." Like most things with such extreme descriptions, the truth lies somewhere in between. In fact, Napster is both a client application for the PC and a file-sharing service used for the express purpose of (according to Napster, Inc.) sampling different songs.

Napster is the creation of Shawn Fanning, who created the application to go out and hunt down music files out on the Internet. The file format he targeted was the MP3 format, which, due to its great compression-to-quality ratio, is the best format for squeezing music down to a manageable file size and still maintaining good acoustical values.

The Joy of Tech   by Nitrozac and Snaggy

There have been applications like this before, of course. Known as "robots," the traditional form of this application goes out, finds selected files, and then creates a database of Web links to all the files. The disadvantage to this older system is that unless it's updated a lot, it gets out of date very quickly. Another problem was that many MP3 music files were not even on the Web at all—they were sitting on users' home or office PCs, well away from any Web server.

Fanning's approach was to reverse the robot methodology and give users a tool that would not only allow them to find and acquire fellow users' music files, but would also report to other users what MP3 files were on their PCs so they could be shared. When Napster is run on client A's PC, client A can see all the music every other client has—and every client can see and share what's on client A's PC. There are limitations to this orgy of music sharing, of course. Napster can only see and grab MP3 files, and even then only the files the host user wants to share.

Fanning started developing this application soon after he began attending Northeastern University in the fall of 1998. By the following spring, he was driven to make it work and dropped out of school to do so. In May of 1999, he and his uncle incorporated Napster, Inc. That same summer, Fanning released an early beta version of the Napster client for Windows. To say his idea took off would be an understatement. Napster *exploded*. By October 2000, Fanning reported 32,000,000 users of Napster and a growth rate of 1,000,000 additional users per *week*.

Linux users knew a good thing when they saw it. Once they figured out what Fanning had done, Linux programmers quickly built their own clients to tap into the Napster virtual community. Today there are about 10 free Napster clients of varying degrees of quality available on the Internet. Several of them are indistinguishable in functionality from the original Windows client.

> When coupled with the myriad music-ripping applications for Linux, any Linux user can quickly set up their own recording studio, just like anyone else's platform.

When coupled with the myriad music-ripping applications for Linux, any Linux user can quickly set up their own recording studio, just like anyone else's platform. But herein lies the rub of using Napster.

Fanning, and Napster, Inc., immediately came under fire by the one industry that potentially stands to lose a lot from the existence of such wide-spread sharing: the recording industry. Traditionally, recording studios have kept a firm lock on the distribution and copyrights of their artists' music. Some would argue a tight chokehold, but so far it's all been legal. To the recording industry, the advent of Napster represents the end of the world as they know it. The thought of CDs getting bought, copied, and distributed without collection of royalties makes recording executives, and not a few artists, weak and short of breath. And, in an age where dueling pistols are passé, the Recording Industry Association of America has taken Napster to court to get them to cut it out.

Many of us in the Linux community often feel compelled to defend Napster to the hilt, likening its flaunting of commercial copyrights to the free software and open source movements. In fact, some outside media establishments have started to think of Linux users as some kind of intellectual property thieves ourselves because we seem to be so anti-copyright. In fact, nothing could be further from the truth. Linux, GNU, and the Free Software Foundation are all about removing the principle of copyrights from software, so that everyone can access and use the source code for applications directly. This does not equate to ignoring copyrights altogether, something the mainstream press seems to get wrong from time to time. Pretty much everyone in the Linux community has a healthy respect for copyrights that are already in place.

> Open sourcing someone's intellectual property is always done with the consent and willingness of all parties involved.

We just wish they would go away so we could get on with the business of improving or adding to the code.

There are a lot of reasons to argue for the use of Napster, all of which are pretty compelling. It can be used to listen to new music before purchasing, to find music that is old and out of publication, and to distribute music for artists that otherwise could not through the mainstream recording industry.

Participation in the Napster phenomenon is not the same thing as avocation of open source, however. Open sourcing someone's intellectual property is always done with the consent and willingness of all parties involved. To do otherwise is real theft, which is not what Linux or open source is about. Why, then, do Linux users like Napster so much? Well, why does any user like it? This is one area of use that transcends the bounds of operating systems, much like the Internet itself. Napster has become a common area of music sharing, communication, and contention by users of many operating systems, and does not reflect the values of any one OS.

Maybe it's because we just like the free music.

MOVING ON TO SOMETHING NEW

There is not a lot Linux and Windows users seem to have in common, but there is one unfortunate trend that is still a big problem for the Penguins of the world: Linux users often are Windows users, too.

The massive proliferation of the Microsoft operating system virtually guarantees that most Linux users will be exposed to a Windows machine, often against their wills. It may be the PC at work, the Windows machine in the library, or the laptop your spouse insists on keeping Penguin-free from your vile mechanizations.

So... you've been faithful to Linux, perhaps on a weekend of passion and a promise of more to come. But on Monday, you're back in front of the seductive yet abusive Windows mistress you'd left behind. In Chapter 12, we'll give you some coping tips on making Windows behave more like your true love.

12

Breaking up Is Hard to Do

MY FIRST TIME

It was 1992, and I was a stranger in a strange land, looking at my first X desktop with a feeling akin to horror. There I was, small-town Indiana boy, working in a grungy little office overlooking the United Nations complex on the East River, staring at what appeared to be a windows-like GUI on the flickering monochrome screen.

The view outside was almost as intimidating as the one inside. Across the way I could see the Turkish embassy; out on the East River, the Greenpeace ship *Rainbow Warrior* sat in the middle of the channel, barking megaphoned protests at the U.N. On the way to work that morning, I had passed the Iranian and Iraqi embassies, rather troubling in the post–Gulf War era. I had also passed more adult bookstores, peep shows, and street hawkers than I could count, but given my history with such establishments, I did not linger in front of these for long.

I was a huckster, smelling fresh of corn and Indiana clay, transplanted to this island called Manhattan to work as an academic journal editor. I commuted from our home in New Jersey two hours one way to get to this building; by 9 o'clock on those first days, I was already spent, mostly from culture shock.

Of course, I would soon learn the ways of this city, and start shouting at tourists in the subway turnstiles to get the hell out of the way like the rest of the citizenry. But that was months down the road. Today, I was introduced to X for Solaris, and I was not happy.

> Today, I was introduced to X for Solaris, and I was not happy.

My mentor/editor started to run me through the ins and outs of this system, which she just called UNIX, showing me the two important tools I would need to do my work: the SGML editor used to compile articles and the e-mail application used to communicate with article authors.

E-mail I thought I could handle, because the last place I'd worked had an internal messaging system. SGML, on the other hand, scared the bejesus out of me. They had told me when I interviewed for the position that I would be using desktop publishing; this thing before me looked nothing like Ventura Publisher or Adobe PageMaker, which was what I had seen before.

"No, no," my new boss told me. "Not desktop publishing. *Electronic* publishing." There were no layout capabilities, and no real-time WYSIWYG, either—just a text editor with tags that you had to manually preview every time you wanted to see how the final text would look. This editor also dealt with TeX, another context-sensitive tagging language, which we used to build complex mathematical formulas.

I was in hell.

At home, I was happily chugging away on Windows for Workgroups 3.11. This Sun interface behaved completely differently, with a taskbar, start menu, and pop-up menus. Who would ever use stuff like this? It was weird!

As time went on, I became more adept at maneuvering the interface and managing the rigors of SGML and TeX. I even grudgingly admitted I was starting to like the speed of the Sun workstation, since it was noticeably faster than the 286 I had at home.

Then I had an epiphany.

My workload began to noticeably lessen about three months after I started; my wife was due with our firstborn, and I was prepared to take a leave of absence at basically any moment. Since I had more time on my hands, another editor at the office, who was far more savvy to the ways of the computer world, pointed out how to run this application called Mosaic for X.

"What does it do?" I asked my colleague, Walter.

"It goes out to the Internet and lets you view pages on it," Walter said as he typed a cryptic-looking string of text that began with "http://" in a field on the screen.

"Like e-mail pages?" I replied. "I don't get it."

"No, it's called the World Wide Web. Here, watch," he said, pressing the Enter key.

And there, in 256-level grayscale, were Richard Nixon and Elvis Presley shaking hands in the Oval Office.

Information junkie that I was, I was hooked.

> SGML, on the other hand, scared the bejesus out of me.

The World Wide Web (we hadn't gotten around to just calling it "the Web" yet) in those days was a raw frontier of information appearing on just a few hundred HTML pages. But what pages they were! I could access a computer in the United Kingdom and view pictures of a London street corner. From a computer in Michigan, I could pull hour-old weather satellite photos onto my screen and use them as a background.

The world had just become very small.

In those days, there was no Yahoo to track this stuff down. The entirety of the Web was listed on the NCSA site, the creators of this new "browser" application for X. New Web sites were posted on the site at a rate of about ten a week. (By the time I left the organization, this site was incapable of listing a mere one percent of the new sites that were appearing daily, so great was the growth of the Web.)

Back home, I was no longer happily chugging away on Windows for Workgroups 3.11. I had no connectivity to the Internet. CompuServe was still proprietary content only, and there were no ISPs in north Jersey yet. My super-fast, top-of-the-line PC was now just a glorified typewriter.

Two things happened next. After a hectic and terrifying Saturday, we had our baby girl, and my world became very small indeed. A few weeks later, once I was back at work, our Slavic systems admin burst out of the server room in near tears, pleading with all of us, "Please! Stop vat you are doing! You are bringing too much traffic into the netvork!"

> From a computer in Michigan, I could pull hour-old weather satellite photos onto my screen and use them as a background.

In our desire to explore the Web (for now everyone in the office was surfing), we had inadvertently poured thousands of cached files onto the servers, bringing them to their electronic knees.

The Web, for a time, was off limits. Eventually we got it back, albeit at a much more controlled pace.

I left that organization about a year later, packing up my 286 with all the rest of our possessions to move back home again to Indiana. We carried with us a lot of memories and lessons from the three years we lived and worked near New York, the most important being our daughter's first year. I brought back a few more things as well: the ability to drive like a New Jersey driver on any street or highway in Indiana at any time, thereby scaring the hell out of anyone around me; a healthy respect for gentlemen named Vinnie and Guido; and a firm commitment to get connected to the Internet as soon as I could.

And UNIX?

We did not part as friends, but I had a healthy respect for it, which grew even more the first time I saw a beta version of Windows 95 and its interface with a taskbar, start menu, and pop-up menus...

> **M**y super-fast, top-of-the-line PC was now just a glorified typewriter.

L-O-L-A LOLA

Deception is a big part of the human mating game. If we don't like our self-image, we change it. A whole industry out there devotes itself to enlarging various parts of female and male anatomy alone.

These types of alterations tend to short-circuit the whole point of the mating process. If a woman instinctively desires the strong man she eyes across the room, that is nature's way of getting a stronger set of genes into the gene pool. But if that man's musculature is enhanced and not natural, then a weaker set of genes is passed on.

Muscles aren't everything, of course, but people are attracted to certain things no matter how intelligent and sensitive they claim to be. A Rhodes scholar might be reduced to a slathering idiot when he spies a nice pair of legs. We never really control these physical impulses, but often have to avoid acting on them. Otherwise, long-term relationships would never last. Instead, we try to seek out someone with looks *and* personality.

Some deceptions are not quite so harmful, of course. Put any man in a well-fitting tux, and he looks good—or at least better. A beautiful gown enhances the beauty of most women. This is plumage, the same as makeup, cologne, and hair styles, and certainly no different from the feathers of a peacock. This kind of image-enhancement is more like an advertisement than a whole new set of goods. It says "Hey! Look! I'm over here!"

Somehow, this activity eludes many members of the geek set. Our love for members of the opposite sex is sometimes overshadowed by our driven need to make the machines we work with better. After all, the better the machine, the better quality of nekkid pictures we can download and ogle. Of course, a geek's life is not solely driven by the pursuit of soft-core JPEGs; the true

The Joy of Tech   by Nitrozac and Snaggy

driving force seems to be the chance to make something really special with our hands and minds. In the old days, we'd be the ones whittling, or writing in a journal. Today, we play with computers—or appear to. Geeks are actually not playing, but crafting and building, looking for the next "better solution."

Linux opened a new doorway for many in this social archetype. Here was their chance to not only tweak something to make it better, but get into its guts to change it completely from within. Even non-geeks can appreciate the ease in which the desktop can be altered to their exact needs. Is it any wonder, then, that once bitten, the Linux user finds it so hard to part with her beloved operating system and deal with the ubiquitous Windows?

> **H**ere was their chance to not only tweak something to make it better, but get into its guts to change it completely from within.

The unfortunate reality for lovers of the penguin is that we often are forced to use Microsoft on a regular basis because of the overwhelming pervasiveness of the Windows operating system in business, education, and home situations.

Only the most resolute Linux user can keep his home Windows-free, especially if there're kids around. There are simply too many educational programs built for Windows (and Mac) machines to keep them out of the house. So, the die-hard Linux user grudgingly keeps a small machine or part of a disk drive of a larger machine loaded with Windows—and doesn't breathe a word about it to the folks down at the LUG (the Linux equivalent of Kiwanis).

Work situations are often worse. Corporate America has bought into the Microsoft Way like parents shoving each other for Cabbage Patch dolls or Britney Spears concert tickets. They go out of there way to have the latest and greatest toys from Redmond installed on their computers, and then wonder why they have to keep paying for hardware upgrades every year or so.

It is into this environment that Linux users must trudge every Monday: an office where the IT staff openly professes to despise Linux and everything it stands for, when more than a few of them likely have used it themselves but don't want to break away from the "WinPack." Even high-ranking IT workers have a hard time bringing their beloved Linux into the firm. They face resistance from underlings who've spent all their time and effort learning how to pay homage to Microsoft and resent having to deprogram themselves to use Linux. Alternatively, they must contend with line managers who base all of their employees' IT needs on some magazine article they read and insist on doing things their own way, not IT's. In either situation, Linux gets left behind while the Linux user is forced to make nice with Windows.

Unless the Linux user gets sneaky.

People undergo another type of transformation connected to social interaction, but not mating *per se*. Known as transexuality, it is when a member of one gender decides, fully and completely, to become a member of the other gender. This decision is not made lightly, and the reasons for the change are varied and deeply personal. Many times the change is secretive, since much of society tends to react badly to situations it doesn't understand.

> **A**lternatively, they must contend with line managers who base all of their employees' IT needs on some magazine article they read and insist on doing things their own way, not IT's.

Switching genders is not easy to manage, even in these modern times. Sometimes a less drastic, but still more personal change is done: assuming the outward identity of another gender, which is known as transvestitism.

Again, the reasons for dressing like a member of the opposite sex are varied and personal—but the change is a lot easier to pull off.

Likewise, when Linux users are immersed in an environment of hostile and maladjusted Windows machines, they typically have three options. They can do nothing and be miserable; they can completely and defiantly switch their machine over to Linux, a solution that is often impractical and likely grounds for termination at the workplace; or they can perform an act of electronic transvestitism: Dress the Windows machine like a Linux box.

SO COME UP TO THE LAB AND SEE WHAT'S ON THE SLAB

The idea of adding applications that look and feel like Linux apps to your Windows machine is not exactly the *latest* obsession. After all, Microsoft Windows was just an attempt to run the Mac OS on an Intel machine, once upon a time.

There are several different ways to get Linux stuff on a non-Linux machine—it really just depends on how far you want to take it. For this look, we'll focus on three different levels: Linux applications for Windows, X servers for Windows, and full-fledged

Linux boxes running right on a Windows PC without the need to partition a hard drive. Windows control freaks might call these strategies an Abomination Against the Proper Way of Things, but keep in mind there's nothing illegal or illicit about any of this software. So be open. Be expressive. And show your Windows companions how to loosen up and have a little fun.

A Little Lace

Quite a few Linux applications out there are so loved, so extensively used, that the people who use them cannot bear to part with them for any length of time. Once such application is Emacs, which, according to the GNU Emacs Web site, is an "extensible, customizable, self-documenting real-time display editor." (In English, "a really functional text editor.")

Emacs is a pretty robust application that allows users to create anything from simple text files to sophisticated programming scripts. It is this latter functionality that gives it such appeal to the Linux crowd. After all, if we are going to play with the code, then we need a tool with which to do so!

Emacs revolts against the notion that applications that generate text must be big, slow mega-apps that let you change the font size, typeface, and molecular structure of each and every letter on a page. Even some Linux applications are a bit guilty of this, such as StarOffice and WordPerfect, to name two. Hard-core Linux users reject this pretty-boy view of document creation.

> Windows control freaks might call these strategies an Abomination Against the Proper Way of Things, but keep in mind there's nothing illegal or illicit about any of this software.

Their motto? "Just give the reader something to read; the rest will sort itself out." Emacs is certainly no pretty application. But what it lacks in looks, it more than makes up in raw functionality. It is this functionality that users can install on their Windows machines. Xemacs, a more graphical form of Emacs, is also available for the Windows platform.

After all, if we are going to play with the code, then we need a tool with which to do so!

Another text editor employed heavily by Linux users who shun the graphical interface is VIM. VIM, which actually stands for *vi Improved*, is a complete departure from anything Emacs related. VIM and its predecessor vi are completely text-based editors that work entirely within the console mode of Linux. Where Emacs has menus and shortcut commands, VIM has key commands and that's it.

Because of this seemingly total lack of interface, VIM takes quite a while to get used to. Experienced VIM users, however, can make this application sing. VIM is an excellent alternative to Windows' Notepad and Wordpad applications.

Text editors are not the only things you can export to Windows from Linux. One simple way to create a Linux-like feel in Windows is to install some larger applications that have been available on both platforms for years.

First off, even if you do the kind of work that needs an office-suite application, why spend money on something like Microsoft Office when you can install StarOffice for Windows for free? StarOffice 5.2 duplicates a lot of the functionality of MS Office and is very compatible with all the popular word-processing, spreadsheet, and presentation file formats. For example, when creating a document, you can open or create Word, WordPerfect, text, and AbiWord files...even use the old XYWrite file formats, if you need to deal with something that arcane.

StarOffice is no Office, of course, but in a lot of ways, it's better. The interface on the Windows version is identical to the Linux version, so you need not make any adjustments when switching between the two.

Another major application that is basically identical on both platforms is the Netscape Communicator suite of Internet applications. Comprised of Netscape Communicator, Composer, and Messenger, Netscape 6 for Linux resembles in many ways the functionality of its Windows counterpart.

There are two drawbacks to this option, though. First, Windows makes it very, very difficult to replace Internet Explorer with another browser such as Netscape, no matter what Redmond says. Basically you have to install the additional Netscape browser suite and leave IE on the machine and put up with the latter fighting the former for a couple of sessions until you can tweak the settings to get IE to ignore Netscape. This is not difficult, just a big pain.

A larger problem stems from Netscape's decision to release all its Netscape for Linux source code to the general public a couple years ago. This massive open-source project is known as Mozilla. Although well-intentioned, Netscape failed to assume project ownership as it should have; with no real leadership, various factions started pulling the existing source code into several different programming directions. Eventually, the project imploded, and Mozilla became a complete re-write of the Netscape source code from the ground up. Netscape 6 for Linux, although it resembles the Netscape 6 for Windows counterpart, is still very slow compared to other browsers.

> One simple way to create a Linux-like feel in Windows is to install some larger applications that have been available on both platforms for years.

Open source is not a miracle cure, it seems, for software development. Without effective leadership, any project can go awry,

The Joy of Tech   by Nitrozac and Snaggy

and this one is a classic example. Still, using Netscape on the two platforms will bring you quite a bit of synchronicity and help ease the stress of using Windows.

The Cygwin development tools have been used to port a great many applications to the Windows platform. These tools allow programmers to quickly adapt existing UNIX applications to use the Win32 API. Just a partial list of these ported applications include:

- Apache 1.3.9 and php-4.0b2
- FreeCIV 1.8.0
- gcc 2.95.2
- Gimp for Win32
- Kerberos V4 eBones Distribution
- lynx-2.8.2r1
- perl-5.6.0
- TCL/Tk 8.1
- XChat-text 1.5.7

The Cygwin tools have been a powerful conduit to porting Linux-based software to Win32 platforms. But using Windows versions of your favorite Linux apps may not be enough to satisfy your Linux desire.

Is That a Kilt?

A more drastic change to effect on a Windows machine is to add an application that will allow you to run any Linux application within it. In short, what you need is X Window. Question our sanity if you must, but there is validity in this statement: There are several versions of X out there for the Windows PC.

> Open source is not a miracle cure, it seems, for software development.

One of these products is StarNet's X-Win32. When run on a Windows platform, X-Win32 allows you to connect to a Linux (or UNIX) server and run the applications on the server remotely on your client machine. X-Win32 and similar products do not allow users to run Linux applications natively, however; you must point your Windows machine to a Linux server somewhere on your network. Given the success of Linux on server platforms as opposed to client machines, though, this is not such a daunting task.

When you run a Win32 X server on a Windows system, it's pretty much the same thing as running it on Linux, though there are some speed limitations involved. This is perhaps the best compromise for most people to get Linux functionality on the Windows desktop, because it's small, relatively easy to install, and pretty quick on its electronic feet.

Maxwell Q. Klinger, Reporting for Duty

Another solution is to install a new kind of application on your PC that will effectively let you run a Linux platform right on your Windows machine. Called a *virtual machine*, the application known as VMware allows anyone using it to run a completely separate operating system on his computer—without affecting the existing system. VMware is a great solution for those who need Linux on their PCs, but don't want to deal with the cantankerous task of partitioning a hard drive to do so.

When VMware is installed on your PC, it creates a virtual machine in the active memory of your computer. To any operating system running on the virtual machine, it's as if it's running on a real computer. This is not a hard leap to make, when you realize that operating systems work simply by processing electronic signals from hardware. VMware sends those same signals within the virtual machine, so the operating system is (usually) none the wiser.

Like anything else in the world of software, there are some limitations. This is what computers have in common with cars—the legal limitations mumbled at the end of the commercials.

VMware will run on pretty much any distribution of Linux specified by its developers, and it will run the same distributions within it. Unfortunately, the only Windows platform it will run on is Windows NT/2000. So, if you have Windows 98, you are out of luck for now.

VMware is also on the slow side, since it is borrowing a good chunk of your system's resources to produce this virtual machine. That makes VMware good for casual use, but serious users will be driven to fits by the time it takes to get things done.

What's a user to do? Simple: Install Linux itself.

The typical Linux installation is not something to put *on* a Windows machine. Instead, you must shove the Windows partition aside to make room on a hard drive for a new operating system, such as Linux. The two operating systems then run completely independently of each other.

A select few Linux distributions, however, can run on a Windows partition of a hard drive, just like a Windows application.

All you need is space on your hard drive and you're all set. One of the larger Linux distributions that performs this feat is Corel Linux. Corel Linux is relatively new to the Linux community, but because of its heavily automated installation routines and ease of configuration, it has become fairly popular early in its career, particularly among the newbie Linux users.

Like most other Linux distributions, Corel Linux prefers to roost in its own hard disk partition. But Corel Linux also provides users the choice to install itself directly on a Windows partition. Once Corel Linux is installed in this manner, the user is left with a perfectly normal Windows machine, minus some room on the hard drive. With one command, however, the user's machine is transformed into a true Linux box capable of doing anything a Linux machine can do. It's a tad slow, because of the system resources that are forced to contend with the very inefficient UMDOS file system, but it is fast enough to suit all but the most discriminating user.

> **A** select few Linux distributions, however, can run on a Windows partition of a hard drive, just like a Windows application.

Unlike Corel Linux, one Linux distribution was built for one reason and one reason only: to run straight on a Windows partition. WinLinux 2000 was built by JCRP, a company that sees its distribution as "a bridge that can bring Windows users to the Linux world," according to Technical Director Dinamerico Schwingel. WinLinux 2000 has fewer tools than Corel Linux, but given the space and memory limitations of sharing a Windows partition, this is not such a bad thing. Tools can always be added later, when the mood strikes.

Either one of these two distributions can be installed on an existing Windows platform, changing it into something it's not, but something that is a better expression of what the user wants and needs.

Moving on to Something New

This chapter just touches briefly on the possibilities of getting a Windows PC to behave more like a Linux box. There are a host of other possibilities to explore.

Indeed, there are other avenues to approach on every Linux-related topic. Critics maintain this lack of centralized knowledge is a hindrance to Linux, though a complete centralized Windows support database has yet to emerge, even from Microsoft.

> **I**t takes a village to raise a Linux newbie.

Finding out about things in Linux is sometimes not, admittedly, as simple as picking up a nice book such as this and finding the answer you seek. Help is often buried in a mishmash of online help files, man pages, and Web sites.

The Linux community is, more than anything else, just that: a community. A community that talks and communicates far more than any other user groups. When Hillary Clinton first said it takes a village to raise a child, she could have easily been referring to us.

It takes a village to raise a Linux newbie.

In Chapter 13, we'll sort through some of the chatter and nonsense that's out there about the Linux phenomenon and give you solid guides to find the village elders and avoid the village idiots.

CHAPTER 13

The Linux Sutra: Resources

I JUST ENJOY READING THE ARTICLES

Newbies show up at the Linux doorstep in a variety of ways and for a variety of reasons. Many have some technical knowledge churning about in their brain cells, much of it from using other operating systems. Very few people come into Linux completely inexperienced.

This is a conundrum that few other operating systems must face, since they are often used as starting points for those users completely new to computers. Rare is the new user who gets set down in front of a Linux box to start learning computer technology. Too many times, it's Windows or Macintosh machines that newcomers are exposed to first, which brings a whole new set of problems to the Linux community besides stolen market share.

Here's why: Whenever I hire people to work for me, I like to get someone who is experienced enough to know what's what, but not so experienced that they can do their job right from the start. This may seem counter-intuitive and even counter-productive, but there's a method to my madness. I have found through experience that the more skilled someone is on a new job, the more time I have to spend de-programming any bad habits he or she may have picked up along the way. This is not to say that my employees have to do it all my way or else. Indeed, sometimes I learn new things from them. But invariably, people will pick up some kind of work habit that will completely not gel with what I am trying to accomplish.

The same type of problem exists for Linux newbies—they have picked up habits while learning how to use computers that are incompatible with the way Linux works.

One of the big problems that faces new Linux users is file permissions. This is something Windows users can use, but only the most hard-core Windows users even bother to assign restrictions on their files. (Which is too bad, really, because locking down the important files on anyone's system is a great security measure.)

> Rare is the new user who gets set down in front of a Linux box to start learning computer technology.

In Linux, file permissions are given far more than mere lip service. They are the fundamental way Linux operates. In Windows, it is assumed that any user can get to all files, unless otherwise specified. In Linux, it's the opposite: All files are restricted to those users who created them and no one else, unless otherwise specified. Even more distressing to new Linux users: Applications are handled this way, too.

This is the kind of stuff that trips up people coming over from the Microsoft side of the fence. And invariably they come to the initial conclusion that because Linux behaves in such a bizarre fashion, there must be something wrong with it. Certainly Microsoft itself goes out of its way to promote this notion.

I had the same feelings myself when I really started working with Linux. I could not believe how awkward this OS was. Beyond the file permissions, who could learn the arcane console commands? What was the deal with the X server and why couldn't it switch my screen resolutions in one step? And what in God's name was this penguin for?

> In Linux, file permissions are given far more than mere lip service.

It's enough to make your head explode.

This is a period of Linux use I like to call "Tux adolescence." Like real adolescence, it's an awkward, frustrating time, replete with embarrassing moments and fumbling revelations. The only thing missing are the hormones, but other than that, it's pretty much the same thing. Here are some observations that support this theorem:

Adolescence: You're trying to act all grown-up and everyone around you keeps being condescending and saying stuff like "You'll learn someday."

Tux adolescence: You're trying to act like you know what you're doing and Linux gurus all around you keep being condescending and saying stuff like "You'll learn someday."

Adolescence: You know what you want to say to your girlfriend/boyfriend, but you can't seem to get your mouth and your brain working together.

Tux adolescence: You know what you want to say to Linux gurus, but you can't seem to get your mouth and your brain working together.

Adolescence: You don't know what to touch.

Tux adolescence: You don't know what to touch.

And so on.

What every new Linux user needs is technical assistance in unlearning all the knowledge they've picked up along the way and relearning the knowledge they need to use. This technical assistance should ideally come in the form of a Linux guru—someone in their circle of acquaintances who has already blazed the trail through the jungle of knowledge to find the answers on Linux.

Many new Linux users do not have the luxury of a guru of their own. Indeed, many experienced Linux users may not feel adequate enough themselves to become someone's guru. In that case, the next best source of knowledge is clearly the Internet. Less personal than a guru, but more personal than a book, many Web sites on the Internet contain specific and detailed information about Linux machines. There are also scads of message

boards and newsgroups where new users can post questions about obstacles they've slammed into.

And then there are books. Reams and reams of information exist out there on your local bookstore's shelves about Linux and its myriad components. Granted there's this book, but what other books are out there that are considered to be essential?

Think of this chapter as being your own personal Linux guru, guiding you to the essential, can't-do-without Web sites, documents, and books for the Linux user, beginning or advanced.

If you don't have this material in your repertoire, you're really just faking it.

> What every new Linux user needs is technical assistance in unlearning all the knowledge they've picked up along the way and relearning the knowledge they need to use.

BETTER THAN FIFTH GRADE HEALTH CLASS

Whenever users get started in Linux, there are four places they should point their browsers to get the background on what Linux is and how it works. The content on these sites ranges from learned dissertations to tongue-in-cheek lexicons, but all are vitally important to understanding Linux.

The Cathedral and the Bazaar

Web: http://www.tuxedo.org/~esr/writings/cathedral-bazaar/
Book: *The Cathedral and the Bazaar* (O'Reilly, 1999)

If the world reduced everything to its bare minimums, this might be the way someone would describe Eric Raymond's discussion of open-source software. And, at bare minimums, they would be right.

This paper, first presented at the Linux Kongress in May 1997, is the definitive document that explains the methodology and philosophy behind open-source software. *The Cathedral and the Bazaar* tells the story of how Raymond undertook the task of fiddling with an e-mail client, and how he ended up taking on the development of an entire project, one of whose end results was the hugely popular e-mail client fetchmail. The story of fetchmail is a vehicle outlining Raymond's journey of self-discovery of how open-source development should work. As Raymond becomes more involved in the project that would become fetchmail, he begins to realize how efficient and how powerful the peer review and feedback loops contained within the open-source model are.

> The story of fetchmail is a vehicle outlining Raymond's journey of self-discovery of how open-source development should work.

Raymond derives many of his insights on open source not only from his fetchmail application, but also from observing Linus Torvald's success with Linux. In many ways, then, *The Cathedral and the Bazaar* is a very good commentary on how Linux gets put together by a community of people scattered all over the planet.

One of Raymond's maxims identifies one of the most prominent characteristics of Linux: "Release early. Release often. And listen to your customers." This is certainly how Linus handles Linux, as new beta releases for the kernel come out nearly every two weeks, if not more.

Just how revolutionary is *The Cathedral and the Bazaar*? It is said to have prompted Netscape Communications, Inc. to release the entirety of the source code for the Netscape Communicator browser suite as open source, forming the Mozilla project.

Any developer looking to try open source needs to come here first, as does any new Linux user.

Free Software Foundation
Web: http://www.gnu.org

The FSF is the brainchild of Richard M. Stallman, a name so familiar to the Linux community that he's usually referred to just as RMS. Stallman's premise is essentially this: The practice of copyright, which originated with the paper-and-ink publishing industry, is not especially appropriate for the digital software industry. He considers software creators as being morally wrong in enforcing copyright. Software, he maintains, is free to all: free to use, free to modify, and free to copy.

Having made this decision, Stallman began writing the GNU operating system in the beginning of 1984—well before the 1991 release of Linux. By the time Linux was developed seven years later, Stallman and his fellow GNU Project members had developed and distributed GNU Emacs, a powerful and efficient text-editor application.

The Joy of Tech   by Nitrozac and Snaggy

With just a few changes to the GNU slogan, Richard Stallman's dream of making proprietary software obsolete was almost guaranteed.

Stallman had also devised the GNU General Public License, a legal document that basically inverts the copyright law. Instead of keeping software private, the GNU GPL works to keep software and its derivatives free.

When Linus Torvalds created his Linux kernel, it soon became apparent that he could make use of the tools which Stallman had created, such as GNU Emacs and the GNU C library. In fact, the GNU system Stallman had worked to create was missing one vital element: a kernel.

This was a software match made in heaven. By incorporating these digital tools and keeping Linux under the GNU GPL (also known as a *copyleft*), the FSF maintains that Linux should really be called GNU/Linux.

> The practice of copyright, which originated with the paper-and-ink publishing industry, is not especially appropriate for the digital software industry.

Stallman makes it clear in his writings, available on the FSF's site, that free software is not the same as open source. The term "open source" shifts the focus away from the right ideas, Stallman argues. "Open source," he explains, is just used to focus "on the potential to make high quality, powerful software, but shuns the ideas of freedom, community, and principle."

This distinction is a very important one and it marks a divide between the FSF and the Open Sourcers. This is not a chasm, by any means, as many of the these factions' goals overlap. Still, some friction gets created by the strength of Stallman's beliefs, and reactions from others in the Linux community range from eye rolling to outright vehement attacks on the FSF's ideals.

RMS has pronounced an interesting new philosophy to the world of software development, and although agreement with his ideas are not mandatory to be in the Linux community, knowledge of the FSF goals should be.

Linux Documentation Project

Web: http://www.linuxdoc.org/

When you saunter into your local coffee bar/lounge/bookstore and mosey over to the computer-books section, odds are you are going to find

> **S**tallman makes it clear in his writings, available on the FSF's site, that free software is not the same as open source.

an overwhelming amount of Windows books. Why is it that the Linux sections are typically smaller in bookstores? After all, in terms of user friendliness, only recently has Linux approached the level of ease that Joe Schmoe off the street could feel comfortable with. Your would think, then, that this would create a real market need for books to explain just how the heck you use this thing called Linux.

There are two reasons for this phenomenon. One is money. No big surprise here, of course. If publishers do not smell money in a certain market niche, they are unlikely to put forth more than a token book or two in that niche. And, until recently, no one smelled the money in Linux. (Now, of course, with commercial distributions grabbing up market share away from the Microsoft behemoth, the Linux community looks a little more lucrative, and the how-to books are starting to pour out of the presses.)

The other holdback is more subtle and has to do with the nature of Linux itself. Linux, when you install it on a computer, is a very personal thing. If two customers buy the same Linux distribution off the shelf at the local megastore on the very same day and go home on install it on the same computer models, almost certainly there will be wide differences between the two machines when all is said and done.

Unlike Windows, where one Windows machine pretty much contains the same OS-level tools as another, Linux operating system tools can vary wildly from one box to the next, even with the same distribution. This is due to the modularity of Linux, which lets the user piece together a highly customized, very personal operating system based on what he or she needs, not on what the software manufacturer thinks he or she needs.

Now, Linux's modular nature can make it very hard for an author or publisher to pin down a comprehensive how-to book on every facet of Linux. It's plenty daunting to nail down even the most-used aspects of this OS. Faced with this challenge, and the erroneous early impression that there was no money in a group of people using a "free" operating system, publishers held back their entry into Linux documentation.

> **And, until recently, no one smelled the money in Linux.**

There is a third reason unmentioned until now that may have kept the books on Linux at low numbers for a while: Linux users simply did not need the material. After all, they had the Linux Documentation Project. The LDP is a collection of volunteers located around the world whose sole objective is to create the most comprehensive documentation on Linux. Period.

If you are new to Linux, or an old wizened guru, there is something at the LDP Web site for you. You'll find a dizzying array of FAQs and guides for a wide range of tasks. For the more specific tasks, there are multitudes of HOWTOs and mini-HOWTOs, documents that drill down to the lowest level of Linux minutiae, if need be.

The Linux Documentation Project operates on the principle of open source, so contributors are pouring their knowledge into these documents on a daily basis, making the LDP a model of successful online publishing for any topic, not just Linux.

Getting the Jargon Down

Web: http://www.tuxedo.org/~esr/jargon/

So, you know how to run Linux but you find yourself at odds with the language your fellow enthusiasts use from day to day? Then check out Eric Raymond's Jargon File—the most complete guide to hacker-talk ever known. Through the jargon file, you'll learn about everything from "cargo cult programming" to "bondage and discipline languages."

Although this isn't a Linux-specific resource, you'd be hard-pressed to communicate with long-time Linux enthusiasts and come across some term or phrase that isn't discussed in this work. In addition, spending some time reading through it without any particular goal in mind is a good way to learn a lot of the unreported history of computing.

> **I**f you are new to Linux, or an old wizened guru, there is something at the LDP Web site for you.

Remember the 2000 presidential election's "hanging chads?" The Jargon File can tell you why they're called that.

Peeping through the Windows

The sheer number of Linux interfaces makes it impossible for someone to point at a Linux desktop and say *"That* is Linux." That would be like coming to anyone in a sailor's uniform and saying *"You* are looking for some action." It's ridiculous to place such sweeping stereotypes on any one group of people (though, in retrospect, the sailors may have been a bad example), and it can never be done to the Linux desktop.

The sheer number of Linux interfaces makes it impossible for someone to point at a Linux desktop and say "*That* is Linux."

Linux users can choose from among a staggering array of desktop environments and X window managers—all forms of graphical user interfaces designed to make life easier. They are not the be-all and end-all for Linux, however; in many cases, experienced users view GUIs as a necessary evil to accomplish a certain goal.

Which one is the best? Not a chance we're going to tell you, save to give you one unassailable piece of advice: Whichever environment or GUI you pick, it has to be the one that suits *your* needs.

GNOME

Web: http://www.gnome.org

First off, it's not "gnome," like those goofy little blue-coated, red-hatted critters that run around the Scandinavian countryside. It's "Guh-nome," heavy on the "G" and light on the "uh".

Glad we got that cleared up.

That said, GNOME is the product of one Miguel de Icaza, a Mexican computer-engineering student who took one look at the KDE environment and really liked what he saw—until he discovered the non-free code sitting beneath it.

De Icaza, a devoted follower of the Free Software Foundation's goals, decided that what was needed in Linux was a similar desktop environment that had none of the licensing limitations of KDE.

GNOME debuted in August 1997, when de Icaza announced its existence in the comp.os.linux.announce newsgroup. By December of that same year, the first workable test version was made available to the Linux community. It would not be until March of 1999, however, that version 1.0 would be released to the general public, but by then the word had gotten out and thousands of free software devotees climbed on board the GNOME bandwagon.

GNOME, like KDE, is a desktop environment. It is not a window manager, like Enlightenment, IceWM, or Sawfish. Window managers control the look and feel of the windows, menus, and other visual components of a graphical interface. Desktop environments, on the other hand, provide a specific platform for applications to operate within. If an application is written for a desktop environment it can tap into a wide range of common features with other applications in that environment.

In the Linux community, GNOME is lauded for more than its free software status. It is generally regarded as more aesthetically pleasing than KDE, as the themes available for GNOME have more eye-candy appeal.

Beyond the look of GNOME, de Icaza has pushed new boundaries for the perception of free software in the corporate world. A year after the release of GNOME 1.0, de Icaza partnered with several major corporations to form the GNOME Foundation—a non-profit organization dedicated to the ideal of keeping GNOME development moving forward in a rapid and open way. The GNOME Foundation, with high-power members such as Sun Microsystems, Compaq, and IBM, wants to make GNOME *the* interface for Linux, and to make that interface very easy for users to adapt to.

> Beyond the look of GNOME, de Icaza has pushed new boundaries for the perception of free software in the corporate world.

One of the major hurdles to people using Linux has been the perception that it is too hard to use, a perception the GNOME Foundation wants to change. By offering software developers a stable and communicative environment within which to create new GNOME apps, the GNOME Foundation serves as an incubator of sorts for bringing more user-friendly applications to the GNOME interface.

KDE

Web: http://www.kde.org

KDE was the first desktop environment made for the Linux platform and as such, it is ahead of the game in terms of stability and innovation. But in many ways, KDE has been the most beleaguered application of any kind in the Linux community. The continued presence of non-free code within its architecture really set a lot of people against what was to be the penultimate in Linux GUIs. In sharp contrast to this issue, however, is the fact that surveys show KDE in use on over 70 percent of Linux desktops. Free software or no, clearly KDE is doing something right.

KDE was started in 1996, ten months prior to GNOME's origins. It offered users a very stable interface to the oh-so-mysterious Linux platform, and offered developers an excellent place to start building core applications for Linux.

Free software or no, clearly KDE is doing something right.

KDE began as a mostly volunteer effort, and remains such an effort to this day. It is a less centralized organization than its opposite number GNOME, but this has aided it in making advances in specialized areas far ahead of other development groups.

KDE maintains a rigid standard in working with window managers, so much so that many default installations of KDE use kwm, KDE's own window manager. This is different from GNOME, which is compatible with several window managers.

This seeming lack of flexibility does hold KDE back in the aesthetics department, but it definitely helps make KDE a rock-solid platform. KDE has recently released its 2.0 version, a long-awaited GPL offering that takes some big steps toward making Linux easier to use for everyone.

KDE is also following in the footsteps of GNOME, having recently created the KDE League, which promises to promote KDE to the hilt with the League's new corporate backers. Critics have argued that this is just a knock-off of the GNOME Foundation, but KDE developers assert that unlike the Foundation, the League will only be involved in promoting KDE, not in actual development.

Given its stability and proliferation, KDE is one environment you should take a look at.

X Window Managers
Web: http://www.plig.net/xwinman

Choosing a window manager is never an easy proposition. If you own one of the Linux distributions that includes a number of window managers, you're in luck, because you get to try out different interfaces to see what you like. If you are not so endowed, then research is likely your first step. There are several window managers out there, so where's the best place to start?

The best organized site is the Window Managers for X site, maintained by Matt Chapman. Chapman has carefully maintained a site that features and reviews most of the X window managers out there.

The site also contains information on desktop environments, links to books, and discussions on various aspects of Linux GUIs. It may sound like a techie haven, but the information provided by Chapman is done in a succinct and non-technical way, with plenty of tutorials to get new users up to speed on this window manager world.

The Joy of Tech — by Nitrozac and Snaggy

AT A LINUX USER GROUP MEETING...

Panel 1: HELLO, I'D LIKE TO INSTALL LINUX. / WHICH DISTRO? RED HAT, DEBIAN, SLACKWARE, ...

Panel 2: COREL, CALDERA, MANDRAKE, ELFSTONE, INDEPENDENCE, LINUX PPC, LASER 5, ROCK LINUX, TRINUX, STAMPEDE GNU/LINUX ...

Panel 3: ARMED LINUX, DLX, DRAGONLINUX, FINNEX, STORM LINUX, SUSE, TURBO LINUX, OR YELLOW DOG?

Panel 4: OH, UM, ...WHICHEVER ONE IS *LINUX.*

© 2000 GEEK CULTURE, JOYOFTECH.COM

Linux Distributions

Web: Various

If you think there are just seven or eight Linux distributions out there, boy, are you in for a shock. There are many ways a Linux user can explore the love they have for this operating system, all of them legal.

A whole book could be filled examining the origins and differences between all these distributions, but for now, we'll just list the ones we know about and where you can find out more about them.

- **Amino Communications** (http://www.aminocom.com/) An embedded version of Linux for set-top devices.
- **Apokalypse** (http://www.gate.net/~mclinux/intro.html) A Linux distribution for the Macintosh platform.

- **Armed Linux** (http://www.armed.net/) A Linux distribution that can be installed on top of Windows.
- **Bastille Linux** (http://www.bastille-linux.org/) The premier security platform, based on Red Hat.
- **Best Linux** (http://www.bestlinux.net/) A Finnish-language distribution based on Red Hat.
- **Black Cat Linux** (http://www.blackcatlinux.com/index-eng.html) A Russian- and Ukrainian-language support distribution based on Red Hat.
- **Caldera OpenLinux** (http://www.calderasystems.com/) A powerful server and client Linux distribution. One of the first to use a graphical installation application for ease of use.
- **Conectiva Linux** (http://www.conectiva.com) A Red Hat–based distribution offered in Spanish and Portuguese that is quite popular in Latin America.
- **Corel Linux** (http://linux.corel.com/) A Debian-based distribution built for users coming over from the Windows arena. Highly automated installation and configuration.
- **Debian GNU/Linux** (http://www.debian.org/) A Linux distribution that makes use of the Debian package format. Very configurable and certainly one of the big ones.
- **Definite Linux** (http://www.definitelinux.com) A UK distribution based on Red Hat 6.0.
- **DLD Linux** (http://www.delix.de/) A German distribution featuring a large toolset, based on Red Hat.
- **DLX** (http://www.wu-wien.ac.at/usr/h93/h9301726/dlx.html) A full-featured Linux distribution that is installed with one floppy disk using only source code.
- **DragonLinux** (http://www.c-cubedinc.com/dragon/) A heavyweight Linux distribution to run atop Windows.

- **Elfstone** (http://www.elflinux.com/linux.html) Elfstone "is a highly stable Linux distribution specifically designed for programmers, engineers, and network administrators."
- **Eos Linux Distribution** (http://www.linux.ncsu.edu/eos-linux/) This distribution is based on Red Hat Linux for on-campus use at North Carolina State University.
- **e-smith server and gateway** (http://www.e-smith.net/) A network server distribution based on Red Hat.
- **Eurielec** (http://www.eurielec.etsit.upm.es/linux/) A Spanish language distribution based on Red Hat.
- **Finnix** (http://www.finnix.org/) A self-contained, portable Linux distribution. Based on Red Hat 6.1.
- **HLC-Linux** (http://hpcl.itwm.uni-kl.de/) Linux for high-performance computers.
- **Independence** (http://independence.seul.org/distribution/) Based on Red Hat, this distribution wants to make Linux "easier to use and more attractive for non-nerds."
- **Krud** (http://www.tummy.com/krud/) A Red Hat–based distribution with extra graphics and security features.
- **KSI Linux** (http://www.ksi-linux.com:8101/) A very Russian and Ukrainian distribution with many localized applications.
- **KW Linux** (http://www.kaiwal.com/) A Thai-language distribution.
- **Laser5** (http://www.laser5.co.jp/) A best-selling Japanese distribution based on Red Hat.
- **Learnux** (http://centre.linux.ca/) A Canadian distribution based on Debian used for schools, primarily on older Intel platforms.

- **LibraNet** (http://www.libranet.com) A Debian-based distribution that tries to take the installation headaches away by a highly automated process.
- **Linux/APUS** (http://sunsite.auc.dk/ftp/pub/os/linux/apus/docs/faq.html) A Danish distribution of Linux for Amiga Power Up Systems.
- **Linux CE** (http://www.linuxce.org/) Linux for Windows CE devices.
- **Linux/m68k** (http://www.linux-m68k.org/) A port of Linux to run on systems using Motorola's 68020, 68030, 68040, and 68060 microprocessors
- **LinuxMac** (http://www.macnews.de/_linuxmac/) A German Linux distribution for the PowerPC platform.
- **Linux-Mandrake** (http://www.linux-mandrake.com/en/) A very user-friendly client and server distribution highly lauded by the Linux user community.
- **Linux on RS/6000** (http://www.rs6000.ibm.com/linux/) "Big Iron" Linux for the IBM RS/6000 platform.
- **LinuxPPC** (http://www.linuxppc.org/) A Linux distribution for the PowerPC platform.
- **Linux-SIS** (http://www.school.net.th/linux-sis) A Thai distribution used extensively in Thai schools. Based on Slackware.
- **Linux/Sun3** (http://www.netppl.fi/~pp/sun3/) Linux for the Sun 3/50, Sun 3/60, and Sun 3/160 workstation platforms.
- **LOAF** (http://loaf.ecks.org/) Stands for "Linux on a Floppy"; for use as a portable network client.
- **LoopLinux** (http://www.tux.org/pub/people/kent-robotti/looplinux/index.html) Formerly DosLinux, this Slackware-based distribution can run atop any DOS/Windows partition.

- **LunetIX** (http://www.lunetix.de/) A German-language form of Linux based on Caldera.
- **M.N.I.S.** (http://www.mnis.fr/home/linux/) A French Debian-based distribution that makes use of KDE, traditionally a Debian no-no.
- **NoMad Linux** (http://www.nomadlinux.com/) NoMad is "a distribution based on the encap package managing system for ease of installation and upgrades."
- **PARISC Linux** (http://parisc-linux.org/index.html) Linux for RISC processor platforms.
- **Phat Linux** (http://www.phatlinux.com/) The first Linux distribution designed to run directly on a Windows partition.
- **Plamo Linux** (http://www.linet.gr.jp/~kojima/Plamo/) A Japanese distribution based on Slackware.
- **Power Linux** (http://power.linuxkorea.co.kr/) A Korean distribution based on Red Hat designed to be a Web server platform.
- **PROSA/Debian** (http://www.prosa.it/) An Italian Debian-based distribution.
- **Q40 Linux** (http://www.geocities.com/SiliconValley/Bay/2602/q40.html) Linux for Q40 and Q80 motherboard machines.
- **Red Hat Linux** (http://www.redhat.com) Not the first distribution, but certainly the most popular. Unless you live in a cave, you've heard of this one.
- **ROCK Linux** (http://www.rocklinux.org/index.html) A text-only, pure command-line distribution of Linux. Not for the timid, but very powerful.
- **SGI Linux** (http://www.sgi.com/software/linux/) A Red Hat–based distribution designed solely for SGI 1400L servers.

- **Skygate Linux** (http://www.skygate.co.uk/
skylinux.html) Based on Red Hat, this distribution can
be run on a Windows partition.
- **Slackware Linux** (http://www.slackware.com) The first
commercial Linux distro. One of the majors, this
distribution has led the way in making Linux a commercial success.
- **Slinux** (http://www.slinux.org/) A secure server distri-
bution.
- **Small Linux** (http://smalllinux.netpedia.net/)
How small can you get? Try using Linux on a 386
laptop with 2MB of RAM and a 40MB hard drive.
Small Linux can.
- **Stampede GNU/Linux** (http://www.stampede.org/)
This distribution tries to balance ease of use with a
power user's choice of tools.
- **Storm Linux** (http://www.stormix.com/) Based on
Debian, Storm attempts to fill the server market needs
for Linux.
- **SuSE Linux** (http://www.suse.com) *The* most popular
European application on any platform, SuSE Linux
offers unique tools for setup and configuration that is
making it a hit in the United States.
- **tomsrtbt** (http://www.toms.net/rb/) A self-contained
distribution that fits on one floppy disk.
- **Trinux** (http://www.trinux.org/) A one-floppy version
of Linux that runs entirely within RAM. Used for
security checking.
- **TurboLinux** (http://www.turbolinux.com/) Actually a
variety of distros, the TurboLinux family offers an
operating system for workstations, servers, and cluster-
ing platforms.

- **Turkuaz** (http://www.linux.org.tr/turkuaz/) A Turkish Linux distribution.
- **UltraLinux** (http://www.ultralinux.org/) Linux for the SPARC platform.
- **Vedova Linux** (http://www.vedova.org/) An Italian Debian-based distribution.
- **WinLinux** (http://www.winlinux.net/) A Linux distribution built to run atop Windows.
- **Yellow Dog Linux** (http://www.yellowdoglinux.com/) A popular Linux release for the Macintosh platform.

The More the Merrier

There is always more than one place to get the latest news on any given topic. This is certainly the case for Linux, which has embraced the concept of communications far more than its Windows counterpart. Linux Web sites exist everywhere, both informative and commercial.

Here's where we help you sort through this orgy of information and nail down the Web sites that will keep you in the know 24/7.

Slashdot
Web: http://slashdot.org

There's plenty to say about Slashdot. It's possibly the best known "Linux site" going, though it isn't really about Linux (all the time). The banner sums it up best: "News for Nerds, Stuff that Matters." There's an implicit set of values expressed here, and whether what matters to Slashdot's maintainers matters to you is something you'll have to wrestle with.

Slashdot has one claim to infamy that sends shudders up and down the spines of Webmasters everywhere: the dreaded Slashdot effect. Documented in informal papers, experienced by every site that ever made the mistake of carrying "stuff that matters," the

Slashdot effect is what you get when tens of thousands of Slashdot readers converge on a Web site at once. Some sites cope, others collapse under the strain.

Slashdot's core community is computer hobbyists and professionals. Most seem to claim an allegiance to Linux as their operating system of choice, and of those who don't there's still a general agreement that something UNIX-like is best. Many consider themselves primarily "hackers," and any story that deals with use of the word "hacker" as a pejorative denotation of "computer criminal" (as opposed to "computer problem solver") invites much wrath.

> There's an implicit set of values expressed here, and whether what matters to Slashdot's maintainers matters to you is something you'll have to wrestle with.

Thanks in part to rallying points like Eric S. Raymond's "Portrait of J. Random Hacker," (part of the Jargon File), some of the more authoritarian members of the Slashdot community have laid claim to the right to grant the titles "hacker," "geek," and "nerd." Professions of geek status are frequently met with scorn when they come from the wrong quarter (as regular Slashdot columnist Jon Katz learned when he declared himself a geek during one of his odes to the digital revolution and its Slashdot cadre).

In the past two years, Slashdot has risen from "frequently visited site of the Linux community" to something else as the Linux/Open Source/Free Software star rises. The site's regular readership has shifted dramatically as the curious are attracted from outside the older Slashdot community. The site's appeal is such that, even though the Linux emphasis remains, computer or technical enthusiasts of many stripes find something to keep them coming back. The site also attracts "trolls," content to merely stir up trouble on a primarily Linux-oriented forum, just as they probably do on similar Usenet fora.

From the mix of longtime UNIX fans, Linux devotees, self-proclaimed nerds, trolls, passers-by, and even Microsoft fans comes a community of some pungency.

If Slashdot were yet another news site, no one would care. What makes it what it is are the discussions that accompany each story that appears on its pages. Hundreds of people take

> **If** Slashdot were yet another news site, no one would care.

the time to argue, debate, villify, and troll over the issues. Not surprisingly, some of the more enthusiastic participants get a little carried away from time to time, which has caused the maintainers to introduce a fairly sophisticated peer-based moderation mechanism to make sure the best comments get to the top of the heap and the worst trolls are consigned to the community dungeons. Does it work? Sometimes.

Some would maintain that Slashdot is a stage through which all new Linux enthusiasts must pass, whether they continue to visit it or not later on in their Linux career. The raucousness of the site, combined with a flippant attitude toward what many of the audience excoriate as "old media" attitudes about good journalistic practice can be a little irritating. On the other hand, the maintainers' hearts are in the right place.

Even if you end up hating it, Slashdot is a force to be reckoned with in the Linux community.

Linux Today
Web: http://linuxtoday.com

Linux Today has been cited as the best news site for Linux events and information, a distinction it maintains well. Primarily a newsfeed site, *Linux Today* offers story synopses and links to all things Linux. There are also talkbacks provided for each story link. What differentiates *Linux Today* from Slashdot is the posting of original news content, which *Linux Today* does on a regular basis.

Linux Today can be viewed as is, or customized to display the topics that interest you most. Literally hundreds of site links are made available at any given moment.

Linux Today is the best place to go to get up-to-date news on all aspects of the Linux community.

Freshmeat and LinuxApps.com

Web: http://freshmeat.net; http://www.linuxapps.com

Because of the decentralized nature of Linux, locating new and updated apps could potentially be a real pain in the butt. The existence of these two Web sites, however, alleviates that pain. Freshmeat and LinuxApps provide the most complete libraries of Linux applications available anywhere. Visit either one of these sites, and you'll understand this bold statement.

Organized by categories, applications are arranged into project pages that give users access to not only the latest download version, but to the histories and change logs for that application as well. Any Linux developer who wants his or her application seen and used will post it on one or both of these sites.

These central repositories make finding Linux applications for your box a breeze.

DELIVERED IN BROWN PAPER WRAPPERS

The Web's a great place to find out all sorts of information about Linux. So great, in fact, that at one point during an unhappy time supporting over one hundred Windows users I found myself having to tell search engines to most definitely *not* return information about how to fix a specific problem under Linux.

Sometimes, though, using the Web isn't an option, especially when the problem you're having is getting your Linux machine to talk to the Internet at all.

During times like this, the most comforting thing in the world is a good, thick book you can balance on your lap as you figure out your problem.

Other times, when you can't actually sit down to your computer and play with Linux, it's nice to be able to read about it, and gain a little insight into why things are the way they are. So, presented for your edification, some must-have books for the curious Linux fan. Everything from how to make it run to why it runs the way it does.

Running Linux and *Linux Configuration and Installation*

So, you have Linux on your machine, you're curious about what makes it tick, and you're looking for a book that does more than tell you what you *could* do wrapped up in innuendo. Look no further than *Linux Configuration and Installation* (called *LC&I* by people in the know) and *Running Linux*.

First, a disclaimer: We both work for one of the co-authors of *Linux Configuration and Installation*.

Double backflip disclaimer: Michael used *LC&I* to complete his first real Linux installation lo these many years ago. It's a good book, written in part by none other than Patrick Volkerding, the ever-slackful maintainer of the Slackware distribution. The advice it gives is good, close-to-the-bone, hands-on information for the Linux newbie who wants to figure out how things go together.

LC&I is a popular book among many older Linux users who remember the days when Red Hat was still "the newbie distro" and Slackware was king.

Running Linux is well-known, well-loved, and frequently the first recommendation of many Linux lovers who are trying to help out first-timers as they navigate the rocky waters of, well, running Linux. It's a beneficiary of the wisdom from the Linux Documentation Project's own Matt Welsh, as well as that of Matthias Kalle Dahlmeyer of the KDE project and Lar Kaufman, who's been writing about UNIX for close to 20 years. It's got information on just about every aspect of Linux you could want, from the simplest configuration to tips on Linux programming. Sometimes it's a little over-general, but if you're a self-motivated learner, willing to look up information based on the leads the book gives you, you'll learn a lot with this book as your guide.

Linux in a Nutshell

O'Reilly is famous for its Nutshell series of books. If you're already familiar with the bulk of the issues involved in day-to-day maintenance of your Linux system, but need a quick reference, *Linux in a Nutshell* is the one to go with. It offers a complete listing of the most common commands and programs on a Linux machine with all the gory details of command-line switches and options. Think of it as a Linux command dictionary. Some people say it's the Linux man pages dumped onto paper, but if you like to look up solutions in a book, that's a *good* thing.

UNIX Programming Environment

Want to go all the way back to the time when men were men, women were women, and UNIX scared the pants off of everybody? Written by Brian Kernighan and Rob Pike in 1984, *The UNIX Programming Environment* is one of those texts that will tell you, by virtue of explaining how the newbies were taught to deal with it, exactly where UNIX was at. Kernighan was one of the co-authors of the programming language awk, which is still in use as a general-purpose text file manipulator.

The information in this book is nothing you aren't going to find anywhere else, but it's interesting because it's a look at UNIX from the days when the OS was unvarnished with GUIs. People learned UNIX from the command line and lived their days in front of text terminals. Even more interesting, when you think about it, is the fact that the underlying mechanisms you might not ever see if you stick to the desktop your distribution came with are still at work under there in some form or another.

In addition to the introductory sections on how to live in the UNIX shell from day to day, the bulk of the book is comprised of the sorts of issues unique to UNIX programming.

Through the introduction to UNIX programming, the authors stress time and time again the beauty of UNIX. Its modularity and capability to reuse small, efficient programs provides a remarkable amount of leverage to produce elegant solutions to problems very simply.

The next time you're staring at yet another reinvention of the wheel in the form of some giant program that does everything in one big lump, wondering why it loads so slowly and runs so poorly, consider the advice in this book and remind yourself that there's a better way to do things.

UNIX Philosophy

Where the previous book taught the nuts and bolts of building code in UNIX, *UNIX Philosophy* provides a guide to some of the rallying cries of UNIX enthusiasts everywhere. You won't learn how to do anything with your new Linux system with this book, but you will learn about some of the design ideals common to the many UNIX variants out there. It's readable even to largely non-technical types who are interested in stepping into the shoes of people who spend their days thinking about the best way to build complex computing environments. As you read, you may also find that it helps you understand the reasons behind the somewhat terse and unforgiving environment the Linux shell provides. In turn, it will help you develop your "Linux intuition," and you'll find a lot of answers coming more quickly as you continue to learn.

If there's one downside to this book (and we're mentioning it only in case you ever get into one of those flame wars we were talking about), it's that, like many simple books that spell things out for the uninitiated, it has become a sort of religious text to enthusiastic young computer-science majors everywhere. If ever a branch of the Taliban forms that concerns itself with keeping operating systems pure and simple, this will be its central document. Of course, that isn't all bad. Obviously we think we could do a lot worse than to fall into the clutches of UNIX fundamentalists, especially when you consider the alternatives.

WRAPPING IT ALL UP

Now that we are here at the end, we can only wait with anticipation about what the future of Linux holds. Soon, the Linux 2.4 kernel will be released, giving Linux users and developers a whole new set of tools to play with.

After all, play is really the name of the game in the Linux community. Everyone, from the multi-millionaire CEO to the curious newbie, has a sense of fun when they use Linux. This is not an operating system that makes you use one set of rules—it's something that will let you make up your own rules and play your own game.

> After all, play is really the name of the game in the Linux community.

This is the secret of the Linux community: the overwhelming sense of play that permeates every aspect of the user's experience. Do you think we would subject ourselves to some of these shenanigans otherwise?

This is why we can smile when facing unsupported allegations from yet another Microsoft flunky; we know that ultimately, we have already won the OS wars, since we are having the most fun. And as long as it's fun, Linux will continue to grow and prosper.

Appendix

GNU GENERAL PUBLIC LICENSE

Version 2, June 1991

PREAMBLE

The licenses for most software are designed to take away your freedom to share and change it. By contrast, the GNU General Public License is intended to guarantee your freedom to share and change free software—to make sure the software is free for all its users. This General Public License applies to most of the Free Software Foundation's software and to any other program whose authors commit to using it. (Some other Free Software Foundation software is covered bythe GNU Library General Public License instead.) You can apply it to your programs, too.

When we speak of free software, we are referring to freedom, not price. Our General Public Licenses are designed to make sure that you have the freedom to distribute copies of free software (and charge for this service if you wish), that you receive source code or can get it if you want it, that you can change the software or use pieces of it in new free programs; and that you know you can do these things.

To protect your rights, we need to make restrictions that forbid anyone to deny you these rights or to ask you to surrender the rights. These restrictions translate to certain responsibilities for you if you distribute copies of the software, or if you modify it.

For example, if you distribute copies of such a program, whether gratis or for a fee, you must give the recipients all the rights that you have. You must make sure that they, too, receive or can get the source code. And you must show them these terms so they know their rights.

We protect your rights with two steps: (1) copyright the software, and (2) offer you this license which gives you legal permission to copy, distribute and/or modify the software.

Also, for each author's protection and ours, we want to make certain that everyone understands that there is no warranty for this free software. If the software is modified by someone else and passed on, we want its recipients to know that what they have is not the original, so that any problems introduced by others will not reflect on the original authors' reputations.

Finally, any free program is threatened constantly by software patents. We wish to avoid the danger that redistributors of a free program will individually obtain patent licenses, in effect making the program proprietary. To prevent this, we have made it clear that any patent must be licensed for everyone's free use or not licensed at all.

The precise terms and conditions for copying, distribution and modification follow.

GNU GENERAL PUBLIC LICENSE TERMS AND CONDITIONS FOR COPYING, DISTRIBUTION AND MODIFICATION

0. This License applies to any program or other work which contains a notice placed by the copyright holder saying it may be distributed under the terms of this General Public License. The "Program", below, refers to any such program or work, and a "work based on the Program" means either the Program or any derivative work under copyright law: that is to say, a work containing the Program or a portion of it, either verbatim or with modifications and/or translated into another language. (Hereinafter, translation is included without limitation in the term "modification".) Each licensee is addressed as "you".

Activities other than copying, distribution and modification are not covered by this License; they are outside its scope. The act of running the Program is not restricted, and the output from the Program is covered only if its contents constitute a work based on the Program (independent of having been made by running the Program). Whether that is true depends on what the Program does.

1. You may copy and distribute verbatim copies of the Program's source code as you receive it, in any medium, provided that you conspicuously and appropriately publish on each copy an appropriate copyright notice and disclaimer of warranty; keep intact all the notices that refer to this License and to the absence of any warranty; and give any other recipients of the Program a copy of this License along with the Program.

You may charge a fee for the physical act of transferring a copy, and you may at your option offer warranty protection in exchange for a fee.

2. You may modify your copy or copies of the Program or any portion of it, thus forming a work based on the Program,

and copy and distribute such modifications or work under the terms of Section 1 above, provided that you also meet all of these conditions:

a) You must cause the modified files to carry prominent notices stating that you changed the files and the date of any change.

b) You must cause any work that you distribute or publish, that in whole or in part contains or is derived from the Program or any part thereof, to be licensed as a whole at no charge to all third parties under the terms of this License.

c) If the modified program normally reads commands interactively when run, you must cause it, when started running for such interactive use in the most ordinary way, to print or display an announcement including an appropriate copyright notice and a notice that there is no warranty (or else, saying that you provide a warranty) and that users may redistribute the program under these conditions, and telling the user how to view a copy of this License. (Exception: if the Program itself is interactive but does not normally print such an announcement, your work based on the Program is not required to print an announcement.)

These requirements apply to the modified work as a whole. If identifiable sections of that work are not derived from the Program, and can be reasonably considered independent and separate works in themselves, then this License, and its terms, do not apply to those sections when you distribute them as separate works. But when you distribute the same sections as part of a whole which is a work based on the Program, the distribution of the whole must be on the terms of this License, whose permissions for other licensees extend to the entire whole, and thus to each and every part regardless of who wrote it.

Thus, it is not the intent of this section to claim rights or contest your rights to work written entirely by you; rather, the intent is to exercise the right to control the distribution of derivative or collective works based on the Program.

In addition, mere aggregation of another work not based on the Program with the Program (or with a work based on the Program) on a volume of a storage or distribution medium does not bring the other work under the scope of this License.

3. You may copy and distribute the Program (or a work based on it, under Section 2) in object code or executable form under the terms of Sections 1 and 2 above provided that you also do one of the following:

a) Accompany it with the complete corresponding machine-readable source code, which must be distributed under the terms of Sections 1 and 2 above on a medium customarily used for software interchange; or,

b) Accompany it with a written offer, valid for at least three years, to give any third party, for a charge no more than your cost of physically performing source distribution, a complete machine-readable copy of the corresponding source code, to be distributed under the terms of Sections 1 and 2 above on a medium customarily used for software interchange; or,

c) Accompany it with the information you received as to the offer to distribute corresponding source code. (This alternative is allowed only for noncommercial distribution and only if you received the program in object code or executable form with such an offer, in accord with Subsection b above.)

The source code for a work means the preferred form of the work for making modifications to it. For an executable work, complete source code means all the source code for all modules it contains, plus any associated interface definition files, plus the scripts used to control compilation and installation of the executable. However, as a special exception, the source code distributed need not include anything that is normally distributed (in either source or binary form) with the major components (compiler, kernel, and so on) of the operating system on which the executable runs, unless that component itself accompanies the executable.

If distribution of executable or object code is made by offering access to copy from a designated place, then offering equivalent access to copy the source code from the same place counts as distribution of the source code, even though third parties are not compelled to copy the source along with the object code.

4. You may not copy, modify, sublicense, or distribute the Program except as expressly provided under this License. Any attempt otherwise to copy, modify, sublicense or distribute the Program is void, and will automatically terminate your rights under this License. However, parties who have received copies, or rights, from you under this License will not have their licenses terminated so long as such parties remain in full compliance.

5. You are not required to accept this License, since you have not signed it. However, nothing else grants you permission to modify or distribute the Program or its derivative works. These actions are prohibited by law if you do not accept this License. Therefore, by modifying or distributing the Program (or any work based on the Program), you indicate your acceptance of this License to do so, and all its terms and conditions for copying, distributing or modifying the Program or works based on it.

6. Each time you redistribute the Program (or any work based on the Program), the recipient automatically receives a license from the original licensor to copy, distribute or modify the Program subject to these terms and conditions. You may not impose any further restrictions on the recipients' exercise of the rights granted herein. You are not responsible for enforcing compliance by third parties to this License.

7. If, as a consequence of a court judgment or allegation of patent infringement or for any other reason (not limited to patent issues), conditions are imposed on you (whether by court order, agreement or otherwise) that contradict the conditions of this License, they do not excuse you from the conditions of

this License. If you cannot distribute so as to satisfy simultaneously your obligations under this License and any other pertinent obligations, then as a consequence you may not distribute the Program at all. For example, if a patent license would not permit royalty-free redistribution of the Program by all those who receive copies directly or indirectly through you, then the only way you could satisfy both it and this License would be to refrain entirely from distribution of the Program.

If any portion of this section is held invalid or unenforceable under any particular circumstance, the balance of the section is intended to apply and the section as a whole is intended to apply in other circumstances.

It is not the purpose of this section to induce you to infringe any patents or other property right claims or to contest validity of any such claims; this section has the sole purpose of protecting the integrity of the free software distribution system, which is implemented by public license practices. Many people have made generous contributions to the wide range of software distributed through that system in reliance on consistent application of that system; it is up to the author/donor to decide if he or she is willing to distribute software through any other system and a licensee cannot impose that choice.

This section is intended to make thoroughly clear what is believed to be a consequence of the rest of this License.

8. If the distribution and/or use of the Program is restricted in certain countries either by patents or by copyrighted interfaces, the original copyright holder who places the Program under this License may add an explicit geographical distribution limitation excluding those countries, so that distribution is permitted only in or among countries not thus excluded. In such case, this License incorporates the limitation as if written in the body of this License.

9. The Free Software Foundation may publish revised and/ or new versions of the General Public License from time to time. Such new versions will be similar in spirit to the present version, but may differ in detail to address new problems or concerns.

Each version is given a distinguishing version number. If the Program specifies a version number of this License which applies to it and "any later version", you have the option of following the terms and conditions either of that version or of any later version published by the Free Software Foundation. If the Program does not specify a version number of this License, you may choose any version ever published by the Free Software Foundation.

10. If you wish to incorporate parts of the Program into other free programs whose distribution conditions are different, write to the author to ask for permission. For software which is copyrighted by the Free Software Foundation, write to the Free Software Foundation; we sometimes make exceptions for this. Our decision will be guided by the two goals of preserving the free status of all derivatives of our free software and of promoting the sharing and reuse of software generally.

NO WARRANTY

11. BECAUSE THE PROGRAM IS LICENSED FREE OF CHARGE, THERE IS NO WARRANTY FOR THE PROGRAM, TO THE EXTENT PERMITTED BY APPLICABLE LAW. EXCEPT WHEN OTHERWISE STATED IN WRITING THE COPYRIGHT HOLDERS AND/OR OTHER PARTIES PROVIDE THE PROGRAM "AS IS" WITHOUT WARRANTY OF ANY KIND, EITHER EXPRESSED OR IMPLIED, INCLUDING, BUT NOT LIMITED TO, THE IMPLIED WARRANTIES OF MERCHANTABILITY AND FITNESS FOR A PARTICULAR PURPOSE. THE ENTIRE RISK AS TO THE QUALITY

AND PERFORMANCE OF THE PROGRAM IS WITH YOU. SHOULD THE PROGRAM PROVE DEFECTIVE, YOU AS-SUME THE COST OF ALL NECESSARY SERVICING, REPAIR OR CORRECTION.

12. IN NO EVENT UNLESS REQUIRED BY APPLICABLE LAW OR AGREED TO IN WRITING WILL ANY COPY-RIGHT HOLDER, OR ANY OTHER PARTY WHO MAY MODIFY AND/OR REDISTRIBUTE THE PROGRAM AS PER-MITTED ABOVE, BE LIABLE TO YOU FOR DAMAGES, IN-CLUDING ANY GENERAL, SPECIAL, INCIDENTAL OR CONSEQUENTIAL DAMAGES ARISING OUT OF THE USE OR INABILITY TO USE THE PROGRAM (INCLUDING BUT NOT LIMITED TO LOSS OF DATA OR DATA BEING REN-DERED INACCURATE OR LOSSES SUSTAINED BY YOU OR THIRD PARTIES OR A FAILURE OF THE PROGRAM TO OPERATE WITH ANY OTHER PROGRAMS), EVEN IF SUCH HOLDER OR OTHER PARTY HAS BEEN ADVISED OF THE POSSIBILITY OF SUCH DAMAGES.

END OF TERMS AND CONDITIONS

How to Apply These Terms to Your New Programs

If you develop a new program, and you want it to be of the greatest possible use to the public, the best way to achieve this is to make it free software which everyone can redistribute and change under these terms.

To do so, attach the following notices to the program. It is safest to attach them to the start of each source file to most effec-tively convey the exclusion of warranty; and each file should have at least the "copyright" line and a pointer to where the full notice is found.

Copyright (C) <year> <name of author>

This program is free software; you can redistribute it and/or modify it under the terms of the GNU General Public License as published by the Free Software Foundation; either version 2 of the License, or (at your option) any later version.

This program is distributed in the hope that it will be useful, but WITHOUT ANY WARRANTY; without even the implied warranty of MERCHANTABILITY or FITNESS FOR A PAR-TICULAR PURPOSE. See the GNU General Public License for more details.

You should have received a copy of the GNU General Public License along with this program; if not, write to the Free Soft-ware Foundation, Inc., 59 Temple Place, Suite 330, Boston, MA 02111-1307 USA

Also add information on how to contact you by electronic and paper mail.

If the program is interactive, make it output a short notice like this when it starts in an interactive mode:

Gnomovision version 69, Copyright (C) year name of author

Gnomovision comes with ABSOLUTELY NO WARRANTY; for details type 'show w'.

This is free software, and you are welcome to redistribute it under certain conditions; type 'show c' for details.

The hypothetical commands 'show w' and 'show c' should show the appropriate parts of the General Public License. Of course, the commands you use may be called something other than 'show w' and 'show c'; they could even be mouse-clicks or menu items—whatever suits your program.

You should also get your employer (if you work as a pro-grammer) or your school, if any, to sign a "copyright disclaimer" for the program, if necessary. Here is a sample; alter the names:

Yoyodyne, Inc., hereby disclaims all copyright interest in the program 'Gnomovision' (which makes passes at compilers) written by James Hacker.

<signature of Ty Coon>, 1 April 1989

Ty Coon, President of Vice

This General Public License does not permit incorporating your program into proprietary programs. If your program is a subroutine library, you may consider it more useful to permit linking proprietary applications with the library. If this is what you want to do, use the GNU Library General Public License instead of this License.

Index